DRUG REGULATORY AFFAIRS

For B. Pharm. & M. Pharm. Students

Dr. N. S. VYAWAHARE
M. Pharm., Ph.D.
Principal
Dr. D.Y. Patil Pratishthan's,
Padmashree Dr. D.Y. Patil College of Pharmacy
Akurdi, **PUNE** – 411044

Mr. SACHIN C. ITKAR
B. Pharm, M.B.A. (International Business)
Bilcare Limited, **PUNE**

N1629

DRUG REGULATORY AFFAIRS
Third Edition   :   July, 2012
©   :   **Authors**

The text of this publication, or any part thereof, should not be reproduced or transmitted in any form or stored in any computer storage system or device for distribution including photocopy, recording, taping or information retrieval system or reproduced on any disc, tape, perforated media or other information storage device etc., without the written permission of Author with whom the rights are reserved. Breach of this condition is liable for legal action.

Every effort has been made to avoid errors or omissions in this publication. In spite of this, errors may have crept in. Any mistake, error or discrepancy so noted and shall be brought to our notice shall be taken care of in the next edition. It is notified that neither the publisher nor the author or seller shall be responsible for any damage or loss of action to any one, of any kind, in any manner, therefrom.

ISBN 978-93-80064-68-0

Published By :
NIRALI PRAKASHAN
Abhyudaya Pragati, 1312, Shivaji Nagar,
Off J.M. Road, PUNE – 411005
Tel - (020) 25512336/37/39, Fax - (020) 25511379
Email : niralipune@pragationline.com

Printed By :
Repro Knowledgecast Limited,
Thane

DISTRIBUTION CENTRES

PUNE
Nirali Prakashan
119, Budhwar Peth, Jogeshwari Mandir Lane
Pune 411002, Maharashtra
Tel : (020) 2445 2044, 66022708
Fax : (020) 2445 1538
Email : bookorder@pragationline.com

MUMBAI
Nirali Prakashan
385, S.V.P. Road, Rasdhara Co-op. Hsg. Society Ltd.,
Girgaum, Mumbai 400004, Maharashtra
Tel : (022) 2385 6339 / 2386 9976,
Fax : (022) 2386 9976
Email : niralimumbai@pragationline.com

DISTRIBUTION BRANCHES

NAGPUR
Pratibha Book Distributors
Above Maratha Mandir, Shop No. 3, First Floor,
Rani Jhanshi Square, Sitabuldi, Nagpur 440012,
Maharashtra, Tel : (0712) 254 7129

BENGALURU
Pragati Book House
House No. 1,Sanjeevappa Lane, Avenue Road Cross,
Opp. Rice Church, Bengaluru – 560002.
Tel : (080) 64513344, 64513355,
Mob : 9880582331, 9845021552
Email:bharatsavla@yahoo.com

JALGAON
Nirali Prakashan
34, V. V. Golani Market, Navi Peth, Jalgaon 425001,
Maharashtra, Tel : (0257) 222 0395
Mob : 94234 91860

KOLHAPUR
Nirali Prakashan
New Mahadvar Road,
Kedar Plaza, 1st Floor Opp. IDBI Bank
Kolhapur 416 012, Maharashtra. Mob : 9855046155

CHENNAI
Pragati Books
9/1, Montieth Road, Behind Taas Mahal, Egmore,
Chennai 600008 Tamil Nadu, Tel : (044) 6518 3535,
Mob : 94440 01782 / 98450 21552 / 98805 82331
Email : bharatsavla@yahoo.com

RETAIL OUTLETS
PUNE

Pragati Book Centre
157, Budhwar Peth, Opp. Ratan Talkies,
Pune 411002, Maharashtra
Tel : (020) 2445 8887 / 6602 2707, Fax : (020) 2445 8887
Pragati Book Centre
Amber Chamber, 28/A, Budhwar Peth,
Appa Balwant Chowk, Pune : 411002, Maharashtra,
Tel : (020) 20240335 / 66281669
Email : pbcpune@pragationline.com

Pragati Book Centre
676/B, Budhwar Peth, Opp. Jogeshwari Mandir,
Pune 411002, Maharashtra
Tel : (020) 6601 7784 / 6602 0855
Pragati Book Centre
917/22, Sai Complex, F.C. Road, Opp. Hotel Roopali,
Shivajinagar, Pune 411004, Maharashtra
Tel : (020) 2566 3372 / 6602 2728

PBC Book Sellers & Stationers
152, Budhwar Peth, Pune 411002, Maharashtra
Tel : (020) 2445 2254 / 6609 2463

MUMBAI
Pragati Book Corner
Indira Niwas, 111 - A, Bhavani Shankar Road, Dadar (W), Mumbai 400028, Maharashtra
Tel : (022) 2422 3526 / 6662 5254
Email : pbcmumbai@pragationline.com

Preface

Pharmaceutical Industry is one of the most intense "Knowledge Driven" industry, which is continually in a state of dynamic transition. This industry will always remain a growing industry and will thrive in the future due to demands of a globally enlarging and aging population with diverse disease profiles and changing life styles. The process of "New Drug Discovery & Development" is very complex, expensive, time consuming that require on an average 12-15 years at a cost of over US$ 1BN to produce a new drug to the market. This entire activity is carried out under strict regulatory supervision. The regulatory Authorities of different countries are actively involved in monitoring and controlling Quality, Safety and Efficacy of drugs developed as well as manufactured by Pharmaceutical sector.

In today's era, Drug Regulatory Affairs is gaining wide importance in all major Pharmaceutical operations like research and development, manufacturing, quality, distribution and dispensing, exports etc. in short, anything and everything in Pharma companies is now governed by regulations and has to be done as per the framed guidelines and laws.

This book has been written with an objective of providing critical and updated information about laws and regulations governing pharma operations in a simple and user-friendly manner. We are indeed delighted to present the book 'Drug Regulatory Affairs' which will be good help to Pharmacy professionals working in different facets of Pharmaceutical sectors like industry, trade, academia and students studying pharmacy at undergraduate as well as at Post graduate level.

We would like to thank everyone who directly or indirectly helped us in compilation of this book. We would like to thank 'Perfect Consultants' Pune for sharing valuable information on drug regulations. We request readers to point out mistakes if any in the book and send their valuable suggestions which will help us in improving the content of the book in next edition.

Looking Forward!

Authors

Contents

1. Regulatory Affair and its Importance — 1.1 - 1.10
2. Drug Discovery and Development — 2.1 - 2.10
3. Regulatory Strategy — 3.1 - 3.6
4. Investigational New Drug Application (IND) — 4.1 - 4.10
5. New Drug Application (NDA) — 5.1 - 5.10
6. Abbreviated New Drug Application (ANDA) — 6.1 - 6.4
7. Drug Master File (DMF) — 7.1 - 7.10
8. Orphan Drug — 8.1 - 8.4
9. Biological Licensing Application (BLA) — 9.1 - 9.6
10. Registration of Drug Products in Overseas Markets – Pharmaceutical Export — 10.1 - 10.16
11. Regulatory Authorities and Agencies — 11.1 - 11.30
12. Overview of Drug and Cosmetic Act — 12.1 - 12.32
13. Regulatory Guidelines — 13.1 - 13.130
14. Useful Information — 14.1 - 14.40

❖❖❖

Chapter 1...
REGULATORY AFFAIR AND ITS IMPORTANCE

Regulatory affair is a dynamic and challenging profession which helps to protect public health by constant monitoring and controlling the safety and efficacy of healthcare products like pharmaceuticals, veterinary medicines, medical devices, pesticides, agrochemicals, cosmetics and complementary medicines. The main objective and motive of regulatory affairs professionals is to ensure availability of safe and effective healthcare products worldwide.

Protection of public health is a prime responsibility of the Government and they do so by controlling the safety, efficacy and quality of the products in areas of pharmaceuticals, veterinary medicines, medical devices, pesticides, agrochemicals, cosmetics etc.

Government ensures and controls the quality supply of healthcare related products to the community by way of framing new rules and regulations as and when required and by way of amending the current regulations. The companies responsible for the discovery, development, manufacture and marketing of these products also want to ensure that they supply products that are safe and effective. Most companies, whether they are major multinational pharmaceutical corporations or small-medium enterprises, innovative biotechnology companies etc. have specialist departments of Regulatory Affairs professionals. Many companies hire services of regulatory consultants in order to comply with the regulations.

Almost every company has regulatory department to keep track on the legislations of countries where companies wish to market their products. This track includes collection and analysis of legal as well as scientific requirements of particular country to obtain and maintain marketing authorizations of healthcare products.

Regulatory Affairs encompasses a variety of disciplines and job responsibilities, which starts during the product development, its manufacture and continue till the product is widely available for use.

Individuals who ensure regulatory compliance and prepare submissions as well as those whose main job function is clinical affairs or quality assurance are all considered Regulatory Affair professionals.

RA professionals are employed in industry, government and academia and are involved with a wide range of products, including :
- Pharmaceuticals
- Medical devices
- In-vitro diagnostics
- Biologics and biotechnology
- Nutritional products
- Cosmetics
- Veterinary products.

The regulatory authority must critically assess the technical reports generated during the development of product and proposed procedures of its manufacturing, quality control. Overall assessment is a close interaction between the staff of regulatory authority (assessor) and regulatory affair department.

The assessment report is a reflection of critical review of scientific evidences presented by the department of regulatory affair to establish products quality, safety and efficacy within acceptable limit. In pharmaceutical company, regulatory affair play vital role in overall development of product including selection of method of initial toxicology, design of clinical trials, compilation of data in prescribed format of market authorization etc. The compilation of data obtained from different departments either within the company or by external contractors into logical way is a key to success. This compilation should be placed in a reviewer friendly way so that the proposal can be processed at a faster rate which in turn reduces company's financial burden. The proper justification for the presented data as well as omitted information is a mandatory part of ideal submission. The approval of product and its compliance is sole responsibility of regulatory department.

The Regulatory Affairs professional's roles and responsibilities often begin in the research and development phases, moving into clinical trials and extending through pre-market approvals, manufacturing, labeling and advertising and post-market surveillance.

Importance of Regulatory Affairs

Regulatory Affair is an important profession that plays a very important role in the journey of a product from laboratory to Pharmacy shop (discovery to market). Pharmaceutical/biotech companies spent huge amount of money and time in developing new pharmaceutical products. It requires over 1 BN US$ (5000 crore rupees) and 12 to 15 years to commercialise new pharmaceutical product. A new pharmaceutical product has to undergo clinical trials and several important regulatory approvals. No new product enters the market without the new drug approval from respective competent regulatory authorities like USFDA (United State Food & Drug Administration), MHRA (Medicine & Healthcare Regulatory Authority), TGA (Therapeutic Goods Administration) or CDSCO (Central Drug Standard Control Organization).

In order to secure the intellectual property rights, innovator company applies for the new products intellectual property protection (patent) to the patent office at the time of discovery phase of the product. It takes over 10 years for the innovator company to launch the product in the market after securing the patent which leaves the company with only 8 to 10 years of monopoly period as the patent protection period is of 20 years. In today's competitive environment, the reduction of the time taken to reach the market is critical to a product's and hence the company's success. The proper conduct of its Regulatory Affair activities is therefore of considerable economic importance for the company.

Inadequate reporting of clinical data may prevent a timely positive evaluation of a new drug application. Even a month delay in bringing new product to the market has severe financial considerations. Even worse, failures to fully report all the available data, or the release of product bearing incorrect labelling, may easily result in the need for a product recall. Either occurrence may lead to the loss of several millions rupees or dollars of sales. Hence, a sound regulatory department or professionals with a 'right first time' approach is a necessity of all the Pharmaceutical companies. They are the first point of contact between the government authorities and the company. Regulatory Affair departments or professionals plays a very important part in coordinating scientific endeavors with regulatory demands throughout the life of the product and helps the companies meet all the regulations and guidelines and in turn maximize the profits.

Functions of Regulatory Affairs Department/Professional

The Regulatory Affairs Department/professional's job is to keep track of the ever-changing legislation, amendments in existing rules and regulations in all the countries in which the company wishes to distribute its products. These responsibilities mainly include collection, analysis and subsequent negotiation required to obtain and maintain market authorization for the product. For this regulatory affair professional need to study the process of drug development, data generated during preclinical as well as clinical studies, quality control procedures, safety and efficacy of the product etc. This complete process is usually known as assessment.

Regulatory affair within any pharmaceutical company plays an important role in the overall development process ranging from strategic decisions like design and timing of clinical studies to compilation, submission of marketing authorization application followed by dealing with the regulatory authorities until approval. Moreover they have to work for the products compliance for its lifetime.

Regulatory Affairs professional's main function is to advise on the legal and scientific restraints and requirements, and collect, collate, and evaluate the scientific data generated by the research and development department.

RA professionals give strategic and technical advice to all the concerned departments like R&D, manufacturing, marketing etc. in relation to the product rules and regulations.

It may take anywhere upto 15 years to develop and launch a new pharmaceutical product and many problems may arise in the process of scientific development and because of a changing regulatory environment. Regulatory Affairs professionals help the company avoid problems caused by badly kept records, inappropriate scientific thinking or poor presentation of data.

The Regulatory Affairs department will take part in the development of the product marketing concepts and is usually required to approve packaging and advertising before it is used commercially.

Many Pharmaceutical companies export range of products to various overseas markets. Their Regulatory Affairs departments must be aware of the regulatory requirements in all the export markets.

However, Regulatory Affairs role and responsibility doesn't just stop after a successful approval. The majority of regulatory submissions involve the maintenance of existing marketing authorizations, compiling and submitting so called variation applications to update authorizations as a result of modifications and amendments to manufacturing processes, extending product indications as a result of additional clinical trials, updating product literature and labeling, and filing renewals. Product license maintenance is usually the introduction to regulatory affairs for most regulatory professionals, and provides a solid grounding in the interpretation and application of regulatory guidelines.

Regulatory Affairs professionals with their vast knowledge of global markets and the regulations, act as advisors to the company on critical matters related to the product registrations. Despite recent international efforts towards harmonization of requirements, the regulations laid down by different regulatory authorities rarely match. Hence the registration data prepared for one country frequently fails to meet the requirements for another. Therefore, great care has to be taken in drawing up efficient and economical research and development programmes whose results may be used as widely as possible.

A good Regulatory Affairs professional requires qualities like communicative competency both written & oral, analytical abilities, presentation skills before a panel of experts such as scientists, pharmacists, doctors and lawyers, considerable understanding of both legal and scientific matters etc. to name a few. A high degree of sensitivity is required when proposing and executing the strategy and tactics needed to obtain approvals/permissions/licenses in a way which will satisfy the authorities and serve the best needs of the company.

Chapter 2...
DRUG DISCOVERY AND DEVELOPMENT

Pharmaceutical Industry is one of the most intense "Knowledge Driven" industry, which is continually in a state of dynamic transition. This industry will always remain a growing industry & will thrive in the future due to demands of a globally enlarging and aging population with diverse disease profiles & changing life styles. Innovation will continually drive this industry. The drug discovery and development is a major aspect of pharmaceutical business. It can be safely said that the pharmaceutical industry is more research-intensive, as compared to any other sector industry. The process of "new drug discovery & development" is elaborate requiring on an average 12 to 15 years at a cost of over US$ 1 BN (over 5000 crore rupees) to produce a new drug to the market. The whole activity of new drug discovery & development is very complex, expensive & time consuming which necessitates the creation of "Proprietary Knowledge" which is of paramount importance in establishing and sustaining a global competitive posture.

The process of drug discovery involves the identification of candidates, synthesis, characterization, screening, and assays for therapeutic efficacy. Once a compound has shown its value in these tests, the process of drug development starts which involves pre-clinical testing and clinical studies including regulatory approvals for commercialization of the new chemical entity/new biological entity. Introduction of ICH-GCP guidelines have phenomenally changed the entire process of drug discovery and development and have brought in standards which are largely accepted all over the world and have streamlined the entire process of drug discovery & development.

In the past most drugs have been discovered either by identifying the active ingredient from traditional remedies or by serendipitous discovery. A new approach has been to understand how disease and infection are controlled at the molecular and physiological level and to target specific entities based on this knowledge.

The innovator company synthesises a New Chemical Entity (NCE) or New Biological Entity (NBE), which can probably be a cure for a disease. The synthesis of a

NCE/NBE takes place in the pre-clinical testing period. The innovator company, after synthesising a NCE, files an Investigational New Drug (IND) application, and requests the FDA to grant permission to conduct clinical trials. Clinical trials today have become one of the most important aspects of modern medical research & drug development.

After studying the IND application, FDA grants permission to conduct clinical trials which involves studies in phases like phase 1, phase 2, phase 3 & phase 4. After successful completion of Phase 3 trials, the innovator company files NDA (New Drug Application) and requests the FDA to grant permission to commercialize the product. After scrutiny of the application, FDA grants permission to launch the new drug in the market. The company continues clinical trials of the same molecule in Phase 4 called as product surveillance studies.

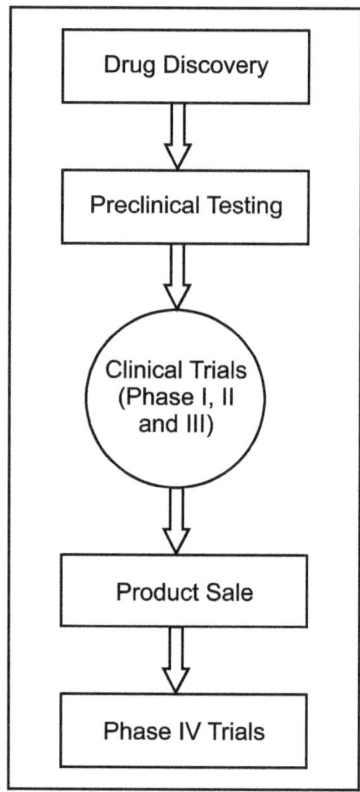

Fig. 2.1 : Summary of drug discovery and development

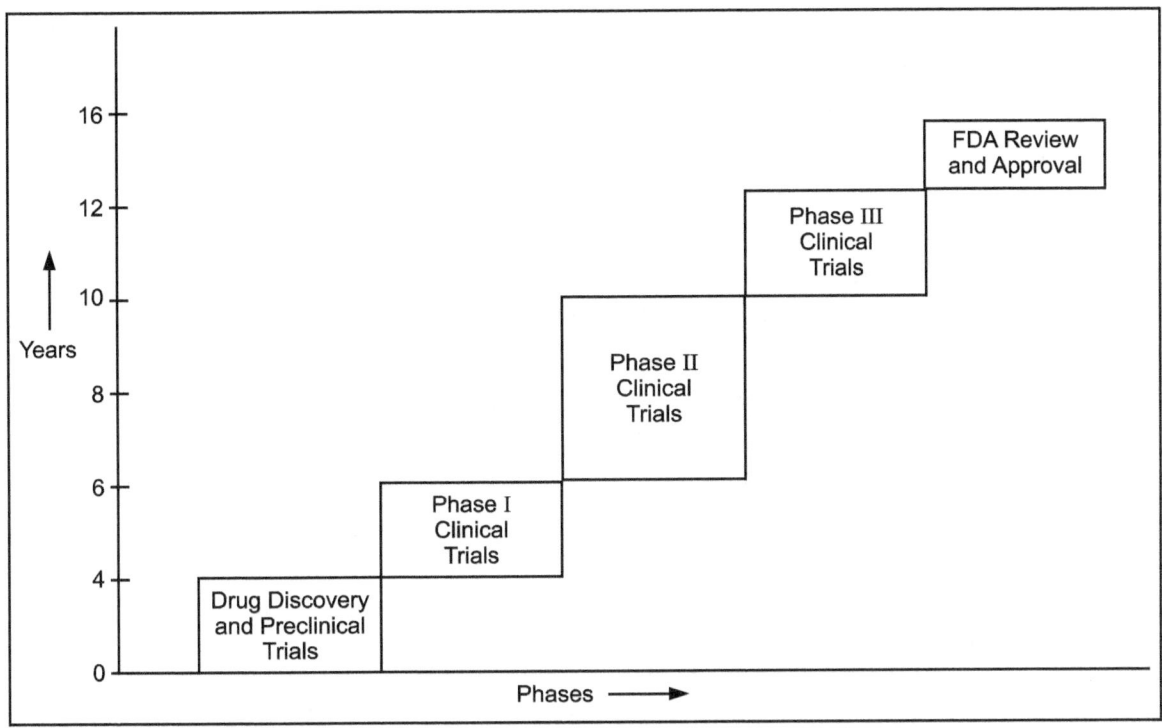

Fig. 2.2 : Approximate step wise duration for drug discovery and development

The process of drug discovery & development is a complex process and involves various activities like introduction of new products, formulations, modifications in existing products or formulations and its manufacturing process, basic and advance research, toxicity testing etc. to name a few.

Research and development in pharmaceutical/biotech sector is of two types:

1. **Basic Research :**

This type of research deals with the development of lead molecule and usually starts from cellular level. It also includes screening of newly synthesized molecule for its therapeutic effectiveness. Basic research is time consuming, very complex and highly expensive and hence is dominated by global multinationals Pharma companies.

2. **Applied Research :**

It is an application of identified chemistry to find new processes (manufacturing & other) for known molecules. In the past (before introduction of TRIPS regulations); majority of the Indian pharma companies were engaged in carrying out applied research activities.

Most of the new drugs and drug products are discovered or developed using one or more of the following approaches:

1. Identification of new drug target.

2. Drug design of new drug based upon disease mechanism, receptor structure and structure of drug.
3. Chemical alteration in the existing known molecule.
4. Screening of already discovered chemical entities, natural products, peptides, nucleic acids etc.
5. Biotechnology and cloning techniques.
6. Preparation and evaluation of new combinations of known drug.

The majority of Indian companies do not necessarily carry out the entire process of drug discovery & development. Rather they prefer to sale the lead molecule to leading MNCs on milestone payment basis at a stage of filing IND (investigational new drug) application.

The innovator company synthesises around 5000 to 7000 compounds out of which approximately 03 to 05 synthesised compounds reach to clinical level and out of which only one come to the market as a drug. The success rate is very low and it is also estimated that only 03 out of 10 newly introduced drugs are able to recover the R&D investments and can generate profits.

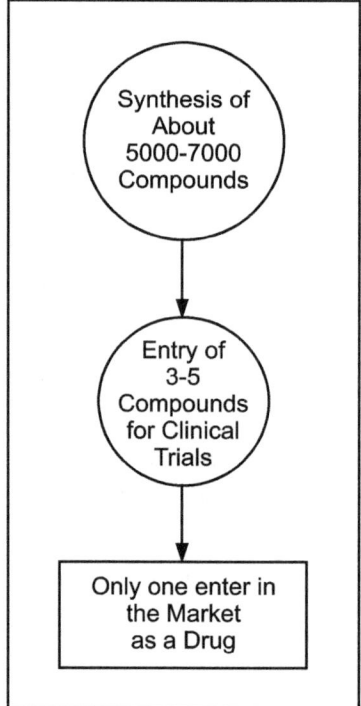

Fig. 2.3 : Journey of new chemical entity to drug

The overall NDDD (New drug discovery & development) process is as follows:

1. **Drug Discovery:**
   (a) **Target identification:** Every drug has specific target in the body. These targets are believed to be associated with disease and/disorders. The detailed study about functions of this target in normal physiology and pathophysiology is very helpful to discover the compound that can interact with them to show particular effect.
   (b) **Target validation:** The selection of target is most vital step towards development of treatment for particular disease or disorder. It involves critical analysis and comparison of various targets and their association with specific diseases. Moreover it discusses the ability of targets to regulate biological and chemical compounds present in the body. In these step, certain tests are conducted to confirm interactions of these targets and its impact on the behavior of diseased cells.
   (c) **Lead identification:** A lead compound or substance is one that is believed to have potential to treat or modify the disease or disorder. The lead compound is tested compared with known substance, using suitable techniques available to confirm predicted effect.
   (d) **Lead optimizations:** It is a comparison between different compounds for its potential to treat disease. The information is quite useful to pharmaceutical companies to select proper compound.

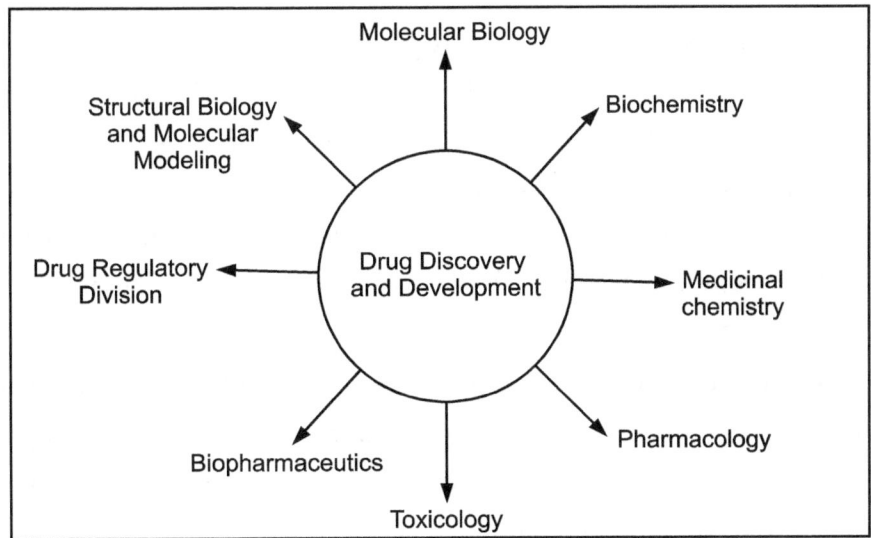

Fig. 2.4 : Major departments involved in drug discovery and development

2. Drug Development Process :

Once the lead optimization is completed the drug development process starts which is further divided into two types i.e. preclinical and clinical studies. Former one is assessment of safety and efficicacy in animals while later is conducted in human volunteers and patients. The innovator company may involve specialized CROs (contract research organizations) to improve the overall quality and efficiency of these activities. Many innovator companies outsource clinical studies to specialized CROs in order to reduce the time required to launch the product in the market. Many CROs have the competency and set ups to perform the clinical studies with required speed without compromising the quality.

(A) Preclinical Evaluation :

It is a study to define pharmacological profile to lead molecule using suitable animal model. In this the screening is either disease oriented or organ oriented which is further extended to cellular or molecular level.

The preclinical evaluation mainly consist of :

(i) **Toxicological study :** To evaluate toxicity of the lead molecule to a particular organ, system or whole body with respect to duration and dose of compound. It is conducted as acute, subacute, chronic and special toxicity.

(ii) **Pharmacodynamic study :** It is evaluation of action produced by the lead molecule that is relevant to the proposed therapeutic use. The normal course of study is targeted to particular generalized condition (e.g. Arrythmia by reporting heart rate, ECG etc.) followed by organ specific exvivo or in-vitro studies (e.g. Isolated heart, aortic strip, ventricular strip, in-vitro cultured cells etc.). Finally the study is extended to molecular level like recording receptor affinity, receptor binding studies on cell membrane fractions from organs or cultured cells.

(iii) **Pharmacokinetic study :** The promising lead molecule emerged after above two studies, is subjected to pharmacokinetic evaluation (including absorption, distribution, metabolism, excretion) in different experimental animals. Beside ADME, bioavailability, bioequivalence, etc. are also recorded.

From above different tests, safety index of the molecule is calculated.

Table 2.1 : Various Safety Tests in Preclinical Phase Development Process

Sr. No.	Type of Test	Description of Approach
1.	Acute toxicity	Usually tested in two species, by two route and single dose to record lethal dose in 50% of animals and maximum tolerated dose.
2.	Subacute toxicity	To identity toxicity on longer use (01-03 months). Generally two species and three doses are used.
3.	Chronic toxicity	To identify toxicity upon long-term use (more than 06 months). Usually tested in rodent as well as non-rodent species. Simultaneously with clinical trial.
4.	Reproductive toxicity	To record effect on reproductive systems like reproduction, pregnancy, birth defects post natal development etc.
5.	Carcinogenicity	To check carcinogenic potential of drug. It is conducted when drug is intended for long term are usually 02 species are used and tested for 02 years.
6.	Mutagenicity	To evaluate effect on genetic stability and mutations in bacteria and mammalian cells in cell culture. Usually rodents are used.

Once the preclinical data shows promising results, the lead molecule is then tested in human volunteers and patients called clinical trials or human studies.

(B) Clinical Tests :

Upon satisfactory completion of preclinical studies, the new compound is subjected to clinical studies through proper application known as Investigational New Drug (IND) application to respective regulatory authorities. In United State, it is Food and Drug Administration (FDA) whereas in India it is Drug Controller General, Govt. of India (DCGI).

The IND application consist of preclinical data, chemical structure, source, manufacturing details, specification of dosage form, investigational protocol, details of investigators involved, informed consents of participants, other various agreements etc.

The entire clinical trial is expected to achieve a well balance between ethical and scientific issues. The ethical aspects look for the maintenance of "right to autonomy" of participants (healthy volunteers or patients) whereas scientific section is dedicated to assume authenticity and statistical significance of the generated data.

An Institutional Review Board (IRB) or Ethical Advisory Board (EAB) an independent committee consisting of physicians, community advocates, socially aware persons are responsible to protect the right of study of participants. For any IND protocol, IRB approval in addition to permission from regulatory authorities is mandatory.

The clinical trial consist of four different phases with specific objectives :

Phase I : It is conducted in small number of healthy volunteers (except in specific conditions like testing of anticancer drugs, where significant toxicity is expected) that usually range from 20 to 100 for short duration of compound administration. The entire study usually completed within 06-09 months.

The major objectives of this phase include determination of pharmacokinetic difference between animals and humans, determination of safe and tolerable dose to human and documentation of any predictable toxicity.

Phase II : This phase is designed to determine effectiveness and safety of candidate drug in patients with target disease. Based upon type of candidate drug and condition it treat, the duration range between 06 months to three years.

The study is further divided as :

Early phase : It is conducted in comparatively small number of patients (20-200) and mainly observe potential therapeutic benefits versus risk. It is usually single blind study (subject does not know what he/she is taking) and prepare platform for later phase.

Late phase : It is conducted in comparatively larger number of patients (50-300) to ensure safety and efficacy of candidate drug in patients. This phase is usually double blind controlled type to rule out the influence of preconvinced notion or communication of investigator. However in rare cases single blind study can also be conducted.

The entire phase II may include placebo or marketed standard or both groups for comparison.

Phase III : This is conducted in still larger number of patients (200-1000 plus) to further establish safety and efficacy of candidate drug. It is usually a double blind randomized type of study. The minimization of error on the data generated in phase I and II studies is another objective of this phase. The usual duration of this phase is between 01-04 years.

Once phase III studies are completed the sponsor files New Drug Application (NDA) with respective regulatory authorities to market this drug. The NDA consist of complete monograph of the product, proposed brand name, package inserts, detailed drug development data etc. This application is then thoroughly reviewed by the regulatory department. There may be several correspondences between sponsor and regulatory department for clarification, if required. Once NDA is acceptable then drug enter in the market with New Drug Status i.e. available for controlled marketing.

This phase is further extended to phase III (b) which usually begins before approval to supplement additional safety data. In some cases, it may be conducted upon approval of drug to produce more data that may prove useful. It also includes comparative analysis about cost and effectiveness of drug against other available drugs in the market.

Phase IV : It is started once drug is marketed and also called a post market surveillance and hence generally do not have specific time period. It is mainly focused on identification of rare side effect, previously unknown side effects and even therapeutic indications. During new drug status, it is expected that manufacturer should gather and report such new information to respective regulatory authorities until it is released to unrestricted marketing.

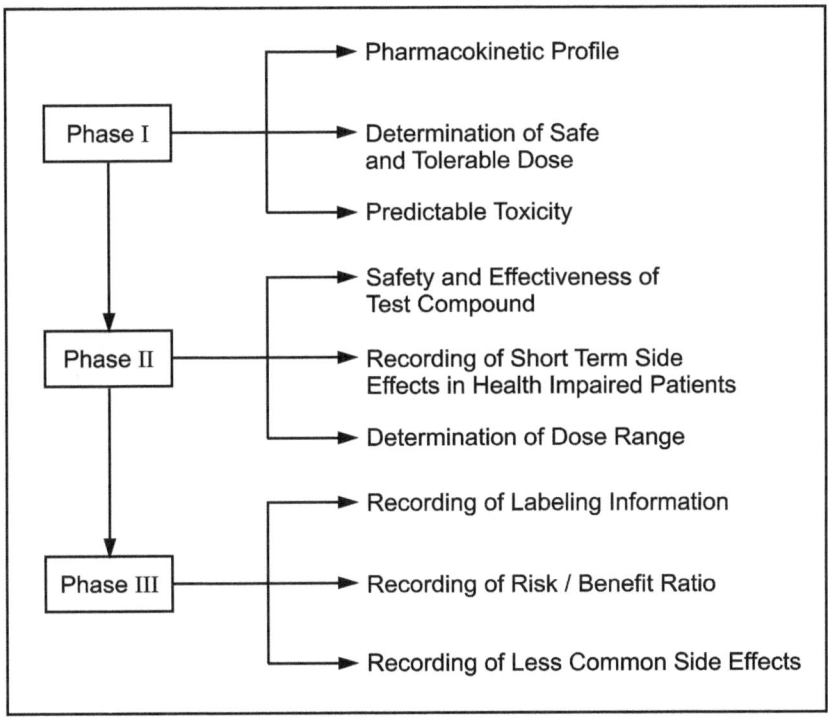

Fig. 2.5 : Major phase wise objectives of clinical trials

Non-Clinical Development Activities

The innovator company also carries out number of non-clinical development activities while the clinical studies are performed. These research activities are essentially carried out in-house and includes studies like

- Establishing pharmacokinetics and pharmacodynamics (ADME)
- Assess safety

- Develop formulations for clinical trials
- Assess efficacy (where possible)
- Develop analytical and chemical methods
- Evaluate product stability
- Develop manufacturing process

These non clinical research activities are of paramount importance as they support the clinical studies and commercialization of new drug also depends on success of these studies.

Chapter 3...
REGULATORY STRATEGY

Regulatory strategy is a plan that identifies the steps to be completed to generate optimum data to obtain or maintain regulatory approval for marketing a pharmaceutical product.

As the total span of drug development (including additional indications for use and post approval changes in the dosage form) may extend up to twenty years, a product requires series of regulatory strategies for the commercial success and to prolong the life cycle. During this, adequate changes in the next strategy based upon previous are possible. However, there are some general principles that apply to any strategy to achieve determined regulatory milestones. The common regulatory milestones are described in following in Table 3.1.

Table 3.1 : Regulatory Milestones

Sr. No.	Regulatory Milestones
1.	Assignment of an established name by respective regulatory authority.
2.	Assignment of international non-proprietary name by WHO.
3.	Agreement of regulatory authority regarding initiation / start-up of clinical study research program following submission clinical trial application or notification.
4.	The approval of inclusion of the drug product in a special category like orphan drug to hasten regulatory review process.
5.	The approval specific benefits of regulatory procedure like accelerated approval special protocol assessment, if applicable.
6.	Certification of quality compliance after regulatory inspection or audit.
7.	Certification of regulatory inspection before marketing approval.
8.	The marketing authorisation approval by regulatory authorities.
9.	The approval of a regulatory submission regarding beneficial changes to expand label claim like additional therapeutic indications or extended safety profile.
10.	The approval of a regulatory submission for changes in nonclinical information like stability data or chemistry of product.

Regulatory affairs professionals are required to apply their knowledge and experience before and during various phases of product development and its marketing. The appropriate implementation of aforementioned parameters can speed-up drug development programme leading to successful filing of required regulatory applications and final marketing approval.

Pharmaceutical product development plan is a multi-step procedure wherein identification of critical steps and the resources required to meet the goals of marketing a product has great importance. The regulatory strategy is a fundamental part because clinical testing and marketing of product is totally dependent on regulatory approval. This strategy may need intermittent modification with respect to changes in legislation, requirements by regulatory authority for clinical trials, increasing information about the knowledge etc.

The success of regulatory strategy is dependent upon ability of regulatory professional to research, analyze, and interpret the literature as well as result obtained and communication with other discipline professionals involved directly or indirectly in the drug development process.

The regulatory strategy preparation must consider current and proposed regulations for pharmaceuticals products of the applicable class, regulatory requirements and trade organizations in respective countries. This information can be directly obtained as paper copies or electronic files from regulatory agencies or related other organizations.

In addition, through literature surveys, useful available information on the plans, companies and research institutes which is relevant to the product shall be obtained. The selection of key word is another important parameter which shall provide limited but valuable information.

Once the aforementioned information is gathered, then a complete background report summarising the key features of regulatory environment in which the product is being developed shall be prepared. It shall also include the information about the drugs that are being developed by other organizations that come in same class or for similar indications called "competitive intelligence".

The time is one of the important features of any pharmaceutical development plan and regulatory strategy. The regulatory strategy should identify the key information, adequate data and detailed study reports sufficient for regulatory submission. The persons involved in the preparation of strategy can suggest realistic timelines so as to achieve the desired pace for the regulatory submission.

The time required to prepare a regulatory strategy must also be considered as its delay may affect the overall process.

The frequent review and revision of regulatory strategy is important and should be carried out at designed time intervals.

In fast changing area of research and development, rapid refinement of clinical research study designs and regulatory strategy is mandatory to keep the product being developed ahead of competition.

Looking at the goal to be achieved, multiple parallel strategies may be followed. These strategies may have different outcomes however all of them will meet the same business goal.

In case of multiple pharmacological activities of drugs, organizations have to decide on the typical therapeutic areas where research is to be carried out. Moreover preference to be given is another key parameter because it may influence many business decisions which could generate funding for further needs. e.g. If product's possible indications includes cancer and immuno supression then the selection for indication for which it will seek marketing approval is major step which further can influence the entire plan.

Regulatory Strategy during Preclinical Development Phase

The preclinical phase deals with generation of preliminary data on chemistry, manufacturing, quality control and stability of the drug substance and drug product. In-vivo and in-vitro pharmacological studies including toxicology profile are also carried out to record the effect of the drug and to establish possible mechanism of action.

This data is evaluated, verified and used to prepare proposed clinical research study design according to the regulatory requirements and submitted to one or more regulatory authorities to initiate clinical research studies. The regulatory authorities acknowledge the receipt and indicate whether or not clinical study or studies may proceed.

As permission of conducting clinical trials is totally dependent upon quantum of preclinical evidences provided, hence regulatory strategy must focus on assembling appropriate data that is helpful to obtain regulatory clearance.

The preparation of regulatory strategy is essential at early stage especially when compound has passed from discovery research to pharmacological screening. Early preparation results in opening of channels of communication with all disciplines involved in the product development about type, scope and quality of data required for regulatory submission.

Table 3.2 : Major Factors that have an Impact on Regulatory Strategy

Sr. No.	Major Factors
1.	Need of IND for the product.
2.	Need of more than one IND submission.
3.	Need of pre-IND meeting with FDA.
4.	Need of DMF.
5.	Need of use of available trade name for the drug product in the IND.
6.	Quality of substance required and available to meet GMP requirement.
7.	Quantity of available data on the chemistry, characterisation, quality control testing and stability of drug substance and drug product.
8.	Quantity of data from the pharmacology studies sufficient to establish scientific rationale for the product to show progress in clinical studies.
9.	Relevance of pharmacological data to a human disease or target population for the intended therapeutic use.
10.	Quantum of information available from animal studies to predict dose as well as dose regimen safe for first human use during clinical study.

An estimate of time required for meeting regulatory and product development objectives may influence regulatory strategy and helps in resource planning and cost management.

Regulatory Strategy during the Clinical Phase

The regulatory strategy in this phase deals with characterisation of drug substance, improve in the manufacturing processes, scale up of product, testing for consistency and reproducibility. Moreover testing of analytical methods used for quality control, newer analytical methods may be developed for routine tests and quality control of the drug substance and drug product.

Clinical research studies are conducted to determine dose regimen, safety and efficacy of drug product in humans for particular therapeutic indication. Clinical research study is usually conducted in three different phases as follows:

> **Phase I** : This is usually conducted in healthy human volunteers with the objective to obtain safety, pharmacokinetic, pharmacodynamic and tolerability data. The early benefit of therapeutic action is also documented. Statistics may or may not be applied. The decision is taken on the basis of design of the study.

Phase II : This phase has primary objective of exploration of therapeutic effectiveness in patient with the help of variety of uncontrolled or controlled study designs. Determination of dose and dose regimen for phase III clinical studies is another aim of this phase.

Evaluation of potential study end points, comparison of therapeutic regimens and collection of safety as well as efficacy data are not mandatory but can be secondary objectives of this phase.

Phase III : It is extension of phase I and II knowledge with the objective of confirmation of therapeutic effectiveness of the drug and collection of safety data in intended indication.

The study may be of self control or drug or placebo control type with quite larger number of subjects as compared to phase I and II. A comprehensive statistical analysis is carried out to minimise error or false results. The level of documentation and verification of its accuracy is highest in this phase.

The audit of phase III by representative of the sponsor or staff from compliance monitoring groups of regulatory agencies is frequently done. The significant deviation from regulatory reporting or compliance requirement may result into heavy penalties or substantial delay in approval. In some cases outright rejection of a marketing authorisation application may be the type of penalty.

The regulatory strategy for this phase must work upon short term and long term goals and milestones.

Table 3.3 : Common Regulatory Goals in Phase III

Sr. No.	Goals
1.	Maintenance of effective and active clinical trial application
2.	Relevant revision of submitted information
3.	Addition of new information pertinent to ongoing clinical investigations
4.	Maintenance of regulatory compliance
5.	Updation of documentation and data management
6.	Maintain availability of clinical study material
7.	Identification and verification of current regulatory authorities' requirements for approval of marketing authorisation application
8.	Identification of regulatory requirements for launch of the product
9.	Application for consideration of product under special regulatory initiatives
10.	To adopt regulatory practices which will help in speedy preparation of market authorization application
11.	To adopt techniques to enhance the regulatory authorities review cycles.

Periodic analysis of the regulatory environment is essential for development of an effective regulatory strategy for clinical phases otherwise as impact of changes in regulatory requirements, guidelines or its interpretations by the regulatory agencies may result in tremendous increase in cost of study design. In addition, an in depth analysis of competitive intelligence is also required to compete with similar products. Different points mentioned in following Table 3.4 must be considered while preparing regulatory strategy.

Table 3.4: Major points to be considered to prepare Regulatory Strategy

Sr. No.	Parameters
1.	Need of legal corporate entity with respect to the country
2.	Number of well controlled clinical studies required
3.	Existence of therapeutic indication in the country where marketing authorisation application to be submitted
4.	Number of therapeutic indications for which approval to be sought
5.	Number of dose and dosage form for which approval be sought
6.	Simultaneous application for multinational applications
7.	Time slot for project review procedure at each stage of the process for each regulatory agency
8.	Local regulatory requirements for each agency
9.	Identification of data, information and documents required on critical path to meet the regulatory goals.
10.	Detailed track log of completion of study reports, availability of specific data, document management issues

Regulatory Strategy for the Post Approval Phase

This phase start after first approval for marketing and prominently work to provide data for revised labelling for line extensions to extend market share. Normally, non-clinical information such as chemistry, manufacturing, quality control testing etc. are submitted to revise original marketing application.

The clinical studies to explore new indications, doses, dosage form, patient populations are carried out as per the same format discussed earlier and submitted to the regulatory authority under the existing or new clinical trial application.

The other administrative type of regulatory submissions is made in case of transfer of ownership or responsibility in case of closure or mergers, etc., change in trade name or co-marketing agreements. Moreover change in legal status of the product in case of product recall or withdrawal requires regulatory submissions.

Chapter 4...

INVESTIGATIONAL NEW DRUG APPLICATION (IND)

An Investigational New Drug application is a submission to the respective government authority (e.g. FDA in United States) requesting permission to start clinical study of a new drug product.

Investigational New Drug is an exemption from the law which otherwise requires that a drug (biologic, device) be approved before it can be transported to different places. If IND is approved, it is an evidence of safety and efficacy. The IND exemption is granted for purposes of clinical investigation (research) which are carried out in different places of the world.

The Investigational New Drug application allows the company to legally ship/transport an unapproved drug or import a new drug from other country. In addition, this submission to regulatory authorities gives an idea regarding possible risk to the subjects participating in the clinical studies. FDA or other regulatory authorities may keep the trial on hold (called clinical hold), if reasonable risk in the proposed, assured safety is observed. Clinical hold is an order issued to the sponsor either to delay the proposed trial or to suspend ongoing investigations. The subject may not be provided with the drug or may require stopping new enrollment.

The Investigational New Drug application is required whenever sponsor or Innovator Company wants to conduct a clinical trial of an unapproved drug. IND is also required in cases where composition of the drug is such that the drug is not recognized as safe and effective in prescribed, suggested or recommended conditions on label.

Table 4.1 : Do's and Don'ts of Investigational New Drug

Need of Investigational New Drug	Don't need Investigational New Drug
1. For new chemical entity. 2. For a drug not approved for the indication under investigation. 3. For a new dosage form. 4. For a new combination to be approved.	1. For a drug not intended for human use but for in-vitro testing. 2. For non-clinical studies (laboratory research animals) 3. For study of an approved drug for approved indication.

Before conducting clinical studies, investigators or sponsors shall consult the staff of their regulatory department and if required can consult with the Institutional Review Board (IRB) followed by FDA.

Institutional review board is formally designated by an institution to review and approve the initiation of research involving human subjects with the primary intention of protecting rights as well as welfare of human subjects.

A meeting between sponsor and statutory agency (e.g. FDA) can be very useful to aid solutions of scientific and technical problems with the help of available resources.

The content and format of an Investigational New Drug Application shall be as per the key guidance documents published by the statutory agency like FDA.

Importance of IND

- Discloses knowledge about the manufacturing, pharmacology, and toxicology of the drug to support its use in human testing.
- Requires that the clinical investigation(s) be performed in accordance with Good Clinical Practice (GCP).
- Provides an additional level of protection through FDA oversight.

Basic Components of investigational New Drug Application (INDA)

Preclinical investigation i.e. animal experimentation is a step to generate required data regarding potential therapeutic effects of the substance on living organisms. This data is useful to present strong evidence regarding reasonable/anticipated safety in humans and thereby to start human testing. Though FDA requires no prior permission for investigators or sponsors to conduct preclinical testing however insist to follow Good Laboratory Practices (GLP) regulations. Normal duration of preclinical investigation ranges from 01-03 years. Once sufficient data is collected to reach the goal of potential therapeutic effect and adequate safety, then sponsor can formally notify FDA about their wish to conduct clinical trials by filing Investigational New Drug Application (INDA).

Table 4.2 : Basic components of Investigational New Drug Applications

Sr. No.	Components
1.	Detailed cover sheet
2.	Table of contents
3.	An introductory statement
4.	Basic investigate plan
5.	Investigators brochure
6.	Detailed investigation protocols
7.	Actual and proposed chemistry of compound
8.	Pharmacological and toxicology information of compound
9.	Details of previous human experience with compound (If any)
10.	Any other information asked by FDA.

Cover sheet consists of details of any investigational new drug application that includes basic information like name of sponsor, investigational new drug number, name of drug, type of submission, serial number and content of application.

IND sponsors are required to obtain a signed FDA Form "1572" from each clinical investigator, containing :

- Name and address of CI
- Name and code number of any protocol(s)
- Name and address of research facility and any clinical labs
- Name and address of responsible IRB
- Names of sub investigators
- Signed commitment by the investigator

The initial investigational new drug application is numbered as 0000 while subsequent number should be 0001. These serial numbers are important and will be filed accordingly for each and every further corresponding should be mentioned.

In case of conduction of any part of the study by contract research organization (CRO) and if any obligations are transferred to CRO, then it is necessary to mention in the form 1572. In any case, the sponsor of the investigational new drug is ultimately responsible for the conduct of the clinical investigation, the regulatory and other requirements related to the clinical trial.

Table 4.3 : Commitment of Sponsor in form 1571

1.	The sponsor should not initiate clinical study until 30 days after the FDA receives the investigational new drug.
2.	The sponsor should not start clinical study unless notified by the FDA or when placed on clinical hold.
3.	The sponsor shall see that IRB do initial and continue approval of each study proposed in the trial.
4.	Conduction of investigation in accordance with all other applicable regulatory requirements.

Note : Deviation from above mentioned commitments or inclusion of any false statement in form 1571 is a criminal offence.

Review of Investigational New Drug

When initial investigational new drug submission is made, then it is kept in the records room and numbered. This number can also be obtained in advance to the submission and used within the submission documents. Once investigational new drug is stamped as received then it is sent for critical review by several reviewers from different branches like chemistry, pharmacology, toxicology, biopharmaceuticals etc. in order to ensure safety of the individuals who will be enrolled in the study.

Once investigational new drug is submitted, then the permission of initiate the trial, or issues related to safety or clinical hold will be informed to the sponsor and will be resolved.

Contents of Investigational New Drug

1. **Introductory Statement :** This provides an overview of the investigational drug and plan of investigation. It should begin with a description of the drug and the indication(s) to be studied followed by structure, pharmacological class, dosage form, route of administration etc. In addition, it include rationale for the proposed study plan, type of clinical studies to be conducted, number of patients that will receive the drug and anticipated risk based on non-clinical studies.

If drug is used previously in humans then brief summary of this human experience specially safety of the drug should be included.

If the drug was withdrawn from investigation or marketing, then details regarding country and reasons for withdrawal should be discussed.

The investigator's brochure (IB) is a key document that present summary form, clinical as well as non-clinical and CMC (Chemistry Manufacturing and Control Information) data that support the clinical study. This also helps to make unbiased risk-benefit assessment of the trial. The type and extent of information provided in IB is variable with respect to the stage of development however it must contain minimum required information mentioned in Table 4.4.

Table 4.4 : Minimum required information in Investigator's Brochure

1.	Physical, Chemical and Pharmaceutical properties of the drug.
2.	Supply, Storage and Handling information of the drug.
3.	Chemical name and chemical structure of the drug.
4.	Summarised relevant information about non-clinical pharmacology toxicology, pharmacokinetics aspect of the drug.
5.	Summary of safety and efficacy profile of the drug (if studied earlier in humans).
6.	Guidelines regarding management of subject participating in the trial.

2. Protocol of Clinical Study : It is an information regarding the conduction of proposed clinical study including objective, trial design, selection of subjects. The Phase I protocol is less detailed as compared to phase II and III. Although phase I is less detailed it cannot be substituted by protocol summary. The essential part of phase I protocol includes estimate of number of subjects to be enrolled, dosing plan and safety exclusions. The elements that are critical to the patients (e.g. monitoring of vital signs dose adjustments rules) must be included in detail.

The essential contents of any protocol are mentioned in Table 4.5.

Table 4.5 : Essential Contents of Any Protocol

1.	Name, address and qualification of each investigator and co-investigator.
2.	Name and address of each clinical site.
3.	Name and address of each institutional review board.
4.	Copies of case report form with the 1572 (in case of phase II and III).
5.	Inclusion and exclusion criteria of subjects.
6.	Estimate of the number of subjects to be enrolled.
7.	Study design, methods employed to minimize bias on the part of subjects and investigators.
8.	Maximum proposed dose and duration of exposure to the subjects.
9.	Method of measurements and observations to be made.
10.	Clinical procedures and laboratory tests planned to monitor the effects of drug in the subjects.
11.	Methods to be used to determine the doses to be administered.

Pharmacology and Toxicology Information

The review of data obtained from non-clinical in-vivo and in-vitro studies determine the administration of the investigational drug to humans. This data must provide a good level of confidence that the new drug is safe to administer to the human subject at proposed dosage levels. The non-clinical safety information is also useful to determine initial safety starting dose for human trials. The quantum of non-clinical data required to support a new product depends on the class of new drug, duration of proposed clinical trials and patient population. The common non-clinical safety studies required to start phase I studies are mentioned in Table 4.6.

Table 4.6 : Common Non-Clinical Safety Studies

1.	Safety pharmacology.
2.	Single dose and repeated dose toxicity studies.
3.	Genotoxicity study to evaluate mutuations and chromosomal damage.
4.	Reproduction toxicity study.
5.	Other supplementary studies based upon identified safety concern.

The pharmacology and toxicology section should describe pharmacologic effects, mechanism of action, and pharmacokinetic profile of the drug. If this information is not known then it should be mentioned accordingly, however, it may lead to clinical hold. In addition, an integrated summary of toxicologic effects of the drug in pre-clinical phase that support the safety of the proposed human investigation should be prepared. The content of summary is abstracted in Table 4.7.

Table 4.7 : Content of Integrated Summary

1.	Brief description of the design of the trial.
2.	Details of deviation from the design in the conduct of the study.
3.	A systematic presentation of the findings.
4.	Organ or System wise presentation of data.
5.	The names and qualifications of evaluators alongwith their reports.
6.	Animal safety data.
7.	Name of the place where studies are conducted and study reports are stored.
8.	A declaration regarding performance of the study in accordance with GLP.

For the initial submission of investigational new drug, final fully quality assured individual study report is not required and integrated summary report can be developed based upon unaudited draft of toxicology reports of the completed preclinical studies. However, finalized summary report should be submitted within 120 days after previous summary report. If there is difference in these two reports, should be mentioned and if not, such statement should be included.

This section should also include full data tabulations including individual animal data report, brief technical report, abstract of each study and amendments.

If drug is exposed to human earlier or if clinical investigations have been conducted in any country other than U.S., then related extensive information should be given as previous human experience. If it will be administered to human volunteers for the first time in proposed study then this information is not required.

The information must include pharmacokinetic, pharmacodynamic reports and observed adverse events. In addition, any published information regarding safety of the drug must also be provided in the investigational new drug. The list of countries, other than U.S. where drug is marketed (if any) or was withdrawn from the market due to safety or effectiveness issues should be mentioned.

Certain specific information like drug dependence, drug abuse potential, radioactive substance dose, safety as well as effectiveness in pediatric population etc. should be included as additional information section.

Some important information of investigational new drug :

1. Financial disclosure information collected from each investigator or co investigator involved.
2. Revised financial disclosure information, within one year if any changes occur during the course of investigation.
3. Copy of informed consent form.
4. List of reference previously submitted to FDA and used in present in the investigational new drug application.
5. Drug master file.

Maintenance of Investigational New Drug

Clinical development of drug is long-term process which usually take 10-12 years and hence it is necessary to continuously update investigational new drug application. The continuous updating may be in the form of new information or new protocols as drug moves from one phase to another. The various common types of amendments and reports are discussed below :

1. The Investigational New Drug Safety Report :

The sponsor of investigational new drug shall continuously review the safety of the investigational drug(s) obtained from various sources like preclinical studies, clinical investigations, scientific journals, marketing feedback etc. The ongoing safety review is another tool to update the drug information specially its adverse events and serious adverse drug reaction. The later is defined any reaction that involves life threatening reaction that need hospitalization or results in either significant disability or death. In addition, unexpected adverse event (of which the specifically and severity is not consistent with the current investigator's brochure) is another constituent of safety report.

The non-serious or those reactions which are already included in the brochure are not required immediate reporting to FDA however all such reports must be included in the sponsor's safety database.

Normally, the investigational new drug regulations discuss two types of safety reports as follows :

1. **15 day report :** It is a report of serious and unexpected event with the use of investigational drug that should be submitted to FDA in prescribed form (e.g. 3500 A or CIOMS form) within 15 calendar days.

2. **7 day report :** It is more urgent report wherein serious and unexpected event is observed with the use of drug. In this case it is mandatory to inform to the FDA by telephone followed by submission within the 7 calendar days. If these safety report does not match the requirements, then it should be submitted to the investigational new drug in an information amendment or in the annual report. The sponsor must continue to investigate further adverse drug events even after investigational new drug safety report submission and additions to FDA in due course of time. The submission of safety report does not mean that the event is caused by the drug.

As per the modified rules set by FDA for the minimum data set of investigational new drug safety reports include identifiable patient, identifiable reporter, a suspect drug and suspected adverse drug reactions that defined as any noxious or unintended response to any dose of a drug product for which there is reasonable possibility that the product caused the response.

The Protocol Amendment

It is submitted to initiate a new clinical study that is either not described in the existing investigational new drug or sponsor make some changes like addition of investigator to the existing protocol.

Usually new protocol are submitted during advancement of study from one phase to another; however, in some cases it may be required within a phase to conduct additional study. (example, evaluation of differences in pharmacokinetic profile with respect to changes in route of administration).

A protocol amendment includes copy of new protocol and brief summary of differences between old and new protocol. A method of data collection in amendment may be asked by the FDA to ensure the amendment specifications e.g. Protocol Amendment: New protocol, Protocol Amendment: New Investigator.

Information Amendment

This is the process of submission of important information to the investigational new drug that is not within the scope of a protocol amendment, annual report or investigational new drug safety report. This may consist of information related toxicology, pharmacology, chemistry manufacturing, discontinuation of clinical study etc. This submission should be identified clearly on the cover e.g. Information Amendment : Toxicology. This may be submitted as per the need but not more than once every 30 days.

Sometimes information submitted in an information amendment may require to support other type of amendment.

Example : Change in formulation may require additional CMC information in new product.

In such case, it is not mandatory to submit separate protocol and information amendment rather can be submitted together in the same amendment with one serial number. However from inside it must be labeled and clearly separated.

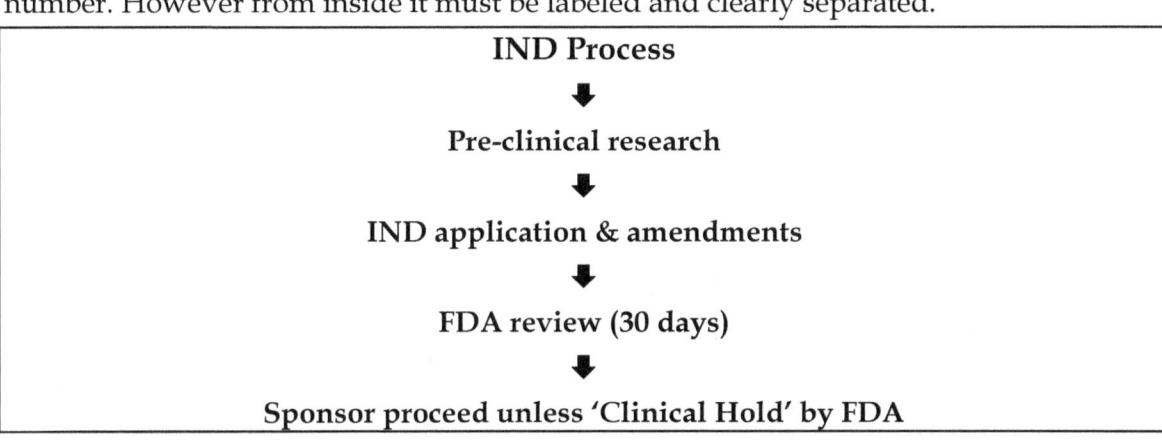

Annual Report

It is submission of brief update on the progress of all investigations included in the investigational new drug as per its specific format. The information to be included in annual report is as follows :

1. Individual study information including total number of subject enrolled participated, dropped and completed the study along with brief description of study results, if known.
2. Summary information including a non-clinical and clinical information obtained during the previous year like most serious and frequent adverse drug events, mechanism of drug action, bioavailability profile of the drug, details of ongoing as well as completed non-clinical studies, dose responses etc.
3. General investigation plan for next year.
4. List of changes made (if any) in investigator's broucher.
5. Significant marketing developments like approval, withdrawal or suspension in particular country.

The annual report should not be used as substitute for an information amendment. It should not be used to inform about new adverse event that can change risk-benefit profile of the investigation. In short annual report is a summary of the progress of the study over the past year and provides the general investigational plan for the coming year.

Review of IND Application

As per GCP guidelines, FDA conducts review of IND application with the focus on safety for human research subjects and ensuring that the studies will produce useful information to assess safety and efficacy of the test product

The reviews are conducted by team of experts which includes

- Medical Officer
- Consumer Safety Officer/Project Manager
- Statistician
- Chemist
- Pharmacologist
- Human Biopharmaceutics
- Microbiologist

IND Forms Available on-line through:

www.fda.gov/cder/regulatory/applications/

Chapter 5...

NEW DRUG APPLICATION (NDA)

New Drug Application (NDA) is a submission to the USFDA (United States Food & Drug Administration) or concerned regulatory authority of the country containing clinical and non-clinical test data / analysis reports along with drug chemistry information. NDA is submitted by Innovator Company to the FDA for the purpose of review of the various activities carried out during the various phases of clinical studies before final marketing authorization to the new pharmaceutical product.

The FDA constitutes different teams with relative expertise to review the thousands of pages of above submission. For the ease of review process for such huge information, certain guidelines for formatting, assembling and submission have been established. The failure to prepare submission as per the set guidelines may lead to delay in review, amendment of application or refusal.

The information contained in the NDA should satisfy FDA review team to reach the following key decisions :

- The new drug is safe and effective in its proposed use(s), and whether the benefits of the drug out past the risks.
- The new drug's proposed labeling and package insert (info in insert) is appropriate.
- The methods used in manufacturing of the new drug and the controls used to maintain the quality are adequate to preserve the drug's identity, strength, quality and purity.

The NDA document should explain everything about the new drug including detailed information of clinical trials and the data generated results of animal studies, ingredients of the new drug, its manufacturing process, labeling/packaging, how the drug behaves in the body etc.

The guidelines regarding preparation and submission of NDA were written and implemented in early eighties. The said guidelines were amended from time to time. Now NDA shares many common elements with the standard common technical documents developed by the International Conference on Harmonization (ICH) to maintain uniformity for getting registration in different ICH regions across the globe.

The NDA to be submitted to FDA is prepared in multiple copies as follows :

1. **Archival copy :** It contains all sections of the NDA including cover letter, form FDA-356 h (Application to market a new drug for human use) administrative section, NDA index and all technical sections. It is the only copy that contains the case report tabulation and case respect form.
2. **Review copy :** It contains the NDA's technical sections along with the cover letter, form FDA-356 h, NDA index as well as individual table of content, the labeling section and application summary.
3. **Field copy :** This is required by the FDA inspectors during pre-approval facilities inspections. In addition to the content of review copy it includes the CMC and methods validation package. The field copy preparation is implemented since 1993.

Now-a-days NDA submission is been done electronically.

The total number of copies in each section of US-FDA is mentioned in Table 5.1.

Table 5.1 : Details of Applications Copies to be submitted to Different Sections

NDA Section	Number of copies of to be submitted
Cover letter, 356 h form, section 13 – 20 (#)	07 (08*)
Index	07 (08*)
Labeling	07 (08*)
Application Summary	07 (08*)
CMC and method validation package	03
Non-clinical Pharmacology and Toxicology	02
Human Pharmacokinetics and Bioavailability	02
Microbiology	02
Clinical	02
Safety updates	02
Statistical	02
Case report tabulation	01
Case report forms	01

[(*) indicates number for anti-infective drug application only]

(#) Sections   13   Patient information
                  14   Patent certification
                  15   Establishment description (if applicable)
                  16   Debarment certification
                  17   Field copy certification
                  18   User free cover sheet
                  19   Financial disclosure
                  20   Other / Pediatric

The NDA may have as many as 20 different sections in addition to the form FDA-356 h itself. The content of every NDA may be variable based upon nature of drug and volume of information available at the time of submission. However, components are uniform.

The form FDA-356 h serves as a checklist as well as certification that the sponsor agrees to comply with all legal and regulatory requirements. The applicant must mention residence address or business center address of United States (US) in the form; if he doesn't have then shall include name, signature and address of applicant's authorized US agent.

The NDA has total 12 sections with particular specification for each. The details of each section are discussed below.

Section I (Index) :

It is a comprehensive table of contents placed immediately after the form FDA-356 h in order to review the specific information with ease. It must show the location of each section by volume and by page number. Each separately bound technical section should have individual as well as overall index.

Section II (Labeling) :

It includes all draft labeling that is intended for use on the container, cartons and packages (including the proposed package insert) of the product. There should be four copies, each placed in archival copy and in clinical, chemistry and pharmacology section of review copy.

Section III (Application Summary) :

It is an abbreviated version of the entire application that give clear idea of the drug and its application to the reviewer. The content of the draft product labeling is mentioned in Table 5.2. The summary should also include details of individual sub-sections discussed in Table 5.3.

Table 5.2 : Draft Product Labeling Sections

1.	Description
2.	Clinical Pharmacology
3.	Indications and Usage
4.	Contraindications
5.	Warnings
6.	Precautions
7.	Adverse Reactions
8.	Drug Abuse and Dependence
9.	Overdosage
10.	Dosage and Administrations
11.	How supplied

Table 5.3 : Details of Individual Subsections

1.	Basic information summary	Include Pharmacologic class, scientific rationale, intended use and potential clinical benefits.
2.	Foreign marketing history	Include list of country in which the drug is or was marketed, withdrawn for any reason relating to safety or efficacy or in which an application has been rejected.
3.	Chemistry, Manufacturing and Controls (CMC) summary	Include an abbreviated version of CMC information on the drug substance or drug product from NDA Section 4.
4.	Non-clinical pharmacology and toxicology summary	Include an abbreviated version of the NDA Section 5. i.e. information on pharmacology, toxicology and pharmacokinetics (See Table 5.4 for more details).
5.	Human Pharmacokinetics and Bioavailability (HPKB) summary	Include tabular listing alongwith brief description of each HPKB study and integrated summary of drug products. Pharmacokinetic characteristics, differences in pharmacokinetics in various subgroups, drug products bioavailability with other dosage forms.
6.	Microbiology summary	Include results of microbiology studies conducted and is applicable only for antibiotics.
7.	Clinical data summary and statistical analysis	Include information on clinical pharmacology, overview of clinical studies, controlled and uncontrolled clinical studies, general safety conclusions, overdose and drug abuse.
8.	Benefit risk relationship	Brief report of benefit and risk assessment based upon ISE to ISS and clinical studies and proposal of postmarketing studies.

Table 5.4 : Specific tables for the Sections to be included as per FDA Guidelines in non-clinical Pharmacology and Toxicology Summary

1.	Pharmacology
2.	Acute toxicity
3.	Subchronic, Chronic, Carcinogenecity
4.	Special toxicity
5.	Reproduction studies
6.	Mutagenecity
7.	Absorption, Distribution, Metabolism, Excretion (ADME)

Section 4 (Chemistry, Manufacturing and Controls – CMC)

The chemistry includes information on composition, manufacture and specifications of the drug substance and the drug product. The stability and physical as well as chemical characteristics like appearance, colour, odour, melting point, boiling point, refractive index, viscosity, specific gravity, thermodynamic stabilities etc. are included. Moreover it must provide generic or common name, chemical name (IUPAC, USAN, CAS) and internal code for the ease of review. The deficiencies may arise if multiple internal code numbers do not match with the codes used in the documents. The structural overview including molecular structure, empirical formula, molecular weight and elemental composition is another part of CMC. It should also provide a reference standard to elucidate the drug substance's chemical structure including major measures like X-ray, UV/visible spectrum, FTIR spectrum, NMR spectrum, high resolution mass spectrum etc. It must also include names, addresses and functions of each site where the drug substance is manufactured or tested.

Information on the drug product component / composition should include qualitative and quantitative listings of each drug product component used in the clinical formulation when filing IND whereas marketed formulations when filing NDA. In addition it should include drug product packaging information (container summary, closure system, list of packaging components along with their specifications, test methods, packaging process description etc.), drug product analytical controls (specifications, methods, method validations, batch analytical data, sampling plan etc.) drug product stability data (unstressed or stressed data, expiration dating, statistical analysis to establish data consistency, post approval stability commitment etc.).

Every NDA must include either an Environmental Assessment (EA) or claim for an exemption to its requirement. As EA is an analysis of the manufacturing process and ultimate use of the drug product and its effect on the environment and hence also called as environmental impact analysis report.

Section 5 (Non-clinical Pharmacology and Toxicology)

This include summary of in-vivo (animal studies) and in vitro studies with the drug. The table of content should clearly identify all studies not previously submitted to the IND. It also includes narrative summary of notable findings followed by its discussion including intra and inter species similarities or differences. It also provides individual study reports including pharmacology, toxicology and ADME studies with specified presentation pattern. This report should present effects related to the therapeutic indications (e.g. ED 50, mechanism of action) secondary pharmacological actions and drug interactions.

In the non-clinical pharmacology data provide structural formula for all names by which the compound is referred. Identify all metabolites and reference compounds by either chemical name or structural formula. Specify all animal strains used and name of all animal suppliers.

Section 6 (Human Pharmacokinetics and Bioavailability)

It include complete phase I safety and tolerance data observed in healthy volunteer's and ADME studies. The tabulated summary of in vivo studies performed arranged in descending order of importance shall be the first content followed by summary of data and overall conclusion. In addition, it includes drug formulation. Information consisting of list of all formulations used in clinical trials and in in-vivo bioavailability and PK studies (Table 5.5, 5.6).

Table 5.5 : Contents of in-vivo Study Data Summary

1. Study number
2. Route of administration
3. Dose
4. Peak concentration (C_{max})
5. Time to reach peak concentration (t_{max})
6. Distribution volume (V_d)
7. Area under the curve (AUC)
8. $t^1/_2$
9. Urinary excretion
10. Comments

Table 5.6 : Contents of Drug Formulation Development Summary

1. Study number
2. Lot number
3. Dosage Form and Strength
4. Formulation Change (if any)
5. Reason for Formulation change
6. Effect of change

The summary of analytical methods used including major emphasis as sensitivity, linearity, specificity and reproducibility must be included.

The technical section must include individual study reports from any of five types of major biopharmaceutic studies that are :
1. Pilot or background studies.
2. Bioavailability or bioequivalence studies.
3. Pharmacokinetic studies.
4. Other in vivo studies.
5. In vitro studies.

The essential parameters to be included in the aforementioned O5 studies are summarized in Table 4.7

Table 4.7 : Contents of Major Biopharmaceutics Studies

Sr. No.	Name of study	Contents
1.	Pilot or background studies	Preliminary assessment of ADME information to design further kinetic studies and early clinical trials.
2.	Bioavailability or bioequivalence studies	Establishment of rate and extent of absorption, equivalent extents, dosage strength equivalence studies etc.
3.	Pharmacokinetic studies	Design to define time course, major metabolite concentration of drug, rate of elimination, dose dependent changes in particular kinetic parameters. Influence of demographic factors (e.g. Age, gender, race, disease etc.), binding to different biological constituents (e.g. plasma protein binding).
4.	Other in vivo studies	To employ pharmacological or clinical measurements or endpoint in animals or humans.
5.	In vitro studies	Design to define drug release pattern, from batch to batch to assure consistency and characterization of drug moiety.

Section 7 : Microbiology

It is applicable to any anti-infective agents as these drugs affect pathogens, physiology and not that of patient. It is design to check effectiveness of the drug moiety itself, its comparison with closely related established antimicrobial drug and potential to develop the resistance. The section consist of description of following areas :

(a) Biochemical basis of drug action.

(b) Antimicrobial spectrum of the drug.

(c) Any known mechanism of resistance to the drug and epidemiology regarding prevalence to resistance factor.

(d) Clinical microbiology laboratory methods.

Section 8 : Clinical Data

This information is submitted to understand overall safety and effectiveness of the compound. It is further divided into following sections.

(a) List of investigators, list of INDs and NDAs : It includes alphabetical list along with their address, study identifier and its location in NDA of all investigator who have used any dosage form. Also provides list of all known IND under which the drug in any dosage form has been investigated and other relevant NDA of which the applicant is aware.

(b) Background or overview of clinical investigations : It should discuss general approach and rationale used like number of patients, duration, selection criteria etc. in the development of clinical data. Also provide relevant references if study deviated from FDA clinical guidelines. The reason for selection of particular area (e.g. Drug interactions or gender specificity) shall be addressed along with discussion on safety issues raised by other drugs from the same pharmacologic class. It shall also answer the typical queries raised during clinical trails of similar drug conducted earlier.

(c) Clinical pharmacology : It should include brief synopsis followed by overall summary (including name of investigator, study number, start up date, location, etc.) for pharmacokinetic, pharmacodynamic and dose response studies in appropriate format. The control clinical trials section should be submitted in its designated format. The uncontrolled clinical trials may be used as supporting documents to controlled trials and to provide critical safety information as it usually doesn't contribute to any substantial evidence for the effectiveness of the drug.

(d) Other studies and information : It includes description and analysis of any additional information that applicant has obtained from any other source.

The information that is to be incorporated includes list of countries wherein drug is approved, rejected, copies of approved labeling from major regions of the globe and reports from the literature, not provided elsewhere in the NDA.

- **(e) Integrated summary of effectiveness data :** It is information to demonstrate appropriate evidences of effectiveness for each claimed indication. These evidences must include well controlled studies followed by their analysis. If the results don't support the anticipated conclusion, then explanation for the same shall be included. The detailed preclinical data (pharmacokinetic as well as pharmacodynamic) and its use for the various parameters like dose, dose interval, selection method of titration etc. must be incorporated.
- **(f) Integrated summary of safety information :** It include safety data from all sources consisting of preclinical as well as clinical studies and foreign marketing experience. The details of patients related factors like dose and duration of exposure, gender, groups and sub-groups etc. must be included in tabular format. It also describe demographic characteristics of entire population used, followed by narrative discussion of adverse events observed in entire studies. The analysis and comparison of these adverse events with respect to dose, duration, cumulative dose and other variables is also a part of this section.
- **(g) Drug abuse and overdose :** It include detailed description of studies regarding abuse of the drug. It is necessary to include proposal for scheduling as per controlled substances act, if the drug has potential for abuse.

Section 9 : Safety Update Reports

The newly available safety data must be included in pending application, if the data could affect statement of draft labeling, warnings, contra indications, precautions and adverse events. These reports are used to submit any new final report which may impact review time. Safety report updates are submitted 120 days after the initial application, following the receipt of an approval letter.

Section 10 : Statistics

It includes description and documentation of the statistical analysis carried out to evaluate controlled clinical trials and other safety information. This section must include copies of all controlled clinical trial reports, integrated summary of efficacy, safety and risk benefits ratio.

Section 11 : Case Report for Tabulations

It includes complete tabulation for each patient from phase I clinical pharmacology study to phase III efficacy study. It must also include tabulations of safety data from all clinical studies.

Section 12 : Case Report forms

It is mandatory to include complete case report forms for each patient who either have died during the study or dropped from the study due to an adverse event regardless of whether patient was receiving drug or placebo. Additional CRF's (CRO's) must be provided if requested by the FDA.

Recently ICH has developed a Common Technical Document (CTD) to stream-line regulatory submission in three major regions of the globe i.e. Europe, United States and Japan. It includes data related to clinical, non-clinical and manufacturing of the drug.

There are well-defined modules with a specific structure and numbering of sections within the modules. Module 1 is not harmonized and contains separate document for each of the above mentioned region.

The use of CTD format provides benefit to the industry as well as regulatory agency as it enhances communication; simplify exchange of information between regulatory authorities as well as applicant and regulatory agency. In addition, it reduces time courses and resources necessary for sponsor to compile global registration applications. Flexible but comprehensive utilization of multi-regional resources is an added advantage of this CTD.

Chapter 6...

ABBREVIATED NEW DRUG APPLICATION (ANDA)

A generic drug has similar effects in terms of its rate and extent of absorption of an approved product, which has to be proved by the generic company. In other words the generic drug has similar effects in curing a disease as the approved product. The generic approval process is called Abbreviated New drug Application (ANDA).

ANDA approval for a pharmaceutical product authorizes and certifies an entry of a generic version of innovator product into the market. ANDAs are used when the patent of a innovator drug is expired or is scheduled to expire. The Pharmaceutical companies are continually working on discovering & developing new drugs to treat diseases. The process of drug discovery and development is complex, elaborate and requires huge investment in terms of money and time. It is estimated that innovator Pharma company spends over 1BN US$ (over 5000 crore rupees) and 12 to 15 years to discover & develop a new drug. In nutshell, a journey of a new Pharmaceutical product from laboratory to pharmacy shop requires 12 to 15 years and over 5000 crores rupees. This journey starts with synthesizing 5000 to 7000 compunds out of which one becomes a successful drug after lengthy preclinical and clinical trials.

At the successful completion of lengthy human clinical trials, the innovator files a New Drug Application (NDA) submission with the FDA seeking to bring the new compound to market. In order to recapture the investment, the innovator company seeks the intellectual property rights in terms of patents for the developed product. Patent right for the product gives the innovator company an assurance of return on investment and time which is been spent while developing the product.

As discussed in above paragraph, after the IND (investigational new drug) filing with the FDA, it takes around 10 years for a NCE (new chemical entity) to pass through the three phases of clinical trials and get the final FDA (Food & Drug Administration) approval to market the product. The innovator company applies for the patent (exclusive right to manufacture & market) to USPTO (United States Patent & Trademark Office) or concerned patent authority of the country of origin at the time of the IND filing and receives the grant for the patent which has a life of 20 years. In this context, a drug ultimately enjoys patent protection after its market launch for only around 10 years. During this 10 years period, the innovator company enjoys the monopoly and tries to recover the cost of development of the product and earns moderate profits.

The generic pharmaceutical company, seeking to market an equivalent to an innovator's product (once the market exclusivity on the innovator's product has expired), uses a significantly less costly and faster process, the Abbreviated New Drug Application (ANDA) process. It is essential to understand that the generic manufacturer relies on the safety and efficacy data supplied by the innovator, and only has to prove to the FDA that its product is equivalent to the innovator product.

The ANDA should propose the same active ingredient without any change in the conditions originally approved. Moreover the generic companies filing ANDAs are required to prove that this generic version of the innovator product meets bioavailability, bioequivalence, pharmaceutical equivalence dose, dosage form, strength etc. of the standard.

When processing an ANDA, the FDA waives the requirement for conducting complete clinical studies as safety and efficacy have already been established by the innovator company. However, it usually requires the generic manufacturer to conduct bioavailability and/or bioequivalence studies.

Bioavailability studies assess the rate and extent of absorption and levels of concentration of a drug in the blood stream needed to produce a therapeutic effect. Bioequivalence studies compare the bioavailability of one drug product with another, in this case the innovator's product. When bioequivalence is established, it indicates that the rate of absorption and the levels of concentration of a generic product are substantially equivalent to the innovator product.

The ANDA process eliminates the lengthy and costly clinical research phase of development. As a result, generic pharmaceutical product development takes approximately 18 to 24 months.

The FDA also requires that a company's manufacturing methods conform to current Good Manufacturing Practices (cGMP), as defined by regulatory authorities. The company must follow the cGMPs in all phases of the manufacturing process, and must continually monitor compliance and measure quality control. If the FDA believes that a company is not in compliance with cGMP, it can impose sanctions including initiating an action that can result in the recall of products already sold into the marketplace, withholding new product approvals, disqualifying a company from supplying products to federal agencies, or preventing a company from exporting products.

ANDA - Growth Opportunity to Generic Pharmaceutical Companies :

ANDA filings are turning out to be big growth opportunity to many generic Pharma companies. Under the provisions, first to file generic company gains 180 days exclusivity if the patent expiry is due for innovator product (where the patent expiry is due). The 180 days exclusivity can help the generic company earn millions of dollars. (During the exclusivity period, only innovator and first to file generic company is allowed to sale the product).

The "Waxman-Hatch Act" provides this exclusivity provision as an incentive for generic firms to invest in the lengthy and expensive process of challenging suspect patents that protect innovator drug product. This benefit is passed along to the consumer by having access to high quality and cost effective drugs.

After the expiry of a patent, generic companies immediately launch the products and consequently, there is a sharp downward correction in the price of the particular drug. The fall in prices can be as much as 90% depending upon the number of generic manufacturers and the nature of the drug. The fall in prices also result in a fall in the margins for the innovator drug. The generic market has witnessed significant growth over the years all over the world.

Requirements for Filing an ANDA

At the time of filing an AND application, the applicant seeking approval of a particular drug (innovator drug or patent expired drug) make one of four certifications about the legal status of patent status. They are :

- The required patent information has not been filed.
- That the patent has expired.
- That the patent has not expired, but will expire on a particular date.
- That the patent is unenforceable, invalid or will not be infringed by the drug for which the ANDA applicant seeks approval (paragraph IV).

What happens if there are more than one ANDAs for a Particular Drug ?

In instances where more than one ANDA has been filed on a particular drug, the first filed ANDA may be entitled to 180 day of marketing exclusivity following approval against later filed ANDAs. It is usually the case that the first generic company to market will acquire a larger market share. Therefore, an important marketing benefit is provided to the first ANDA applicant who is entitled to 180 day marketing exclusivity.

Types of ANDA Filing

While filing an ANDA, the generic company has to choose one of the following four options (referred to as paras) :

- **Para I :** The drug has not been patented.
- **Para II :** The patent for the drug has already expired.
- **Para III :** The patent for the product exists but the generic company wants to enter the markets after the date of patent expiry passes.
- **Para IV :** Patent is not infringed upon or is invalid.

In case of Para I and Para II filing, once the application is deemed complete, it is simply processed for approval. In case of Para III the application is processed for approval, however its approval status depends upon the products patent expiry. Apparently Para IV filings are the most lucrative, tedious, time consuming and expensive of the above.

In a Para III filing the company acknowledges the patent of the approved drug and intends to enter the market after the patent for the approved product expires and there exists a scenario of falling prices for the drug, whereas in Para IV filing the company claims that the generic product of the company does not infringe upon the existing patent or the patent of the branded product is invalid and the company strives to win an exclusivity of 180 days during which the margins for the product are very high.

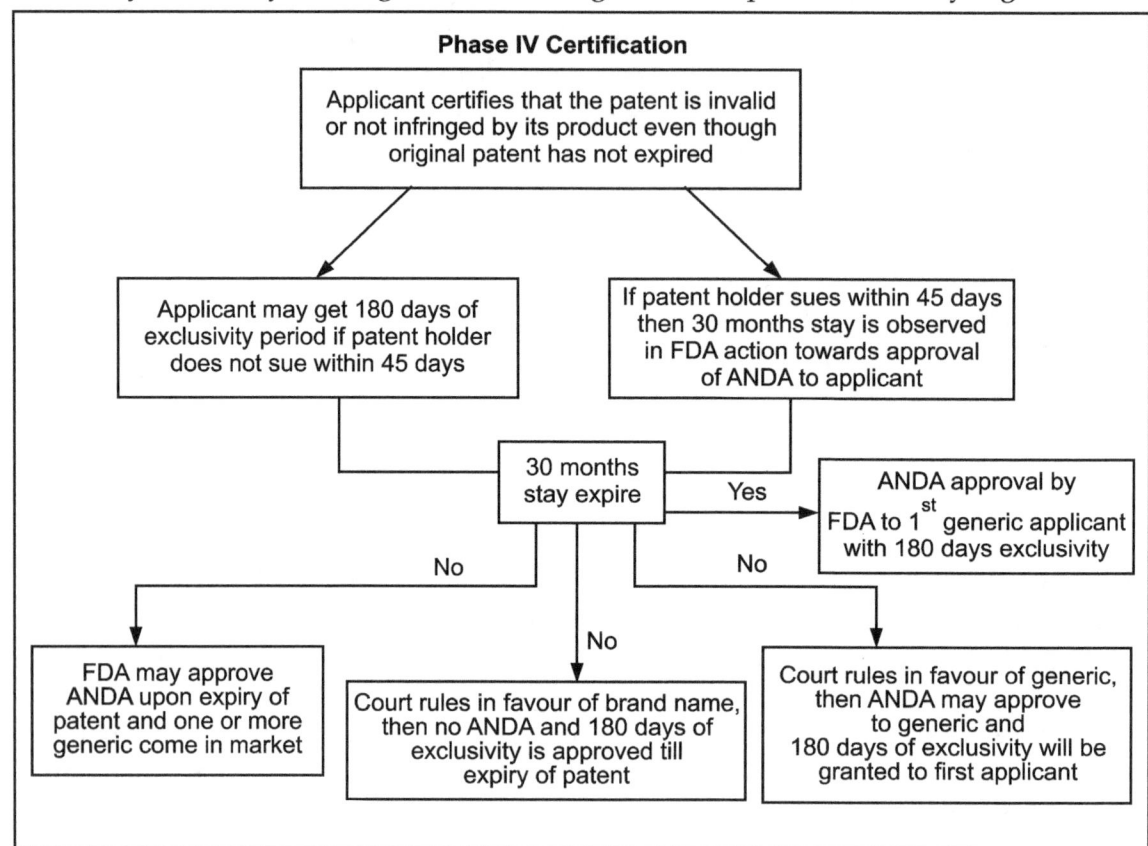

Fig. 6.1 : The approval process of the Para IV

Chapter 7...
DRUG MASTER FILE

A Drug Master File (DMF) is a submission to the United States Food and Drug Administration (USFDA) or to the concerned regulatory authority that may be used to provide confidential and detailed information on facilities, processes or articles used in the manufacturing, processing, packaging or storing of one or more human drugs.

Submission of DMF is not mandatory by law or FDA regulations, however offers guidance on acceptable approaches to meet the regulatory requirements, but submitted solely at the discretion of the holder. The information contained in the DMF may be used to support an Investigational New Drug Application (IND); a New Drug Application (NDA) and Abbreviated New Drug Application (ANDA), another DMF, an export application or amendments and supplements to any of these.

The DMF is not substitute for an INDA, NDA, ANDA or export application. In addition, it is not approved or disapproved. Technical contents of a DMF are reviewed only in connection with the review of an INDA, NDA, ANDA or an export application.

In general, DMFs are usually created to allow the agency other than holder of the DMF to refer to the material without disclosing the content of the file.

Types of drug master files:

There are five types of DMFs each containing only one type of information and all supporting data. This data can be cross referenced to any other DMF. The details are explained in Table 7.1.

Table 7.1 : Types of Drug Master File

Type	Essential Content
I.	Manufacturing site, facilities, operating procedures and personnel.
II.	Drug substance, drug substance intermediate, drug material used and drug product.
III.	Packing material.
IV.	Excipient, flavour, essence, colorant and material used in the preparation.
V.	FDA accepted reference information.

Submission of DMF

Each submission must contain a transmittal letter and adequate administrative information. It must be written in English. If it contains information in another language, then must be supported with accurate certified English translation. Each page of every copy of the DMF should be dated and consecutively numbered along with updated table of contents.

The essential contents of transmittal letter and administrative information are discussed in Table 7.2.

Table 7.2 : Essential Contents of Transmittal letters

Sr. No.	Content	Details
1.	Original Submissions	Name and address of each sponsor, applicant or holder.
		Signature of the holder or authorized representative.
		Typewritten name and title of the signer.
2.	Amendments	The DMF number, type of DMF and the subject of the amendments.
		Short description of the purpose of submission like update revised formula or process.
		Signature of the holder or authorized representative.
		Typewritten name and title of signer.

Table 7.3 : Essential Contents of Administrative Information

Sr. No.	Content	Details
1.	Original Submissions	Name and addresses and specific responsibilities of DMF holder, corporate headquarter, manufacturing or processing facility, contact of FDA correspondence and agent(s), if any.
		Statement Commitment
		A signed statement by the holder certifying that the DMF is current and that the DMF holder will comply with the statement made in it.
2.	Amendments	Name of DMF holder, DMF number, name and address of correspondence affected section and/or page number of the DMF.
		The name and address of each person whose IND, NDA, ANDA, DMF or export applications relies on the subject of the amendment for support.

Types of Drug Master Files :

Type I : Manufacturing Site, Facilities, Operating Procedures and Personnel :

Type I is recommended for a person outside the United States to assist FDA conducting on site inspections of their manufacturing facilities. This DMF shall describe manufacturing site including acreage, site address, map showing location with respect to nearest city, equipment in terms of capabilities, application location and operational layout.

Domestic facilities need to be described in special cases like when person is not either registered or routinely inspected. Making of model is required only when apparatus is unique.

A diagrammatic presentation of major corporate elements of organization, key position in the area of quality control, quality assurance and manufacturing may be given to ease the process.

Type II : Drug Substance, Drug Substance Intermediate and Material Used in Their Preparation or Drug Product :

It should be limited to single drug intermediate, drug substance, drug product and drug materials used in their preparation. It shall summaries all significant steps in the manufacturing and controls of the drug intermediates substance.

Manufacturing procedures and controls for finished dosage forms shall be submitted here if earlier not submitted in INDA, NDA, ANDA or export application.

Type III : Packing Material :

Each packaging material shall be identified by the intended use, components, composition controls for its release. The names of the suppliers or fabricators of the component of packaging material along with accepted specifications should be mentioned. The relevant data supporting the acceptability of the packaging material for its intended use shall be submitted as mentioned in the standard guidelines.

Toxicological data on these materials would be included under this type of DMF, if not otherwise available by cross reference to another document.

Type IV : Excipient, Colorant, Flavors, Essence or Material Used in Preparation :

Each additive should be identified and characterised by its method of manufacture, release specifications and testing methods along with its toxicological data should be submitted.

Once the submission is over, then regulatory department act, as a connecting bridge between company and reviewing agency wherein it has to reply to queries and questions raised by the agent within demanding time frame.

Type V : FDA Accepted Reference Information

FDA discourages the use of Type V DMFs for miscellaneous information, duplicate information, or information that should be included in one of the other types of DMFs. If any holder wishes to submit information and supporting data in a DMF that is not covered by Types I through IV, a holder must first submit a letter of intent to the Drug Master File Staff. FDA will then contact the holder to discuss the proposed submission.

General Information and Suggestions

(a) Environmental Assessment :

Type II, Type III, and Type IV DMFs should contain a commitment by the firm that its facilities will be operated in compliance with applicable environmental laws. If a completed environmental assessment is needed, see 21 CFR Part 25.

(b) Stability :

Stability study design, data, interpretation, and other information should be submitted, when applicable, as outlined in the "*Guideline for Submitting Documentation for the Stability of Human Drugs and Biologics.*"

(c) Format, Assembly and Delivery :

An original and a duplicate copies are to be submitted for all DMF submissions.

Drug Master File holders and their agents/representatives should retain a complete reference copy that is identical to, and maintained in the same chronological order as, their submissions to FDA.

The original and duplicate copies must be collated, fully assembled, and individually jacketed.

Each volume of a DMF should, in general, be no more than 2 inches thick. For multivolume submissions, number each volume. For example, for a 3 volume submission, the volumes would be numbered 1 of 3, 2 of 3 and 3 of 3.

U.S. standard paper size (8-1/2 by 11 inches) is preferred.

Paper length should not be less than 10 inches nor more than 12 inches. However, it may occasionally be necessary to use individual pages larger than standard paper size to present a floor plan, synthesis diagram, batch formula, or manufacturing instructions. Those pages should be folded and mounted to allow the page to be opened for review without disassembling the jacket and refolded without damage when the volume is shelved.

Drug Master File submissions and correspondence should be addressed as follows :

Drug Master File Staff
Food and Drug Administration
5901-B Ammendale Rd.
Beltsville, MD 20705-1266

Letter of Authorization to FDA

Before FDA can review DMF information in support of an application, the DMF holder must submit in duplicate to the DMF a letter of authorization permitting FDA to reference the DMF. If the holder cross references its own DMF, the holder should supply in a letter of authorization the information designated by items 3, 5, 6, 7, and 8 of this section. The holder does not need to send a transmittal letter with its letter of authorization.

The letter of authorization should include the following:
1. The date.
2. Name of DMF holder.
3. DMF number.
4. Name of person(s) authorized to incorporate information in the DMF by reference.
5. Specific product(s) covered by the DMF.
6. Submission date(s) of 5, above.
7. Section numbers and/or page numbers to be referenced.
8. Statement of commitment that the DMF is current and that the DMF holder will comply with the statements made in it.
9. Signature of authorizing official.
10. Typed name and title of official authorizing reference to the DMF.

DMF is never Approved or Disapproved

The agency will review information in a DMF only when an IND sponsor, an applicant for an NDA, ANDA, or Export Application, or another DMF holder incorporates material in the DMF by reference. As noted, the incorporation by reference must be accompanied by a copy of the DMF holder's letter of authorization.

If FDA reviewers find deficiencies in the information provided in a DMF, a letter describing the deficiencies is sent to the DMF holder. At the same time, FDA will notify the person who relies on the information in the deficient DMF that additional information is needed in the supporting DMF. The general subject of the deficiency is identified, but details of the deficiency are disclosed only to the DMF holder. When the holder submits the requested information to the DMF in response to the agency's deficiency letter, the holder should also send a copy of the accompanying transmittal letter to the affected persons relying on the DMF and to the FDA reviewing division that identified the deficiencies. The transmittal letter will provide notice that the deficiencies have been addressed.

Annual Update

The holder should provide an annual report which will describe all the changes and additional information incorporated into the DMF since the previous annual report on the subject matter of the DMF. If the subject matter of the DMF is unchanged, the DMF holder should provide a statement that the subject matter of the DMF is current.

Failure to update or to assure FDA annually that previously submitted material and lists in the DMF remain current can cause delays in FDA review of a pending IND, NDA, ANDA, Export Application, or any amendment or supplement to such application; and FDA can initiate procedures for closure of the DMF.

(Ref. : the above information is derived from the website of USFDA www.usfda.gov)

C. T. D. FORMAT DRUG MASTER FILE

INDEX

Part	Data Module	Page No.
2.0	**Common Technical Document Summaries**	
2.3.S	**Quality Overall Summary**	
2.3.S.1	General Information	
2.3.S.2	Manufacture	
2.3.S.3	Characterization	
2.3.S.4	Control of the drug Substance	
2.3.S.5	Reference Standard	
2.3.S.6	Container Closure System	
2.3.S.7	Stability	
3.0	**Quality (Chemical and Pharmaceutical Information)**	
3.2.S	**Drug Substance**	
3.2.S.1	**General Information**	
3.2.S.1.1	*Nomenclature*	
3.2.S.1.2	Structure	
3.2.S.1.3	General Properties	
3.2.S.2	**Manufacturer**	
3.2.S.2.1	Manufacturer	
3.2.S.2.2	Description of Manufacturing Process and Process Controls	

3.2.S.2.2.1	Flow Chart of Manufacturing Process	
3.2.S.2.2.2	Synthetic Route of Manufacturing Process	
3.2.S.2.2.3	Manufacturing Process Details	
3.2.S.2.3	Control of Raw Materials	
3.2.S.2.4	Controls of Critical Steps and Intermediates	
3.2.S.2.5	Process Validation	
3.2.S.2.6	Manufacturing Process Development	
3.2.S.3	**Characterisation**	
3.2.S.3.1	Elucidation of Structure	
3.2.S.3.1.1	Elemental Analysis	
3.2.S.3.1.2	Infra Red Spectrum of the Drug Substance	
3.2.S.3.1.3	NMR Spectrum of the Drug Substance	
3.2.S.3.1.4	Mass Spectrum of the Drug Substance	
3.2.S.3.1.5	UV Spectrum of the Drug Substance	
3.2.S.3.2	Impurities	
3.2.S.3.2.1	Potential Impurities	
3.2.S.3.2.2	Analysis of Working Standard for Determination of Potential Impurities	
3.2.S.3.2.3	Validation of Analytical Methodology for the Estimation of Potential Impurities	
3.2.S.3.2.4	Residual Solvent Impurities	
3.2.S.3.2.5	Validation of Analytical Methodology for the Estimation of Residual Solvent Impurities	
3.2.S.4	**Control of Drug Substances**	
3.2.S.4.1	Specification	
3.2.S.4.2	Analytical Procedures	
3.2.S.4.3	Validation of Analytical Procedure	
3.2.S.4.4	Batch Analysis	
3.2.S.4.4.1	Certificates of Analysis	
3.2.S.4.5	Justification of specification	

3.2.S.5	**Reference Standards**	
3.2.S.6	**Container and Closure System**	
3.2.S.6.1	Packaging Details	
3.2.S.6.2	Specification for Packaging Materials	
3.2.S.7	**Stability**	
3.2.S.7.1	Stability Summary and Conclusions	
3.2.S.7.2	Post Approval Stability Protocol and Stability Commitment	
3.2.S.7.3	Stability Data	

C.T.D. FORMAT DRUG MASTER FILE
(OPEN PART)
INDEX

Part	Data Module	Page No.
2.0	**Common Technical Document Summaries**	
2.3.S	**Quality Overall Summary**	
2.3.S.1	General Information	
2.3.S.2	Manufacture	
2.3.S.3	Characterization	
2.3.S.4	Control of the drug Substance	
2.3.S.5	Reference Standard	
2.3.S.6	Container Closure System	
2.3.S.7	Stability	
3.0	**Quality (Chemical and Pharmaceutical Information)**	
3.2.S	**Drug Substance**	
3.2.S.1	**General Information**	
3.2.S.1.1	*Nomenclature*	
3.2.S.1.2	Structure	
3.2.S.1.3	General Properties	
3.2.S.2	**Manufacturer**	
3.2.S.2.1	Manufacturer	

3.2.S.2.2	Description of Manufacturing Process and Process Controls	
3.2.S.2.2.1	Flow Chart of Manufacturing Process	
3.2.S.2.2.2	Synthetic Route of Manufacturing Process	
3.2.S.2.2.3	–	
3.2.S.2.3	–	
3.2.S.2.4	–	
3.2.S.2.5	–	
3.2.S.2.6	–	
3.2.S.3	**Characterisation**	
3.2.S.3.1	Elucidation of Structure	
3.2.S.3.1.1	Elemental Analysis	
3.2.S.3.1.2	Infra Red Spectrum of the Drug Substance	
3.2.S.3.1.3	NMR Spectrum of the Drug Substance	
3.2.S.3.1.4	Mass Spectrum of the Drug Substance	
3.2.S.3.1.5	UV Spectrum of the Drug Substance	
3.2.S.3.2	Impurities	
3.2.S.3.2.1	Potential Impurities	
3.2.S.3.2.2	Analysis of Working Standard for Determination of Potential Impurities	
3.2.S.3.2.3	Validation of Analytical Methodology for the Estimation of Potential Impurities	
3.2.S.3.2.4	Residual Solvent Impurities	
3.2.S.3.2.5	Validation of Analytical Methodology for the Estimation of Residual Solvent Impurities	
3.2.S.4	**Control Of Drug Substances**	
3.2.S.4.1	Specification	
3.2.S.4.2	Analytical Procedures	
3.2.S.4.3	Validation of Analytical Procedure	
3.2.S.4.4	Batch Analysis	
3.2.S.4.4.1	Certificates of Analysis	

3.2.S.5	**Reference Standards**
3.2.S.6	**Container and Closure System**
3.2.S.6.1	Packaging Details
3.2.S.6.2	Specification for Packaging Materials
3.2.S.7	**Stability**
3.2.S.7.1	Stability Summary and Conclusions
3.2.S.7.2	Post Approval Stability Protocol and Stability Commitment
3.2.S.7.3	Stability Data

C.T.D. FORMAT DRUG MASTER FILE
(CLOSE PART)
INDEX

3.2.S.2	**Manufacturer**
3.2.S.2.1	Manufacturer
3.2.S.2.2	Description of Manufacturing Process and Process Controls
3.2.S.2.2.1	Flow Chart of Manufacturing Process
3.2.S.2.2.2	Synthetic Route of Manufacturing Process
3.2.S.2.2.3	Manufacturing Process Details
3.2.S.2.3	Control of Raw Materials
3.2.S.2.4	Controls of Critical Steps and Intermediates
3.2.S.2.5	Process Validation
3.2.S.2.6	Manufacturing Process Development
3.2.S.4.5	Justification of specification
3.2.S.5	**Reference Standards**
3.2.S.6	**Container and Closure System**
3.2.S.6.1	Packaging Details
3.2.S.6.2	Specification for Packaging Materials

Chapter 8...
ORPHAN DRUG

Orphan drugs are those which have low commercial value, but are necessary and at times life saving for patient with rare disease. The rare disease is one which the number of people affecting are lower than 2,00,000 in United States. In order to aid the manufacturing of orphan drugs, government of United State signed a law in 1983 wherein attractive financial incentives were offered to the pharmaceutical industry.

The most significant incentive is marketing exclusivity for the period of 07 years for an orphan designated product that receives FDA market approval for same indication followed by tax credits for clinical research expenses, grants to fund investigation of rare diseases treatment studies etc.

Inspite of above promoting aids for orphan drug development process, small size of population available coupled with no opportunity to go back and restudy is a major challenge to get FDA approval. In United States, in 1982 the Office of Product Development (OOPD) continuously assist and encourage the development of orphan drug. It reviews scientific rationale of the proposal, confirm disease prevalence and designate the product that qualify as orphan drug. The grant of funds is another responsibility of OOPD however it is not restrict to drug or biologic product but also include clinical studies for medical foods and devices that meet the criteria of orphan drug. In addition, OOPD brings pharmaceutical company and researcher together to facilitate orphan drug development with alternate sources of funding.

Any product which is previously not approved or having new indication for an already marketed drug can apply for orphan drug designation. It is mandatory to obtain orphan drug designation before sponsor can obtain any direct financial benefit. More than one sponsor may receive designation for same drug indicated for same disease or disorder upon submission of complete request for designation before submission of a marketing application. The common contents of the application is described in Table 8.1.

The drug can be designated as a orphan drug when intended for "medically plausible subset" wherein particular subset is required and not a orbitary subset. e.g. If drug is toxic in patient with specified condition except those who are refractory to other available less toxic drugs, then this refractory patients may be treated as medically plausible subset to get orphan drug designation. Whereas making an orbitary group of patient with hypertension having specified rare condition does not comply the definition of medically plausible subset. Similarly pediatric population may be accepted as a subset for the orphan drug designation for the new drug or already available approved drug for adults. This is due to wide difference in the pharmacokinetic pattern in the pediatric population as compared to the adults.

Table 8.1 : Common Content of Orphan Drug Application

1.	A statement indication request for orphan drug designation for rare disease/disorder.
2.	A description of rare disease or disorder supported with the need of therapy.
3.	Proposed indication (s) for the use of the drug.
4.	A brief description of drug and discussion of the scientific rationale for the use of the drug.
5.	Provide relevant documentation to prove that particular condition for which the drug is intended, affect less than 2,00,000 people in United States.
6.	A summary of the regulatory status and marketing history of the drug in the U.S. and outside the U.S.
7.	Evidence to demonstrate that a proposed indication intended for a subset of person with a particular disease or condition comply the definition of "medically plausible subset".

Although the patient population is the major criteria for the orphan drug designation, it is not a simple job. As per the orphan drug regulation, the prevalence is a number of patients in US who have been diagnosed for particular condition at the time of submission of the application. Moreover, there is no standard.

Source providing prevalence data, rather each indication need independent evaluation of best available source. However, OOPD follows certain principles mentioned below to verify the prevalence estimate submitted in applications for orphan designation.

1. Primary Medical Literature (Referred journals and periodicals).
2. Secondary Medical Literatures (Text books).
3. Federal Agencies (e.g. CDC, HCFA etc.)
4. Rare disease organisations.
5. Affidavits from experts in the specific medical specialty.

The tax credit provisions as per the orphan drugs act is another assistance provided to the sponsor which is monitored by the internal revenue service. The sponsor also provided with the facility of carry back or carry forward of unused credit to carry the excess credit back one tax year if unused either partly or fully. This is possible because of the tax liability limit and to then carry any additional unused credit forward for upto 20 tax years after the year of the credit.

The FDA funds the development of orphan products through its grants program for clinical studies. In response to the announcement regarding the anticipated availability of funds every year, applicants can propose one discrete clinical study intended to facilitate FDA approval of the product. It is mandatory for the applicant to conduct funded study under an Investigational New Drug (IND) or an Investigational Device Exemption (IDE). However, medical food is exempted. In addition, the study must comply all regulatory requirements at the time of submission of application.

Funds for phase I clinical trials that may be granted is upto 1,50,000 US$ per year for a minimum period of 03 years while for that of phase II and III studies, it may be upto 3,00,000 US $. The number of projects funded each year and amount of funds is dependent on wholesome of amount available each year. The studies who are in their 2nd or 3rd year (on going studies) are having preference than that of new studies. The satisfactory progress towards the protocol goal is the major criteria for continuation of funding.

The academic institutes, other foreign or domestic, private or public and profit or non-profit organisations are eligible for the application. Generally phase I and II studies are completed by the academic investigators providing initial data necessary to attract commercial sponsorship for further development.

Once the application is submitted for the grant, it is reviewed for the suitability. The major parameters that are observed are summarised in Table 8.2. If the study do not comply any of the mentioned parameter then termed as non-responsive study which is returned to the applicant without further consideration or review. The acceptable application are then received for its scientific and technical merits by the panel of experts from the respective field. From the review (which also consider recommendations made during level I of review) a rank ordered priority scores and a final awards are made.

Table 8.2 : Major Parameters Required to Grant a Fund

1.	Assurance to conduct the proposed study under an active IND/IDE.
2.	To verify the protocol for its intension to provide safety and/efficacy data of one therapy for one indication which must be rare as per the definition of prevalence.
3.	Availability of minimum required number of patient for the complete study.
4.	Budget proposed for the study is appropriate or not.

Once study is granted, then the regular progress can be monitored by the principal investigator through telephonic or e-communication and/or by personal discussion with the project officers. In addition, officials of grantee organisation conduct periodic visit to the site to know the overall development.

The limited number of patients available for the clinical study is major limitation and hence systematic design of the study, coupled with careful analysis of risk/benefit ratio is required to collect adequate data to demonstrate effectiveness and to determine the optimal dosage.

FDA also serious towards the acceleration of review of drugs and biologics intended to treat serious and life threatening condition. FDA further can designate a drug 'Fast-track" when it is likely to provide significant clinical benefits. The NDA for orphan drugs is also reviewed within accelerated time frame however it do not assure the approval of drug marketing.

Under an accelerated approval procedure, a new drug or biologic can be approved upon sponsor establish that product has an surrogate end point (based upon adequate and well controlled trials) that is likely to predict clinical benefit. The use of surrogate end points in clinical trials hasten the process of new drug development for the treatment of a serious or life threatening condition. Various laboratory tests or physical signs that do not themselves constitutes any clinical effect but when judged by a well qualified scientist are likely to predict clinical benefits are common surrogate end points.

These surrogate end points are helpful to receive "fast track" approval however further post approval studies to validate the end points or confirmation of clinical end point may be required.

■■■

Chapter 9...
BIOLOGICAL LICENSING APPLICATION (BLA)

The classification of a particular product as a biologic is the outcome of more than 100 years of interaction between science and legislation. However, the resultant classification is still inconsistent as well as confusing too.

Initially, i.e. at the start of 20th century, when there were no FDA and its laws for drug product but the research advancement in the field of vaccine production was going on. These vaccines were widely used to protect from small pox, rabies, cholera, typhoid etc. without any concern for its safety, until the incidence of death of 13 children in St. Louis in October 1901, due to administration of unsafe diphtheria antitoxin (that was contaminated with tetanus toxin). Immediately after this, in 1902 the Biologics Control Act was passed by the congress. According to this act, biologics products were defined as "Any virus, serum, toxin, antitoxin, therapeutic serum, vaccine, blood, blood component or derivative, allergenic product or analogous products applicable to prevent, treat or cure diseases or injuries in man". The act further provided provision from licensure requirements to revocation of licenses. This act (with minor changes into Section 351 of the public health service done in 1994) is a current basis for the FDA regulations that cover biologic products as published in the Code of Federal Regulations (CFR).

These regulations were further strengthen and transferred to newly created division of biologics standard, an independent entity with ICH after salk polio vaccine tragedy in 1955, wherein about 200 peoples suffered from paralytic polio who either received vaccine or were in close vaccine contact. The major reason was inadequate inactivation of virus. Further in 1972, congress transferred this responsibility to FDA from NIH with the renaming of division of biologics as Bureau of biologics which in 1982 merged with the Bureau of drugs to form the national center for drugs and biologics. The regulation of drugs and biologics were again separated in the year 1988 into and the Center for biologics evaluation and research (CBER) and the Centre for Drug Evaluation and Research (CDER).

The CBER regulate the market approval of biologic products. The regulations are same as that are for drugs and FD&C act. The FDA uses guidance document to convey their current thinking on various topics along with clarification how to interpret regulations. However neither FDA nor public is legally bound to this document.

Preclinical Issues

The preclinical studies are very important to demonstrate significant benefits by the administration of particular biologics for specific indication and to determine starting dose of clinical study. The in-vivo and in-vitro preclinical studies provide information ranging from toxicological profile of the product to pharmacodynamic picture.

The wide range of biological products like vaccines, therapeutic proteins, blood products, cytokines, monoclonal antibodies, gene therapy products etc. alongwith their diverse chemical composition of each product make preclinical study an essential tool for further research. Moreover due to above mentioned diversity, one toxicological program that fits all is not possible hence usually designed on a case by case basis.

The overall development process of the biologics is abstracted in Fig. 9.1.

```
Demonstrate that the proposed biological product is viable product to develop
                                    ↓
Ensure the company's ability to manufacture the product consistently
                                    ↓
Demonstrate potential benefits for the administration of product to human for a given condition
through detailed preclinical pharmacological studies
                                    ↓
Prepare design for Phase I clinical study based upon preclinical data and sought a permission
                                    ↓
Complete Phase I clinical trials
                                    ↓
Complete additional preclinical general toxicological studies if required
                                    ↓
Complete Phase II and III clinical studies
                                    ↓
Incorporate the results of above studies into the product labeling
```

Fig. 9.1 : General Process of Development of Biological Product

The toxicological profile of any biological product is crucial part in the process of development. Some toxicological studies are compulsory as per the standard guidelines, where some studies need to conduct on case to case basis. The various tests are summarised in Table 9.1.

Table 9.1 : Various Toxicology Test

- Safety pharmacology
- General toxicology
- Local tolerance studies*
- Immunogenicity studies*
- Reproductive toxicology*
- Single / complete genetic toxicology study*
- Additional general toxiclogy*
- Carcinogenecity*

* indicate optional test, design may be variable case to case.

The preclinical pharmacology studies are important especially at the pre IND and Phase I state of development. It includes in-vivo and in-vitro primary pharmadynamics, secondary pharmacodynamic studies and safety pharmacology studies. The selection of proper invitro tests like monoclonal antibodies binding studies and diseased animal model that mimic proposed clinical condition in human are critical parameters. The pharmacodynamic study design shall designed to give clear picture of risk and benefit analysis and suggest whether it should be administered to human volunteer for the first time or not. Secondary pharmacodynamic study do not directly related to the proposed indication but is an attempt to explore additional potential indications for a given biological product. The safety pharmacology study is another important mile stone that is conducted to investigate the potential undesirable pharmacodynamic effect on physiological function in relation to the therapeutic range and above. The core battery of studies includes effect on CVS, CNS and respiratory systems. These reports can be included in an IND submission as an value added information. The safety pharmacology studies can be reduced in number or can be eliminated in certain biotechnology derived product that have highly specific receptor targeting.

The pharmacokinetic studies examines the systemic exposure (Area under the curve) when administered by specific proposed route of administration followed by its comparison with I.V. administration. Other parameters include $t^{1}/_{2}$, T_{max} and C_{max} that are useful to determine the appropriate dosing regimen. Further tissue distribution study is required to find possible site of drug accumulation that may lead to potential organ toxicity. The pharmacokinetic as well as toxicokinetic study design may vary from product to product. For example, this data is very important for product like growth factors, monoclonal antibodies preparation while least useful for prophylactic vaccines.

As per the ICH S6 document, a classical biotransformation studies conducted for pharmaceuticals are not required as metabolic pathways of biotechnology derived products is well understood.

The pharmacodynamics studies usually explain benefits while toxicity studies demonstrate risk of the product and then the product comes to the stage of IND. At this point, preclinical toxicology data is very important to evaluate the risk of administration of the product to the human for the first time. Hence, the plan and execution of toxicological studies as per the FDA regulatory procedures specific to a product class, overall risk/benefit ratio analysis, evaluation of risk on a case by case basis etc. is a critical part.

Once the product is administered to the human in phase I clinical trials, then additional non-clinical general toxicology studies of increasing duration can be required to support Phase II and Phase III clinical trials. In case of occurrence of adverse events, an extended non-clinical toxicological studies may be requested by the FDA to understand its mechanism of action. If the product is to be administered to pregnant or child bearing women, then reproductive toxicology studies are necessary. The duration allotted for submission of the data to the FDA varies with respect to the product class. Ultimately, the entire results of preclinical and non-clinical toxicology must be included into the product labeling.

Overall any toxicology study should be completed in compliance with the GLP requirements and its study design should be based on the proposed clinical protocol. Normally acute and repeat dose toxicology study using two species (Rodent and Non-rodent) is a general requirement however certain parameters like product class, seriousness of product indication and availability of suitable animal model as discussed in Table 9.2 etc. can result in certain modifications. In addition, Maximum Proposed Human Dose (MPHD) and No Observed Adverse Effect Level (NOAEL) in repeat dose study should be included. The usual toxicological study parameters to be evaluated are clinical signs, body weight, food consumption, haematology, clinical chemistry, urinalysis, gross pathology, histopathology and mortality. The special observations include ECG, ophthalmologic evaluation, behavioural recording etc.

Table 9.2 : Relevant Animal Models of Various Product

Sr. No.	Product	Relevant Model Requirement
1.	Vaccine	One in which vaccine is immunogenic
2.	Monoclonal antibody	One in which the appropriate antigenic epitope is expressed in a similar manner to humans.
3.	Cytokine	One in which the cytokine demonstrate biological activity.

Note : In absence of relevant species, an appropriate transgenic animal model expressing the human receptor or use of homologous proteins is recommended by ICH S6 guidance document.

Specific safety considerations for each product class are important for design of a toxicology program. For example, immunogenicity (specific immune response) is essential part of mechanism of action of vaccine while. Same can be limitation (e.g. Inflammation at site of injection) for monoclonal antibody preparation. Such major concerns related to individual class is summarised in Table 9.3.

Table 9.3 : Major concerns of biological products

Sr. No.	Product	Relevant Model Requirement
1.	Prophylactic vaccines	Induction of non-specific antibodies, and IgE. Local site reactions, induction of undesirable cytokine production. Inflammatory response, autoimmunity.
2.	Cytokines	Exaggerated pharmacological response, immunogenecity, inflammation, haematological effects.
3.	Monoclonal antibody	Non-specific binding to tissues other than target tissue, immunogenicity.
4.	Gene therapy	Toxicity due to expression of the intended protein. Integration of DNA sequence into the genome. Distribution to tissues other than target tissues.
5.	Blood products	Formation of adhesions Intravascular clotting.

Overall toxicology study demonstrate possible risk associated with the product whereas pharmacodynamic data suggest potential benefits. At the stage of IND submission, the benefit must overpower the risk aspect. However, the seriousness of the proposed indication, proposed patient population and the availability of other effective treatments may affect the product licensing. In short, comparability more product risk is acceptable for serious and life threatening diseases, especially when there is no other effective treatment available.

BLA

The biologic control act introduced in 1902 and as per this, there were two applications : (1) Product License Application (PLA), (2) Establishment License Application (ELA) required till 1996. Later on, ELA was eliminated and a single form (Form 356 h) was introduced and actual application came in picture in 1999. Now the FDA conducts preapproval inspection to see establishment compliance with GMP prior to final approval of the BLA hence the information to be filled in new BLA form has been reduced drastically. Presently BLA for particular product can be submitted in the CTD format. The current review process is based upon number of guidance documents that provide information about the type of information to be included in the BLA for each biologic product class.

■■■

Chapter 10...

REGISTRATION OF DRUG PRODUCTS IN OVERSEAS MARKETS – PHARMACEUTICAL EXPORT

The Pharmaceutical Industry is one of the fastest growing sectors of the Indian economy and has made rapid strides over the years. From being an import dependent industry in 1950, the industry today, has not only achieved self-sufficiency but has become a major exporter of drugs and pharmaceuticals to more than 150 countries of the world. The leading Indian companies have established infrastructure over 60 plus countries like USA, Europe, Japan etc. who are the front leaders in the Pharmaceutical world.

The Indian Pharma industry has gained a global recognition for producing low cost high quality bulk drugs as well as formulations. The export turnover has reached over Rs. 25,000 crore by the end of year 2008-09 and is growing at a rate of 25% annually. It is predicted that in another 3 to 4 years, the export turnover will surpass the domestic turnover. The Indian drugs and pharmaceuticals are gaining wide acceptance in all the countries. Indian drugs are providing a healing touch not only to our people in India but also to many other developed, developing and underdeveloped countries.

The Indian Pharmaceutical companies are now concentrating on the export markets and are building their marketing network in these markets. Looking at the scenario, export is the biggest growth opportunity for the Indian Pharma Industry in near future.

Stepwise Procedure for Export of Pharmaceuticals Products

Before the Pharmaceutical Company starts actual export of their products to any country, it is very important to understand the pre-requisites like:

- Registration of the products with the respective statutory authority.
- Appointment of agent / representative in that country.

Registration with the respective regulatory authorities like in USA it is USFDA (United States Food and Drugs Administration), in UK it is MHRA (Medicine and Healthcare Regulatory Agency), in Australia it is TGA (Therapeutic Goods

Administration) and so on is must before exporting drugs and pharmaceuticals to these countries. Every country is having their own system and norms for registration of Pharmaceutical products. Either it is Ministry of Health or other independent department who takes care of registration part.

Selection of the Markets for Export

It is necessary to do a proper ground work about the markets and the countries targeted for the export. The markets are thoroughly studied on various aspects like political stability, socioeconomic conditions, Government policies, business environment, investment incentives, status of judiciary etc.

Following are some of the parameters to be studied about the Targeted market :

1. Market potential for the products to be exported.
   (i.e. acceptability of the present composition / strength)
2. Registration requirements, cost of registration and period to complete registration of each product.
3. Labeling and packaging requirements. (pack size, language)
4. Local regulatory guidelines (including those related to the Intellectual Property Rights) and standards practiced.
5. Market distance (by sea / by Air).
6. Marketing costs.
7. Distribution network.

Sequence of Activities in the Pharmaceutical Export

Following is the sequence of activities in Pharmaceutical Exports :

1. Receive orders from overseas agent.
2. Communicate order to the factory.
3. Factory selects relevant batch and complies to special requirements.
4. Documents are prepared by the exports office (refer list below).
5. Documents are passed to CHA (Custom House Agent).
6. CHA prepares shipping bill and does other documentation.
7. CHA books air space or shipping space and communicates the same.
8. Goods are released from factory with relevant excise/other documentation.
9. Goods are handed over to CHA to air-lift or to send by ship.

List of Documents to be passed on to the CHA (Custom House Agent)

1. Invoice
2. Packing List

3. GR form
4. Contract (if required)
5. Letter of Credit
6. DEPB passbook (Duty Entitlement passbook)
7. Certificate of origin (if required)
8. Instruction for shipping bill.

Technical Documentation

To start with actual exports of the Pharmaceuticals, there are number of prior requirement to be completed, including the most important one i.e. preparation and submission of Registration Dossiers for the products to be exported to that country. The registration formats / requirements, cost and period to complete the registration differ from country to country.

However, the following documents/certificate(s) are required to comply with registration requirement:

1. FDA License Copy.
2. Free Sale Certificate.
3. WHO-GMP Certificate.
4. Details of Manufacturing Facilities.
5. Details of Quality Control Systems.
6. Technical details about the product mentioning the following:
    - Pharmacology and Pharmacokinetics.
    - Manufacturing and Packaging process.
    - Quality procedures mainly
        - Method of Analysis of Raw Material.
        - Method of Analysis of Finished products.
    - Stability data of at least three batches of the product.
    - Validation protocol and data of three batches.
    - Summary of clinical trials about the safety and efficacy of the product with published references.
    - Summary of Bio-availability studies.
7. Samples of sales pack with Q.C. test report.

Dossier

The dossier is a complete file containing detailed information about the product for the registration of pharmaceutical products in various countries.

The Dossier should consist the following information as per CTD Guidelines :

1. Administrative and prescribing information
2. Overview and summary of modules 3 to 5
3. Quality (pharmaceutical documentation)
4. Safety (toxicology studies)
5. Efficacy (clinical studies)

Detailed subheadings for each Module are specified for all jurisdictions. The contents of Module 1 and certain subheadings of other Modules will differ, based on national requirements.

After USA, European Union and Japan, the CTD has been adopted by several other countries including Canada and Switzerland.

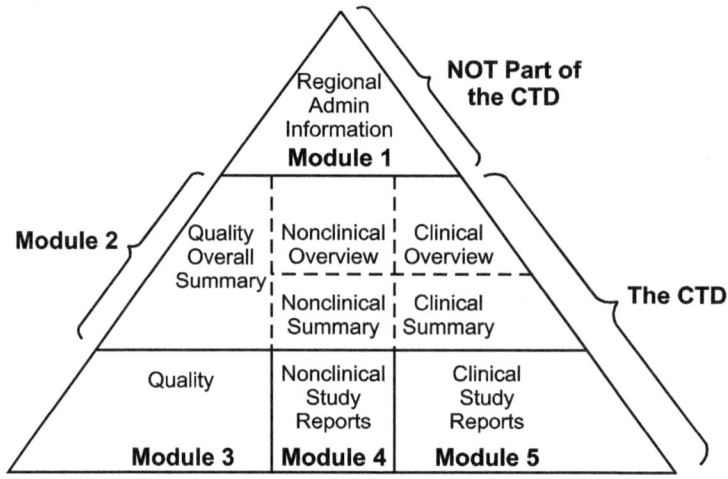

Fig. 10.1

Master Dosseir

INDEX

Sr. No.	Contents	Page no.
Part I	**General Information**	
1.1	Administrative Information.	
1.2	Qualitative and Quantitative Formula.	
1.3	Packaging Details.	
1.4	Summary of Product Characteristics.	
1.5	Pack Insert.	

Part II	**Quality Details.**	
2.1	Nomenclature and Description of Active Ingredient.	
2.2	Specifications of Active Ingredients.	
2.3	Certificate of Analysis of Active Ingredient.	
2.4	Specifications of Excipients.	
2.5	Specifications of Finished Product.	
2.6	Certificate of Analysis of Finished Product.	
2.7	Method of Analysis of Finished Product.	
2.8	Validation of Method of Analysis of Finished Product.	
14.0	Dissolution Studies.	
Part III	**Manufacturing Details.**	
3.1	Flow Chart of Manufacturing Process.	
3.2	Detailed Manufacturing Process.	
3.3	In-process Quality Control.	
3.4	Validation of Manufacturing Process.	
Part IV	**Stability Studies of the Finished Product.**	
4.1	Protocol for Real Time Stability Studies (Storage temperature).	
4.2	Protocol for Accelerated Stability Studies.	
4.3	Actual Stability Data.	
4.4	Conclusion of Stability Studies.	
PART V	**Pharmacological Data.**	
5.1	Pharmacodynamics.	
5.2	Pharmacokinetics.	
5.3	Indications.	
5.4	Dosage and Administration.	
5.5	Contraindications.	
5.6	Precautions.	
5.7	Side Effects.	
5.8	Drug Interaction.	
5.9	Warnings.	
5.10	Overdose.	

Part VI	**Toxicological Data.**	
6.1	Acute Toxicity.	
6.2	Chronic Toxicity.	
6.3	Mutagenicity.	
6.4	Carcinogenicity.	
6.5	Reproduction Toxicity.	
Part VII	**Clinical Data.**	
7.1	Clinical Abstract (Full Text Articles if any).	
7.2	References.	

INDEX FOR CTD DOSSIER

MODULE 1 : ADMINISTRATIVE AND PRESCRIBING INFORMATION

1.0 Cover letter

1.1 Comprehensive Table of Contents

1.2 Application Form

1.3 Product Information

    1.3.1 SPC, Labeling and Package Leaflet

    1.3.2 Mock-up

    1.3.3 Specimen

    1.3.4 Readability Testing

    1.3.5 SPCs already approved in the Member States

1.4 Information about the Experts

    1.4.1 Quality

    1.4.2 Non-Clinical

    1.4.3 Clinical

1.5 Specific Requirements for Different Types of Applications

    1.5.1 Information for Bibliographical Applications

    1.5.2 Information for Abridged Applications

1.6 Environmental Risk Assessment

    1.6.1 Non-GMO

    1.6.2 GMO

MODULE 2 : COMMON TECHNICAL DOCUMENT SUMMARIES

2.1 CTD Table of Contents

2.2 Introduction

2.3 Quality Overall Summary – Introduction

    2.3.S Quality Overall Summary – Drug Substance

    2.3.P Quality Overall Summary – Drug Product

    2.3.A Quality Overall Summary – Appendices

    2.3.R Quality Overall Summary – Regional Information

2.4 Non-clinical Overview

2.5 Clinical Overview

    2.5.1 Product Development Rationale

    2.5.2 Overview of Biopharmaceutics

    2.5.3 Overview of Clinical Pharmacology

    2.5.4 Overview of Efficacy

    2.5.5 Overview of Safety

    2.5.6 Benefits and Risks Conclusions

    2.5.7 Literature References

2.6 Nonclinical Written and Tabulated Summaries

    2.6.1 Introduction

    2.6.2 Pharmacology Written Summary

    2.6.3 Pharmacology Tabulated Summary

    2.6.4 Pharmacokinetics Written Summary

    2.6.5 Pharmacokinetics Tabulated Summary

    2.6.6 Toxicology Written Summary

    2.6.7 Toxicology Tabulated Summary

2.7 Clinical Summaries

    2.7.1 Summary of Biopharmaceutic and Associated Analytical Methods

    2.7.2 Summary of Clinical Pharmacology Studies

    2.7.3 Summary of Clinical Efficacy

    2.7.4 Summary of Safety

    2.7.5 References

    2.7.6 Synopses of Individual Studies

MODULE 3 : QUALITY

- 3.2.S Drug Substance
  - 3.2.S.1 General Information
    - 3.2.S.1.1 Nomenclature
    - 3.2.S.1.2 Structure
    - 3.2.S.1.3 General Properties
  - 3.2.S.2 Manufacture
    - 3.2.S.2.1 Manufacturer(s)
    - 3.2.S.2.2 Description of Manufacturing Process and Process Controls
    - 3.2.S.2.3 Control of Materials
    - 3.2.S.2.4 Controls of Critical Steps and Intermediates
    - 3.2.S.2.5 Process Validation and/or Evaluation
    - 3.2.S.2.6 Manufacturing Process Development
  - 3.2.S.3 Characterization
    - 3.2.S.3.1 Elucidation of Structure and other Characteristics
    - 3.2.S.3.2 Impurities
  - 3.2.S.4 Control of Drug Substance
    - 3.2.S.4.1 Specification
    - 3.2.S.4.2 Analytical Procedures
    - 3.2.S.4.3 Validation of Analytical Procedures
    - 3.2.S.4.4 Batch Analyses
    - 3.2.S.4.5 Justification of Specification
  - 3.2.S.5 Reference Standards or Materials
  - 3.2.S.6 Container Closure System
  - 3.2.S.7 Stability
    - 3.2.S.7.1 Stability Summary and Conclusions
    - 3.2.S.7.2 Post-approval Stability Protocol and Stability Commitment
    - 3.2.S.7.3 Stability Data
- 3.2.P Drug Product
  - 3.2.P.1 Description and Composition of the Drug Product
  - 3.2.P.2 Pharmaceutical Development
    - 3.2.P.2.1 Components of the Drug Product
      - 3.2.P.2.1.1 Drug Substance
      - 3.2.P.2.1.2 Excipients

- 3.2.P.2.2 Drug Product
  - 3.2.P.2.2.1 Formulation Development
  - 3.2.P.2.2.2 Overages
  - 3.2.P.2.2.3 Physicochemical and Biological Properties
- 3.2.P.2.3 Manufacturing Process Development
- 3.2.P.2.4 Container Closure System
- 3.2.P.2.5 Microbiological Attributes
- 3.2.P.2.6 Compatibility

3.2.P.3 Manufacture
- 3.2.P.3.1 Manufacturer(s)
- 3.2.P.3.2 Batch Formula
- 3.2.P.3.3 Description of Manufacturing Process and Process Controls
- 3.2.P.3.4 Controls of Critical Steps and Intermediates
- 3.2.P.3.5 Process Validation and/or Evaluation

3.2.P.4 Control of Excipients
- 3.2.P.4.1 Specifications
- 3.2.P.4.2 Analytical Procedures
- 3.2.P.4.3 Validation of Analytical Procedures
- 3.2.P.4.4 Justification of Specifications
- 3.2.P.4.5 Excipients of Human or Animal Origin
- 3.2.P.4.6 Novel Excipients

3.2.P.5 Control of Drug Product
- 3.2.P.5.1 Specification(s)
- 3.2.P.5.2 Analytical Procedures
- 3.2.P.5.3 Validation of Analytical Procedures
- 3.2.P.5.4 Batch Analyses
- 3.2.P.5.5 Characterization of Impurities
- 3.2.P.5.6 Justification of Specification(s)

3.2.P.6 Reference Standards or Materials

3.2.P.7 Container Closure System

3.2.P.8 Stability
- 3.2.P.8.1 Stability Summary and Conclusions
- 3.2.P.8.2 Post-approval Stability Protocol and Stability Commitment
- 3.2.P.8.3 Stability Data

MODULE 4 : NON-CLINICAL STUDY REPORTS

4.1 Table of Contents of Module 4

4.2 Study Reports

    4.2.1 Pharmacology

        4.2.1.1 Primary Pharmacodynamics

        4.2.1.2 Secondary Pharmacodynamics

        4.2.1.3 Safety Pharmacology

        4.2.1.4 Pharmacodynamic Drug Interactions

    4.2.2 Pharmacokinetics

        4.2.2.1 Analytical Methods and Validation Reports

        4.2.2.2 Absorption

        4.2.2.3 Distribution

        4.2.2.4 Metabolism

        4.2.2.5 Excretion

        4.2.2.6 Pharmacokinetic Drug Interactions (non-clinical)

        4.2.2.7 Other Pharmacokinetic Studies

    4.2.3 Toxicology

        4.2.3.1 Single-Dose Toxicity

        4.2.3.2 Repeat-Dose Toxicity

        4.2.3.3 Genotoxicity

            4.2.3.3.1 In-vitro

            4.2.3.3.2 In-vivo

        4.2.3.4 Carcinogenicity

            4.2.3.4.1 Long-term studies

            4.2.3.4.2 Short- or medium-term studies

            4.2.3.4.3 Other studies

        4.2.3.5 Reproductive and Developmental Toxicity

        4.2.3.6 Local Tolerance

        4.2.3.7 Other Toxicity Studies

        4.2.3.8 Other

4.3 Literature References

MODULE 5 : CLINICAL STUDY REPORTS

5.1 Table of Contents
5.2 Tabular Listing of all Clinical Studies
5.3 Clinical Study Reports
    5.3.1 Reports of Biopharmaceutic Studies
        5.3.1.1 Bioavailability (BA) Study Reports
        5.3.1.2 Comparative BA and Bioequivalence (BE) Study Reports
        5.3.1.3 In vitro-In vivo Correlation Study Reports
        5.3.1.4 Reports of Bioanalytical and Analytical Methods for Human Studies
    5.3.2 Reports of Studies Pertinent to Pharmacokinetics using Human Biomaterials
    5.3.3 Reports of Human Pharmacokinetic (PK) Studies
    5.3.4 Reports of Human Pharmacodynamic (PD) Studies
    5.3.5 Reports of Efficacy and Safety Studies
    5.3.6 Reports of Post-Marketing Experience
    5.3.7 Case Report Forms and Individual Patient Listings
5.4 Literature References

EXPORT REGISTRATION AUTHORITIES IN SOME COUNTRIES

Country	Approving Authority
Abu-Dhabi	Abu Dhabi Center for Herbal Medical Care.
Bangladesh	Ministry of Health and Planning.
Czech and Slovak	State Institute for Drug Control.
Burma/Myanamar	Myanamar Drug Committee.
Eritrea	Pharmacy Dept. of Ministry of Health.
Ethiopia	Pharmacy Dept. of Ministry of Health.
Ghana	The Registrar Pharmacy Board.
Kenya	Pharmacy and Poisons Board.
Kuwait	Drug Controller and Registration Board.
Malaysia	Drug Control Authority.
Philippines	Directorate General of Pharmacy Affairs and Drug Control.

contd. ...

South Africa	Bureau of Food and Drugs.
Sri Lanka	Cosmetics devices and Drug Authority.
Sudan	BADAR Drugs and Chemicals Co. Ltd.
Singapore	Republic of Singapore, Ministry of Health.
Thailand	Drug Controller Division Regulatory Authority, FDA
UK	Medicine and Healthcare Regulatory Agency
USA	Food and Drug Administration (FDA).
Vietnam	Ministry of Health.
Zambia	Pharmaceutical Registration Department.

WORLDWIDE PHARMACEUTICAL REGULATORY AGENCIES

Country wise Regulatory Agencies and their Websites

Argentina
http://www.anmat.gov.ar

Austria
http://www.bmags.gv.at

Austria
http://www.bmsg.gv.at

Australia
http://www.health.gov.au/tga/

Azerbaijan
http://www.medis.az

Bahrain
http://www.batelco.com.bh/mhealth/

Barbados
http://www.uwimona.edu.jm/cesd/barbados/barbados.html

Belgium
http://www.afigp.fgov.be

Belgium
http://www.health.fgov.be

Bolivia
http://www.sns.gov.bo

Botswana
http://www.gov.bw/government/ministry_of_health.html

Brazil
http://www.datasus.gov.br
Brunei
http://www.brunet.bn/gov/moh/
Bulgaria
http://www.bda.bg
Canada
http://www.hc-sc.gc.ca
Chile
http://www.minsal.cl
China
http://www.sda.gov.cn
Colombia
http://www.minsalud.gov.co
Costa Rica
http://www.netsalad.sa.cr/ms/
Croatia
http://www.vlada.hr/english/emin-zdr.html
Cyprus
http://www.pio.gov.cy/cygov/ministry/mhealth/index.htm
Czech Republic
http://www.sukl.cz/defaulte.htm
Denmark
http://www.dkma.dk
Ecuador
http://www.msp.gov.ec
Egypt
http://www.misrnet.idsc.gov.eg/english/minist/health/e-main.htm
Estonia
http://www.sam.ee
Fiji
http://www.health.gov.fj
Finland
http://www.nam.fi/templates/laakelaitos/default/feng.html
France
http://agmed.sante.gouv.fr
Germany
http://www.bfarm.de/gb_ver/

Guam
http://www.admin.gov.gu/pubhealth/
Guyana
http://www.sdnp.org.gy/moh
Honduras
http://206.48.252.66/ssalud.htm
Hong Kong
http://www.info.gov.hk/pharmser/
Hungary
http://www.ogyi.hu/eng011.htm
Iceland
http://www.ler.is
Iceland
http://www.brunmur.stjr.is/interpro/htr/htr.nsf/pages/forsid-ensk/
India
http://mohfw.nic.in
Indonesia
http://www.depkes.go.id
Ireland
http://www.imb.ie
Israel
http://www.health.gov.il
Italy
http://www.sanita.it/farmaci
Japan
http://www.mhlw.go.jp/english/index.html
Jordan
http://www.nic.gov.jo
Kenya
http://www.kenyastatehouse.go.ke/organisation/sect-health.htm#op
Korea
http://www.kfda.go.kr/english/index.html
Latvia
http://www.vza.gov.lv
Lebanon
http://www.public-health.gov.lb
Lithuania
http://www.vvkt.lt/eng/default.htm

Luxembourg
http://www.etat.lu/ms/
Malaysia
http://dph.gov.my
Malta
http://www.magnet.mt/ministries/health/
Mexico
http://www.ssa.gob.mx
Mongolia
http://www.pmis.gov.mn/health
Morocco
http://www.sante.gov.ma
Netherlands
http://www.cbg-meb.nl
New Zealand
http://www.moh.govt.nz
Nicaragua
http://www.ops.org.ni
Norway
http://www.slk.no
Palestine
http://www.pna.org/moh/e-index.htm
Peru
http://www.minsa.gob.pe/index2.htm
Philippines
http://www.doh.gov.ph
Poland
http://www.mzios.gov.pl
Portugal
http://www.infarmed.pt/index.html
Russia
http://www.views.vcu.edu/views/fap/medsoc/medsoc.htm
Singapore
http://www.gov.sg/moh
Slovak Republic
http://www.sukl.sk
Slovenia
http://www.gov.si/mz/organivsestavi2.html

South Africa
http://www.health.gov.za
Spain
http://www.msc.es/agemed/
Sri Lanka
http://www.lk/health/ministry.html
Sweden
http://www.mpa.se
Switzerland
http://www.iks.ch/default_e.asp
Taiwan
http://www.doh.gov.tw/english
Thailand
http://www.fda.moph.go.th
Tunisia
http://www.ministeres.tn/html/indexgouv.html
Turkey
http://www.iegm.gov.tr
UAE
http://www.ecssr.ac.ae/03uae.ministry9.html
UK
http://www.open.gov.uk/mca/mcahome.htm
Ukraine
http://www.health.gov.ua
Uruguay
http://www.msp.gub.uy
USA
http://www.fda.gov
Venezuela
http://www.platino.gov.ve/minfamilia
Vietnam
http://www.batin.com.vn/vninfo/ministry/h.htm
Zimbabwe
http://www.gta.gov.zw/health.html

Chapter 11...

REGULATORY AUTHORITIES AND AGENCIES

There are following main regulatory authorities whose guidelines are globally accepted and followed by the Pharma and Allied industries :

(a) USFDA (United States Food and Drug Administration)
(b) TGA (Therapeutic Goods Administration)
(c) MHRA (Medicines & Healthcare Regulatory Agency)
(d) ICH guidelines (International Conference on Harmonisation)
(e) WHO (World Health Organisation)

(A) USFDA (UNITED STATES FOOD AND DRUG ADMINISTRATION)

FDA ensures that the food we eat is safe and wholesome, that the cosmetics we use won't harm us, and that medicines, medical devices, and radiation-emitting consumer products such as microwave ovens are safe and effective. FDA also oversees feed and drugs for pets and farm animals. Authorized by Congress to enforce the Federal Food, Drug, and Cosmetic Act and several other public health laws, the agency monitors the manufacture, import, transport, storage, and sale of $1 trillion worth of goods annually, at a cost to tax payers of about $3 a person.

USFDA has over 9,000 employees, located in 167 U.S. cities. Among its staff, FDA has chemists, microbiologists, and other scientists, as well as investigators and inspectors who visit 16,000 facilities a year as part of their oversight of the businesses that FDA regulates.

FDA's Mission

The FDA Modernization Act of 1997 (PL 105-115) affirmed FDA's public health protection role and defined the Agency's mission :

- To promote the public health by promptly and efficiently reviewing clinical research and taking appropriate action on the marketing of regulated products in a timely manner;
- With respect to such products, protect the public health by ensuring that foods are safe, wholesome, sanitary, and properly labelled; human and veterinary drugs are safe and effective; there is reasonable assurance of the safety and

effectiveness of devices intended for human use; cosmetics are safe and properly labelled, and; public health and safety are protected from electronic product radiation;
- Participate through appropriate processes with representatives of other countries to reduce the burden of regulation, harmonize regulatory requirements, and achieve appropriate reciprocal arrangements;
- As determined to be appropriate by the Secretary, carry out paragraphs (1) through (2) in consultation with experts in science, medicine, and public health, and (3) in co-operation with consumers, users, manufacturers, importers, packers, distributors and retailers of regulated products.

What FDA Regulates ?

FDA is the federal agency responsible for ensuring that foods are safe, wholesome and sanitary; human and veterinary drugs, biological products, and medical devices are safe and effective; cosmetics are safe; and electronic products that emit radiation are safe. FDA also ensures that these products are honestly, accurately and informatively represented to the public. Some of the agency's specific responsibilities include :

- Biologics
- Product and manufacturing establishment licensing
- Safety of the nation's blood supply
- Research to establish product standards and develop improved testing methods
- Cosmetics
- Safety
- Labelling
- Drugs
- Product approvals
- OTC and prescription drug labelling
- Drug manufacturing standards
- Foods
- Safety of all food products (except meat and poultry)
- Bottled water
- Medical Devices
- Premarket approval of new devices
- Manufacturing and performance standards
- Tracking reports of device malfunctioning and serious adverse reactions
- Radiation-Emitting Electronic Products

- Radiation safety performance standards for microwave ovens, television receivers, diagnostic x-ray equipment, cabinet x-ray systems (such as baggage x-rays at airports), laser products, ultrasonic therapy equipment, mercury vapor lamps, and sunlamps accrediting and inspecting mammography facilities
- Veterinary Products
- Livestock feeds
- Pet foods
- Veterinary drugs and devices

What FDA does not Regulate ?

FDA's responsibilities are closely related to those of several other government agencies. Often frustrating and confusing for consumers is determining the appropriate regulatory agency to contact. The following contact information is for government agencies that have functions related to that of FDA. (Contact information is given for agency headquarters offices, which are located in the Washington, D.C., area. Local offices, listed in the phone book under U.S. Government, may be available to provide assistance as well.)

Advertising

The Federal Trade Commission is the federal agency which regulates all advertising, excluding prescription drugs and medical devices. FTC ensures that advertisements are truthful and not misleading for consumers. Consumers may write to FTC at 6th St. and Pennsylvania Ave., N.W., Washington, DC 20580; telephone (202) 326-2222.

Alcohol

The labelling and quality of alcoholic beverages are regulated by the Treasury Department's Bureau of Alcohol, Tobacco, and Firearms. ATF's address is 650 Massachusetts Ave., N.W., Washington, DC 20226; telephone (202) 927-7777.

Consumer Products

While FDA regulates a large portion of the products that consumers purchase, the agency has no jurisdiction over many household goods. The Consumer Product Safety Commission (CPSC) is responsible for ensuring the safety of consumer goods such as household appliances (excluding those that emit radiation), paint, child-resistant packages, and baby toys. Consumers may send written inquiries to CPSC, Washington, DC 20207. CPSC operates a toll-free hot line at (800) 638-2772 or TTY (800) 638-8270 for consumers to report unsafe products or to obtain information regarding products and recalls.

Drugs of Abuse

Illegal drugs with no approved medical use-such as heroin and marijuana are under the jurisdiction of the Drug Enforcement Administration. FDA assists DEA in deciding how stringent DEA controls should be on drugs that are medically accepted but that have a strong potential for abuse. DEA establishes limits on the amount of these prescription drugs that are permitted to be manufactured each year. Inquiries regarding DEA activities may be sent to the Drug Enforcement Administration, U.S. Department of Justice, Washington, DC 20537; telephone (202) 307-1000.

Health Insurance

FDA does not regulate health insurance, the cost of health care products or procedures, or reimbursement for health and medical expenses. Questions about Medicare should be directed to the Health Care Financing Administration.

Meat and Poultry

The U.S. Department of Agriculture's Food Safety and Inspection Service is responsible for the safety and labelling of traditional meats and poultry. (FDA regulates game meats, such as venison, ostrich and snake.) Consumers with questions regarding meat or poultry, including safe handling and storage practices, should write or call the Food Safety Inspection Service's Meat and Poultry Hotline, Room 2925S, Washington, DC 20250; telephone (800) 535-4555.

Pesticides

FDA, USDA, and the Environmental Protection Agency share the responsibility for regulating pesticides. EPA determines the safety and effectiveness of the chemicals and establishes tolerance levels for residues on feed crops, as well as for raw and processed foods. These tolerance levels (the amount of pesticide allowed to be present in a food product) are normally set 100 times below the level that might cause harm to people or the environment. FDA and USDA are responsible for monitoring the food supply to ensure that pesticide residues do not exceed the allowable levels in the products under their jurisdiction. Public inquiries regarding EPA should be mailed to U.S. Environmental Protection Agency, Office of Pesticide Programs Public Docket (7506C), 3404, 401M St., Washington, DC 20460; telephone (202) 260-2080.

Restaurants and Grocery Stores

Inspections and licensing of restaurants and grocery stores are typically handled by local county health departments.

Water

The regulation of water is divided between the Environmental Protection Agency and FDA. EPA has the responsibility for developing national standards for drinking water from municipal water supplies. FDA regulates the labelling and safety of bottled water.

(Ref. : For more info log on to www.fda.gov)

(B) THERAPEUTIC GOODS ADMINISTRATION (TGA)

(Regulation of Therapeutic Goods in Australia)

The Australian community expects that medicines and medical devices in the market place are safe and of high quality, to a standard at least equal to that of comparable countries. The objective of the Therapeutic Goods Act 1989, which came into effect on 15 February 1991, is to provide a national framework for the regulation of therapeutic goods in Australia and ensure their quality, safety and efficacy.

The regulatory framework is based on a risk management approach designed to ensure public health and safety, while at the same time freeing industry from any unnecessary regulatory burden.

Essentially, any product for which therapeutic claims are made must be entered in the Australian Register of Therapeutic Goods (ARTG) before the product can be supplied in Australia. The ARTG is a computer database of information about therapeutic goods for human use approved for supply in, or exported from, Australia.

The Therapeutic Goods Act 1989, Regulations and Orders set out the requirements for inclusion of therapeutic goods in the ARTG, including advertising, labeling, product appearance and appeal guidelines. Some provisions such as the scheduling of substances and the safe storage of therapeutic goods are covered by the relevant State or Territory legislation.

The Therapeutic Goods Administration (TGA) is a unit of the Federal Department of Health and Ageing and is responsible for administering the provisions of the legislation.

The TGA carries out a range of assessment and monitoring activities to ensure therapeutic goods available in Australia are of an acceptable standard. At the same time the TGA aims to ensure that the Australian community has access, within a reasonable time, to therapeutic advances.

What is a therapeutic good ?

A 'therapeutic good' is broadly defined as a good which is represented in any way to be, or is likely to be taken to be, for therapeutic use, unless specifically excluded or included under Section 7 of the Therapeutic Goods Act 1989.

For the purposes of evaluation and assessment, a therapeutic good is a product for use in humans that is used in, or in connection with :

- Preventing, diagnosing, curing or alleviating a disease, ailment, defect or injury;
- Influencing inhibiting or modifying a physiological process;
- Testing the susceptibility of persons to a disease or ailment;
- Influencing, controlling or preventing conception;
- Testing for pregnancy; or
- Replacement or modification of parts of the anatomy.

Regulation of Therapeutic Goods

Overall control of the supply of therapeutic goods is exercised through three main processes:

(a) Pre-market assessment
(b) Licensing of manufacturers
(c) Post market vigilance

(a) Pre-market assessment:

Products assessed as having a higher level of risk (prescription medicines, some non-prescription medicines and medical devices) are evaluated for quality, safety and efficacy. Once approved for marketing in Australia these products are included in the ARTG as 'registered' products and are identified by an AUSTR number.

Products assessed as being lower risk (many non-prescription medicines including most complementary medicines and low risk medical devices) are assessed for quality and safety. Once approved for marketing in Australia, these products are included in the ARTG as 'listed' products and are identified by an AUST L number.

In assessing the level of risk, factors such as the strength of a product, side effects, potential harm through prolonged use, toxicity and the seriousness of the medical condition for which the product is intended to be used, are all taken into account.

(b) Licensing of manufacturers:

Australian manufacturers of therapeutic goods must be licensed. Their manufacturing processes must comply with principles of Good Manufacturing Practice (GMP). The aim of licensing and standards is to protect public health by ensuring that medicines and medical devices meet definable standards of quality assurance and are manufactured in conditions that are clean and free of contaminants.

(c) Post marketing vigilance:

Post marketing activities include investigating reports of problems, laboratory testing of products on the market and monitoring to ensure compliance with the legislation.

Further information can be obtained from:

Mail:
The Information Office
Therapeutic Goods Administration
P.O. Box 100
WODEN ACT 2606
Telephone : 1800 020 653
Fax : 02 6232 8605
TTY : 1800 500 236
Email : tga-information-officer@health.gov.au

(C) THE MEDICINES CONTROL AGENCY (MCA) (UK REGULATORY BODY)

Introduction

The Medicines and Healthcare Regulatory Agency (MHRA)

The Medicines Control Agency's (MCA) primary objective is to safeguard public health by ensuring that all medicines on the UK market meet appropriate standards of safety, quality and efficacy. Safety aspects cover potential or actual harmful effects; quality relates to development and manufacture; and efficacy is a measure of the beneficial effect of the medicine on patients.

The Agency achieves its objective through :

- A system of licensing before the marketing of medicines;
- Monitoring of medicines and acting on safety concerns after they have been placed on the market;
    - Introduction
    - Licensing of medicines
    - Monitoring the safety and quality of medicines
    - Ensuring the quality of medicines
    - Regulation of the promotion of medicines
    - Regulation of product information
    - Enforcement of medicines legislation
    - General Practice Research Database (GPRD)

Checking standards of pharmaceutical manufacture and wholesaling; enforcement of requirements; responsibilities for medicines control policy; representing UK pharmaceutical regulatory interests internationally; publishing quality standards for drug substances through the British Pharmacopoeia.

This large section of the MCA site describes how we achieve our objectives and is divided into the following sections :

Licensing of Medicines

The MCA operates a system of licensing before the marketing of medicines. Medicines, which meet the standards of safety, quality and efficacy, are granted a marketing authorization (previously a product license), which is normally necessary before they can be prescribed or sold. This authorization covers all the main activities associated with the marketing of a medicinal product. The MCA carries out pre-marketing assessment of the medicines safety, quality and efficacy, examining all the research and test results in detail, before a decision is made on whether the product should be granted a marketing authorization. This section provides information on all aspects of the licensing system.

Monitoring the Safety and Quality of Medicines

The MCA continually monitors both the safety and quality of the medicines available on UK market. This section of the site explains how the MCA carries out this vital area of work.

Ensuring the Quality of Medicines

Quality underpins both safety and efficacy and the MCA promotes the understanding and development of quality assurance in the development, manufacture and distribution of medicinal products. This section of the site explains how the MCA carries out this area of work.

Regulation of the Promotion of Medicines

This section describes how the advertising and promotion of medicines in the UK is controlled.

Regulation of the Product Information

This section describes how the Medicines Control Agency (MCA) regulates product information.

Enforcement of Medicines Legislation

This section describes how the MCA enforces medicines legislation across the UK including our responsibilities and powers as well as details of our prosecutions from January 2000.

General Practice Research Database

The MCA took over the management of the General Practice Research Database (GPRD) from the Statistics Division of the Department of Health in April 1999.

(D) INTERNATIONAL CONFERENCE ON HARMONISATION (ICH)
Introduction

The International Conference on Harmonisation of Technical Requirements for Registration of Pharmaceuticals for Human Use (ICH) is a unique project that brings together the regulatory authorities of Europe, Japan and the United States and experts from the pharmaceutical industry in the three regions to discuss scientific and technical aspects of product registration.

The purpose is to make recommendations on ways to achieve greater harmonisation in the interpretation and application of technical guidelines and requirements for product registration, in order to reduce or obviate the need to duplicate the testing carried out during the research and development of new medicines. The objective of such harmonisation is a more economical use of human, animal and material resources, and the elimination of unnecessary delay in the global development and availability of new medicines whilst maintaining safeguards on quality, safety and efficacy, and regulatory obligations to protect public health. This Mission is embodied in the Terms of Reference of ICH.

ICH is a joint initiative involving both regulators and industry as equal partners in the scientific and technical discussions of the testing procedures which are required to ensure and assess the safety, quality and efficiency of medicines.

The focus of ICH has been on the technical requirements for medicinal products containing new drugs. The vast majority of those new drugs and medicines are developed in Western Europe, Japan, and the United States of America and therefore, when ICH was established, it was agreed that its scope would be confined to registration in those three regions.

The ICH Process for Harmonisation of Guidelines
   1. Overview
   2. Initiation of ICH Harmonisation Action.
   3. Full ICH Process for Major Harmonisation Topics.
   4. Abbreviated Process for Maintenance of ICH Agreements.
   5. Type of Maintenance: Updating Based on New Information.

1. Overview

In its statement on the future of ICH published at the time of Fourth International Conference on Harmonisation, Brussels, July 1997, the ICH Steering Committee undertook to ensure that, in the second phase of ICH activities :
   (i) There is a mechanism to harmonise new technical requirements resulting from scientific progress and developments in innovative drug research.
   (ii) There is a process for updating and supplementing the current ICH guidelines, when necessary and monitoring their use, so that the benefits of harmonisation achieved so far are not lost.
   (iii) Working procedures have been agreed to ensure that these objectives are met.

Harmonisation initiatives will be designated as "Major" and "Minor". A major topic includes proposals for new guidelines and changes to existing guidelines which involve interpretations of statutory or regulatory requirements, changes in interpretation or policy that are more than a minor nature, usually complex scientific issues. Other changes are considered as "minor".

Major Topics will be handled under the full ICH Process as described in Section 2. This is based on the original "five-step" approach which proved extremely successful for the first phase of ICH activities. Proposals for "Minor" changes to existing ICH tripartite harmonised guidelines will be handled through the abbreviated Maintenance Process.

In the first phase of ICH activities the focus was almost exclusively on the technical requirements for developing and registering products containing new drug substances, in the European Union, Japan and the USA. The Expert Working Groups which worked on over 40 guidelines for new drug products were made up of scientists from six ICH parties 1 - the regulatory agencies and the research-based industry in the three ICH regions.

In revising the ICH procedures, however, account has been taken of the fact that the second phase of ICH activities may cover a wider range of topics and issues which have implications for parties outside the six founder members of ICH.

Although some modifications have been made in the ICH Procedures, the basic principles, which have been the cornerstone of ICH work, are unchanged :
- Development of scientific consensus through discussions between regulatory and industry experts;
- Wide consultation of the draft consensus documents, through normal regulatory channels, before a harmonised text is adopted;
- Commitment by regulatory parties to implement the ICH harmonised texts.

2. Initiation of ICH Harmonisation Action

(i) **Proposals for Harmonisation Action** : Suggestions for new harmonisation initiatives may arise in a number of form including ICH Regional Guideline Workshops; other regional and international conferences, workshops and symposia dealing with R&D and regulatory affairs; recognized Associations, Federations and Societies which represent scientific and technical professionals concerned with the development, testing and registration of medicines.

Formal proposals for ICH action must, however, be channeled through one of the six parties to ICH or one of the observers on the Steering Committee.

Proposals for harmonisation action might fall into one of the following categories :

(a) **New types of medicinal product** : Proposals for guidelines to cover new products resulting from advances in technology and techniques for producing medicines. (e.g., products arising from gene therapy and other developments in biotechnological and genomic research).

(b) **Lack of harmonisation in current technical requirements** : Proposals for further harmonisation of existing requirements (e.g., as a result of work on the Common Technical Document).

(c) **Transition to technically improved testing procedures** : Proposals for action to facilitate the replacement of currently established testing procedures to more efficient and economical methods where these provide equal or better assurance of the safety and/or quality of new drug products.

(d) Review of an existing ICH Guideline : Proposals for significant changes to the technical aspects of an ICH guideline or proposals for a major addition to the guideline.

(e) Maintenance of an existing guideline : Proposals for relatively minor modification, updating clarification or review of ICH agreements to take account of either problems with implementation, new information or new scientific knowledge.

(ii) Preparation of a Concept Paper : The ICH party or Observer proposing a new harmonisation action needs to present the issue in the form of a concept paper. This provides a short summary of the proposal (maximum 2 pages) giving the information indicated below :

(i) Type of Harmonisation Action Proposed (e.g., a new tripartite harmonised guideline /recommendation, or an amendment/update of an existing guideline).

(ii) Statement of the Perceived Problem Brief description with an indication of the magnitude of the problems currently caused by a lack of harmonisation, or in the case of new scientific developments - anticipated if harmonisation action is not taken.

(iii) Issues to be resolved summary of the main technical and scientific issues which require harmonisation.

(iv) Background to the proposal, further relevant information, e.g., the origin of the proposal, references to publications, discussions in other form

(v) Type of Expert Working Group Recommendation on whether the EWG (if needed) should be a six-party group - for topics related to the R and D of new drug substances and products - or an extended EWG - for topics with implications beyond new drug research.

Note : A formal EWG is not required for actions designated as "maintenance" of existing guidelines - see below.

Further documentation and reports may be annexed to the concept paper :

(iii) Selection of Procedure : The proposal and Concept Paper should be sent to members of the Steering Committee. Observers and ICH Coordinators and the copy to the ICH Secretariat should ask for the item to be included on the agenda for the next Steering Committee meeting.

Proposals for maintenance of existing guidelines - type (e) above - where the sponsor feels that an abbreviated process is appropriate, should be sent to the ICH Secretariat with a request that the Maintenance Process be initiated.

3. Full ICH Process for Major Harmonisation Topics

(i) Topic Selection : The Steering Committee Agenda will, routinely, include an item on proposals for new topics. The sponsoring party, or observer will have circulated the concept paper to co-ordinators and the secretariat in advance and the concept paper and any comments will be submitted to the steering committee. A preliminary determination will be made on whether the topic is of sufficient interest to all parties and can be accommodated within the ICH work programme.

As noted, the Concept Paper will indicate the type of EWG that is appropriate for the Topic, i.e., six-party membership only, or with membership extended to other interested parties. In the latter case the following procedure will apply :

Topic Selection and Participation of Interested Parties

Once a preliminary determination has been made that a topic is worthwhile and interested parties beyond the six ICH sponsors and three observers are identified, the steering committee will invite, as appropriate, those additional parties to discussions on the topic, just prior to its acceptance by the steering committee as an ICH Topic.

(ii) Steering Committee Action : When a Topic is adopted for harmonisation action the Steering Committee will :

(a) Confirm the Objectives and Expected Outcome of the harmonisation action;

(b) Confirm the composition of the Expert Working Group (EWG) appointed to discuss the technical issues;

(c) Set a Timetable and Action Plan for the EWG.

The Concept Paper will be revised and updated to reflect these decisions.

(iii) Expert Working Groups : Each of the six ICH parties (EC, EFPIA, MHLW, JPMA, FDA, PHRMA) will be asked to designate a Topic Leader for the new topic. The Topic Leaders will participate in the EWG meetings and be the point of contact for any consultations carried out between meetings by correspondence, fax, e-mail etc. A Deputy Topic Leader may also be designated.

The Observers to ICH will also be invited to nominate an expert to the EWG.

In the case of EWGs with extended membership, the secretariat will invite the designated organizations to nominate an expert to participate in the EWG and act as the contact point for receipt of documents on technical issues.

Organizations that have not previously participated in ICH EWGs should be advised that ICH does not cover the cost of travel or accommodation for EWG participants. Participation is at the expense of the party concerned and a contribution to the expenses of holding the meetings might be requested.

Also, the absence of one of the non-ICH parties from an EWG meeting will not prevent the meeting from taking place.

EWG Reports to the Steering Committee

Other interested parties and their experts will be present and able to express their views to the steering committee when topics in which they have a particular interest are discussed. The agenda for the steering committee will be arranged accordingly.

In order to manage the likely numbers of attendees from interested parties during the discussion of these topics, attendance will be limited to one representative in addition to their expert.

(iv) Timetables and Action Plan : The steering committee will agree a "target" timetable for development of scientific consensus in the Expert Working Group for each new harmonisation topic. This would not normally exceed 2 years.

One of the six ICH parties will be designated to nominate the Rapporteur and all involved parties will be asked to nominate their respective experts within a fixed time limit.

(v) Steps in the ICH Process : The five-step process which proved successful for the first Phase of ICH activities will be maintained, with appropriate modifications to accommodate the extended EWGs:

Step 1 : Consensus Building : The Rapporteur prepares an initial draft of a guideline or recommendation, based on the objectives set out in the concept paper, and in consultation with experts designated to the EWG. The initial draft and successive revisions are circulated for comment, giving fixed dead lines for receipt of those comments.

To the extent possible, consultation will be carried out by correspondence, using fax and E-mail. Meetings of the Expert Working Group will normally take place at the time and venue of the biannual steering committee meetings. Additional, formal meetings of the ICH EWG need to be agreed, in advance, by the steering committee.

Interim reports are made to each meeting of the ICH steering committee. If consensus is reached within the agreed timetable the consensus text with EWG signatures (see below) is submitted to the steering committee for adoption as step 2 of the ICH process.

Where complete consensus has not been achieved within the timetable; a report will be made to the steering committee indicating the extent of agreement reached and highlighting the points on which there are differences between the parties. Experts from all parties represented on the EWG will have the opportunity to explain their position to the Steering Committee. The Steering Committee may then :
- Allow an extension of the time-table, on the basis that the EWG can give assurances that consensus could be reached within a short, specified period;

- Decide to suspend or abandon the harmonisation project;
- Decide to proceed to step 2 on the basis of the current draft, notwithstanding absence of complete consensus in the EWG.

Sign-off by Expert Working Group Members : When consensus is reached on the technical issues all parties represented on an EWG would be invited to sign the document to indicate their agreement to the consensus text which is submitted to the steering committee. Circumstances could be envisaged, however, when not all other parties are present or able to sign the consensus text. It would then be for the steering committee to decide whether to proceed to Step 2.

Step 2 : Start of Regulatory Action : Step 2 is reached when the steering committee agrees, on the basis of the report from the Expert Working Group, that there is sufficient scientific consensus on the technical issues, for the draft guideline or recommendation to proceed to the next stage of regulatory consultation. This agreement is confirmed by steering committee members for each of the six ICH parties signing their assent.

Step 3 : Regulatory Consultation : At this stage, the Guideline or Recommendation embodying the scientific consensus leaves the ICH process and becomes the subject of normal wide-ranging regulatory consultation in the three regions. In the EU it is published as a draft CPMP Guideline, in the USA it is published as a draft guidance in the Federal Register and in Japan it is translated and issued by MHLW, for internal and external consultation.

The difference from normal, national/EU procedures for consultations on guidelines is that the regulatory parties exchange information on the comments they have received in order to arrive at a single, harmonised text. Also, there is an opportunity for industry associations and regulatory authorities in non-ICH regions to comment on the draft consultation documents which are distributed using IFPMA and WHO contact lists.

A regulatory rapporteur is designated to draw up the final document and obtain agreement, in the form of a "sign-off" from the experts representing the other regulatory parties.

Step 4 : Adoption of a Tripartite Harmonised Text : At step 4, the topic returns to the ICH forum where the Steering Committee receives a report from the regulatory Rapporteur. If both, regulatory and industry parties are satisfied that the consensus achieved at Step 2 is not substantially altered as a result of the consultation, the text is adopted by the Steering Committee. This adoption takes place on the signatures from the three regulatory parties to ICH affirming that the Guideline is recommended for adoption by the regulatory bodies in the three regions.

In the event that one or more parties representing industry have strong objections to the adoption of the guideline, on the grounds that the revised draft departs substantially from the original consensus, or introduces new issues, the regulatory parties may agree that the revised text should be submitted to further consultation.

Step 5 : Implementation : Having reached step 4 the tripartite harmonised text moves immediately into the final step of the process which is the regulatory implementation. This is carried out according to the same national/regional procedures that apply to other regulatory guidelines and requirements, in the European Union, Japan and the USA.

Information on the regulatory action taken and implementation dates are reported back to the steering committee and published by the secretariat.

4. Abbreviated Process for Maintenance of ICH Agreements

The "Maintenance" process is intended to provide a rapid and flexible way of making minor changes and revisions to existing ICH Guidelines.

The procedure is intended to provide results quickly and efficiently using the minimum amount of resources consistent with the achievement of a scientifically valid result. As far as possible, maintenance work should be completed via a written procedure with recourse to meetings only in exceptional cases.

(i) Contact Network for Maintenance of Guidelines : Each of the six ICH parties should establish a network of experts for dealing with maintenance issues and should identify one Maintenance Contact for each step 5 ICH guideline or implemented agreement. These Maintenance Contacts in close liaison with their respective ICH coordinators will be empowered to deal with all maintenance issues concerning their respective guidelines.

Coordinators should provide the ICH Secretariat with details of the Maintenance Contacts for each guideline, but the first point of contact on all maintenance issues will be via the ICH coordinators.

(ii) Procedure : Maintenance Network

Concept Paper : Once a maintenance issue has been identified a Concept Paper should be prepared, Item (iii) of the paper - issues to be resolved - should be as specific as possible, for example, giving details of wording to be changed and the proposed new wording. The concept paper is sent to the ICH secretariat and the coordinators.

If the coordinators agree that the proposal constitutes a "minor" change the maintenance process is initiated :

Review and Sign-off

(a) The Secretariat registers the maintenance proposal, designates a code number and prepares a draft sign-off sheet identifying the proposed changes to the Guideline. This is attached to the Concept Paper and sent to the Maintenance Network via the ICH coordinators.

(b) The steering committee members and observers are informed about the proposal.

(c) The maintenance contact from the sponsoring party (i.e., the party which provided the concept paper) acts as topic coordinator and is responsible for circulating comments and further proposals as necessary.

(d) After regional or internal consultation, each of the maintenance contacts indicates whether, he or she can agree or not with the proposal made. Minor changes to the wording may be proposed.

(e) If agreement cannot be reached the matter will be referred to the next steering committee for a decision on establishing and Expert Working Group and initiating the full ICH Process.

(f) If there is agreement by all experts, the completed sign off sheet is returned to the ICH Secretariat. The ICH Secretariat then circulates the signed-off proposal to the Steering Committee, with a request to respond within a month.

(iii) Procedure : Steering Committee : When the steering committee receives notification that a proposal for an amendment to an ICH guideline has been agreed by the maintenance network each party will be asked to give their opinion on whether :

(a) The proposal is accepted and can be implemented immediately, without further consultation. (An example might be changes to the residual solvent lists in the impurity guideline).

Secretariat Action

The text of the ICH Guideline is update and circulated to the Steering Committee and Maintenance Contacts. The revised text is announced and published.

(b) The proposal is accepted but requires wider consultation and should be treated as a Step 2 document for formal regulatory consultation.

Secretariat Action

Signatures for all six parties will be required on the step 2 consultation document, after which the consultation will be announced following normal procedure.

(c) There are further issues to be resolved and the matter should be discussed at the next Steering Committee.

Secretariat Action

The Maintenance Contacts will be informed and the item will be included on the agenda for the next ICH Steering Committee.

5. Type of Maintenance

(i) Proposal of a "Permitted Daily Exposure" (PDE) for a new solvent or a revised PDE for an already classified solvent is submitted directly to the ICH secretariat with supporting information through an ICH regional coordinator.

This information should be based on significant toxicity data from studies such as genotoxicity studies, repeat-dose studies, reproductive toxicity studies, carcinogenicity studies and/or other relevant toxicology studies. Single-dose toxicity data alone are not sufficient. The toxicity data should be of sufficient quality to calculate a PDE.

(ii) Revision of an established PDE will be considered only on presentation of previously unrecognized toxicity data sufficient to result in a significant change, or because of convincing evidence that the existing data used to calculate a PDE are invalid. Minor changes in a PDE will not be considered. The rapporteur, with the consensus of the EWG members, will assign data reviews and request subsequent recommendations to the EWG.

(iii) The ICH secretariat will distribute the proposal to the rapporteur of the ICH Ad Hoc Expert Working Group on Residual Solvents (Q3C EWG). The rapporteur will be one of the regulatory members of the ICH who will be available for two-year terms (e.g., FDA, 1999-2000, MHLW 2001-2002, EU 2003-2004). The ICH Secretariat will also notify the ICH steering committee, coordinators, and observers that the Q3 EWG has been called to consider the proposal. The Q3C EWG will be comprised of two members (one chemist and one toxicologist) nominated by the six sponsors of the ICH and one member nominated by IGPA, WSMI and by each pharmacopeia. As appropriate, ICH observers may be invited to join the working group.

(iv) The regulatory rapporteur will ordinarily rely on correspondence or teleconferencing to avoid unnecessary travel. Based on the discussion, with requests for further information to the proposing group and/or individual as appropriate, the rapporteur will prepare an assessment report based on committee approval with a recommendation to accept, with or without modifications, or reject the proposed PDE. Ideally, this activity would occur at the rate of 2 residual solvents per calendar year. For particular residual solvent, it is anticipated that a period of six months from receipt of the toxicological information by the rapporteur to the recommendation of a step 2 guideline to the steering committee will be necessary.

(v) After endorsement by the ICH Steering Committee, either at the next formal meeting or earlier as feasible, the recommendation of the Q3C EWG will be published in each region for public comment (step 2 ICH process). In addition, the proposal will be provided to each pharmacopeia for their publication.

(vi) After close of the public comment periods, the rapporteur may convene a meeting of the Q3C EWG or will reply on correspondence or teleconferencing to consider the comments and finalize the proposal for the new/revised PDE. The final recommendation for the new/revised PDE and implementation is then forwarded to the ICH steering committee for approval. Implementation will follow regional practices. With approval of the ICH steering Committee, the change will be provided to the pharmacopoeias of the three regions for publication.

(vii) When an existing PDE is revised or a PDE for a new residual solvent is recommended by the EWG, approval by the ICH Steering Committee is required. Once approval occurs, the information should be disseminated as quickly as possible to all ICH participants and other members of the chemical and pharmaceutical communities. It is recommended that the following actions should be taken by the ICH Steering Committee to ensure rapid transmission of the new information :

(a) Publish relevant information on the ICH web site.

(b) Request publication of revisions by the pharmacopoeias of the three regions in their forums or web sites.

(c) Request that each member publish the new solvent PDE information on its respective web sites.

(d) Request WHO to distribute this information to its non-ICH member states.

There are Six Parties directly involved in the decision making process.

The Six Parties are the founder members of ICH which represent the regulatory bodies and the research-based industry in the European Union, Japan and the USA: EU, EFPIA, MHLW, JPMA, FDA and PhRMA.

ICH Parties

(i) European Commission - European Union (EU)

(ii) European Federation of Pharmaceutical Industries and Associations (EFPIA)

(iii) Ministry of Health, Labor and Welfare, Japan (MHLW)

(iv) Japan Pharmaceutical Manufacturers Association (JPMA)

(v) US Food and Drug Administration (FDA)

(vi) Pharmaceutical Research and Manufacturers of America (PhRMA)

(E) WORLD HEALTH ORGANIZATION (WHO)

About WHO : The World Health Organization, the United Nations specialized agency for health, was established on 7th April 1948. WHO's objective, as set out in its constitution, is the attainment of the highest possible level of health by all people. Health is defined in WHO's constitution as a state of complete physical, mental and social well-being and not merely the absence of disease or infirmity.

WHO is governed by 192 member states through the World Health Assembly. The health assembly is composed of representatives from WHO's member states. The main tasks of the World Health Assembly are to approve the 'WHO' programme and the budget for the same and to decide major policy questions.

Constitution of WHO

The States Parties to this Constitution declare, in conformity with the charter of the United Nations, that the following principles are basic to the happiness, harmonious relations, and security of all people.

Health is a state of complete physical, mental and social well-being and not merely the absence of disease or infirmity.

The enjoyment of the highest attainable standard of health is one of the fundamental rights of every human being without distinction of race, religion, political belief, economic or social condition.

The health of all peoples is fundamental to the attainment of peace and security and is dependent upon the fullest co-operation of individuals and States.

The achievement of any state in the promotion and protection of health is of value to all.

Unequal development in different countries in the promotion of health and control of disease, especially communicable disease, is a common danger.

Healthy development of the child is of basic importance; the ability to live harmoniously in a changing total environment is essential to such development.

The extension of the benefits of medical, psychological and related knowledge is essential to the fullest attainment of health to all people.

Informed opinion and active co-operation on the part of the public are of the utmost importance in the improvement of the health of the people.

Governments have a responsibility for the health of their people, which can be fulfilled only by the provision of adequate health and social measures.

Objective :

The objective of the 'World Health Organization' (hereinafter called the organization) shall be the attainment of the highest possible level of health by all people.

Functions :

In order to achieve its objective, the functions of the organization shall be :

(a) To act as the directing and coordinating authority on international health work;
(b) To establish and maintain effective collaboration with the United Nations, specialized agencies, governmental health administrations, professional groups and such other organizations as may be deemed appropriate;

(c) To assist Governments, upon request, in strengthening health services;

(d) To furnish appropriate technical assistance and, in emergencies, necessary aid upon the request or acceptance of Governments;

(e) To provide or assist in providing, upon the request of the United Nations, health services and facilities to special groups, such as the people of trust territories;

(f) To establish and maintain such administrative and technical services as may be required, including epidemiological and statistical services;

(g) To stimulate and advance work to eradicate epidemic, endemic and other diseases;

(h) To promote, in co-operation with other specialized agencies where necessary, the prevention of accidental injuries;

(i) To promote, in co-operation with other specialized agencies where necessary, the improvement of nutrition, housing, sanitation, recreation, economic or working conditions and other aspects of environmental hygiene;

(j) To promote cooperation among scientific and professional groups which contribute to the advancement of health;

(k) To propose conventions, agreements and regulations, and make recommendations with respect to international health matters and to perform such duties as may be assigned thereby to the organization and are consistent with its objective;

(l) To promote maternal and child health and welfare and to foster the ability to live harmoniously in a changing total environment;

(m) To foster activities in the field of mental health, especially those affecting the harmony of human relations;

(n) To promote and conduct research in the field of health;

(o) To promote improved standards of teaching and training in the health, medical and related professions;

(p) To study and report on, in co-operation with other specialized agencies where necessary, administrative and social techniques affecting public health and medical care from preventive and curative points of view, including hospital services and social security;

(q) To provide information, counsel and assistance in the field of health;

(r) To assist in developing an informed public opinion among all people on matters of health;

(s) To establish and revise, as necessary, international nomenclatures of diseases, of causes of death and of public health practices;

(t) To standardize diagnostic procedures as necessary;

(u) To develop, establish and promote international standards with respect to food, biological, pharmaceutical and similar products;

(v) Generally to take all necessary action to attain the objective of the organization.

Membership and Associate Membership

Membership in the organization shall be open to all states.

Governance : The World Health Assembly is the supreme decision-making body for WHO. It generally meets in Geneva in May each year, and is attended by delegations from all 192 member states. Its main function is to determine the policies of the organization. The health assembly appoints the Director-General, who supervises the financial policies of the organization, and reviews and approves the proposed programme budget. It similarly considers reports of the Executive Board, which it instructs in regard to matters upon which further action, study, investigation or report may be required.

The executive board is composed of 32 members technically qualified in the field of health. Members are elected for three-year terms. The main board meeting, at which the agenda for the forthcoming health assembly is agreed upon and resolutions for forwarding to the health assembly are adopted, is held in January, with a second shorter meeting in May, immediately after the health assembly, for more administrative matters. The main functions of the board are to give effect to the decisions and policies of the health assembly, to advise it and generally to facilitate its work.

The secretariat of WHO is staffed by some 3500 health and other experts and support staff on fixed-term appointments, working at headquarters, in the six regional offices, and in countries.

The organization is headed by the Director-General, who is appointed by the health assembly on the nomination of the executive board. The current Director-General is Dr. Gro Harlem Brundtland.

(**Ref.** : for more info, log on to www.who.int)

India - Drug Control Administration

Drug control administration in India is a two tier system with clear division of roles and responsibilities at Central and State level.

Under the Drug and Cosmetics Act, the regulation of manufacture, sale and distribution of Drugs is primarily the concern of the State authorities while the Central Authorities are responsible for approval of New Drugs, Clinical Trials in the country, laying down the standards for Drugs, control over the quality of imported Drugs, coordination of the activities of State Drug Control Organizations and providing expert advice with a view of bring about the uniformity in the enforcement of the Drugs and Cosmetics Act.

Central Drugs Standard Control Organization

Responsible for approval of New Drugs, Clinical Trials in the country, laying down the standards for Drugs, control over the quality of imported Drugs, etc.

State Drugs Standard Control Organization

Responsible for the regulation of manufacture, sale and distribution of Drugs etc.

Drug Controller General of India is responsible for approval of licenses of specified categories of Drugs such as blood and blood products, I. V. Fluids, Vaccine and Sera.

State Drug Control Authority's functions are as follows:

- Licensing of drug manufacturing and sales establishments
- Licensing of drug testing laboratories.
- Approval of drug formulations for manufacture.
- Monitoring the quality of Drugs & Cosmetics, manufactured by respective state units and those marketed in the state.
- Investigation and prosecution in respect of contravention of legal provisions
- Administrative actions
- Pre- and post- licensing inspection
- Recall of sub-standard drugs

STATE DRUGS CONTROLLERS

ANDHRA PRADESH The director, Drugs Control Administration, Drugs Control Bhawan, Vengalrao Nagar, Hyderabad-5000036 Phone : 040-23814357, 23814119, 23707777(R) Fax : 23713563	**ANDAMAN & NICOBAR** Director of Health Services Andaman and Nicobar Islands, Port Blair-744104 Phone : 03192-33331/32709(R) Fax : 32910
ARUNACHAL PRADESH Drugs Controller, Directorate of Health Services, Naharlagun-791119 (Arunachal Pradesh) Phone : 0360-2244248(O) 2244182(R) Fax : 2244105	**ASSAM** Drugs Controller, Directorate of Health Services, Dispur, Hengrabari, Guwahati-38 Phone : 0361-22665276, 22200245(R), Fax : 2261630
BIHAR Drugs Controller, Directorate of Health Services, 4th Floor, Vikas Bhawan, New Secretariat, Patna-800015 Phone : 0612-2221110/ 671389(R), 9431278474(M)	**CHANDIGARH** Drugs Controller & Licensing Authority, Chandigarh Admn., Chandigarh Phone : 780781/ 265640(R) Fax : 780781
CHATTISGARH Drugs Controller, FDA, CGO Nursing Hostel, Near Mantralaya, Raipur-492001 Chattisgarh Phone : 0771-2235226, 2221025 5038202 (R) Fax : 2221625	**DAMAN** Drugs License Authority, Director, Medical & Health Services, Primary Health Centre, Moti Daman, Daman-396220 Phone : 0260-250847/ 254870 Fax : 250870
GOA Director, Foods and Drugs Control Administration, Old GMC Building, Panji Goa-403001 Phone : 0832-2224639, 2220245, 2430948 Resi : 2224638, Fax : 2224639	**GUJARAT** Commissioner FDCA Gujarat State, Old Sachivalya, Block No. 8, 1st Floor, Dr. Jivraj Mehta Bhavan, Gandhi Nagar-382010 Phone : 079-23253400, 9825049232, 26851817(R) Fax : 079-23252417

HARYANA Drugs Controller, Directorate General of Health Services, Sector 20, Punchkula, Haryana Phone : 0172-2551081/ 2584999(R), 9814916180 (M)	**HIMACHAL PRADESH** Drugs Controller, Health & FW Deptt. SDA Complex, Kasumpati, Shimla-170009 (HP) Phone : 0177-2621842/ 2621224/ 2621466 Extn. 232/ 01792-221107(R) Fax : 222508. 9816030033 (M)
JHARKHAND Drugs Controller cum Licensing Authority, Jharkhand directorate of Health Services, Jagarnthpur High School Bldg., Sector -3, Dhurva, Ranchi-834004 Phone : 0651-441886/ 0651-245850(R)	**JAMMU & KASHMIR** The Controller, Drugs & Food Control Organization, Patoli Magotrian PP Janipur Jammutavi-180001 Phone : 080-2538527 2597445
KARNATAKA Drugs Controller, Drugs Control Department, State of Karnataka P B No. 5377, Next to Carito House, Palace Road, Bangalore-560001 Phone : 080-22262846/ 22870943/ 23356134 (R) Fax : 22286492 E-mail : drugscontroller@vsnl.net	**KERALA** Drugs Controller & Licensing Authority, Kerala, Public Health Lab. Campus, Red Cross Road, Thiruvananthpuram-695035 Phone : 0471-2473256/ 2471896/ 2472178(R) Fax : 0471-2473256, 9820710993 (M)
MADHYA PRADESH Controller Food & Drugs Admn. Idgah Hills, Bhopal-462001 Phone : 0755-2665385/5299372(R) Fax : 2665385	**MAHARASHTRA** Commissioner, Food & Drugs Admn., Opp. RBI Building, Bandra, Mumbai-400051 Phone : 26590548/ 22844903(R) Fax : 26591959, 26591820, 9820530690 (M)
MANIPUR Drugs Controller & Director, Medical & Health Services, Lamphlept, Imphal-795004 Manipur Phone : 0385-2310283/ 2221848 (R) Fax : 2310964	**MEGHALAYA** Director of Health Services, Government of Meghalaya, Shillong-793001, Meghalya Phone : 0364-2225709/ 225375 (R) Fax : 2228493

MIZORAM Director of Health Services, Mizoram, Chaltlang, Aizwal-796001 Phone : 0389-2323452/ 2328053(R) Fax : 2320169	**NAGALAND** Dy. Drugs Controller, Directorate of Health Services, Nagaland, Kohima-797001 Phone : 0370-2222626/ 2243409 (R) Fax : 2243887
NEW DELHI Drugs Controller, Drugs Control Department, Govt. of National Capital Territory of Delhi, 15, Shamnath Marg, Delhi-110054 Phone : 011-233922018/26492365 (R) Fax : 22393704	**ORISSA** Drugs Controller , New Nandankanan Road, Bhubaneshwar-751017 Phone : 067-2300494/ 2564878 (R) Fax : 2300494
PONDICHERRY Asstt. Commissioner, FDA, 102-C, Chellan Nagar, Pondicherry-605011 Phone : 0443-340193/332849(R)	**PUNJAB** State Drug Controlling Authority, Sector 34-E, Chandigarh-160016 Phone : 0172-604657 Extn. 399 Fax : 609142
RAJASTHAN Drugs Controller, Directorate of Medical & Health Services, Swasthya Bhawan, Tilak Marg, Jaipur-302004 Phone : 0141-2381670/ 2336280 (R) Fax : 2310447	**SIKKIM** State Drugs Controller, Deptt. of Health & FW, Govt. of Sikkim, Gangtok-737101 Phone : 03592-222633 Fax : 224481
SILVASSA Asstt. Drugs Controller, Medical & Public Health Department, Dadra & Nagar Haveli, Silvassa-396230 Phone : 0260-2642961/ 642940/ 642947(R)/642264(R) Fax : 642961	**TAMILNADU** Drugs Controller, 258-261, Anna Salai, Tahampet, Chennai-600006 Phone :044-24321830/ 22440043 (R) Fax : 24321830
TRIPURA Controlling Authority & Deputy Drugs Controller, Garkha Basti Office Complex, P.O. Kunjaban, Agartala-799006, Tripura Phone : 0381-2325868/ 23250166 (R) Fax : 2225001	**UTTAR PRADESH** Drugs Controller, Satya Seva Mahanideshalya (UP) Swasthya Bhavan, Aushadhi Kaksha, Lucknow-226006 Phone : 0522-2221115/22385156 (R) Fax : 2219503/2619503/ 9839080795 (M)

UTTARNCHAL	WEST BENGAL
State Drugs Controller Cum Licensing Authority, Directorate General of Health Services, Chandra Nagar, Dehradun-248001, Uttaranchal Phone : 0135-2720311/ 2622125/ 3102607 (R) Fax : 2729897	Director, Drugs Control, West Bengal, 141, A J C Bose Road, 3rd Floor, Kolkata - 700014 Phone : 033-22412905/22412887/ 22446100 24778710(R) Fax : 22412905

CDSCO Zonal Offices

NORTH ZONE	SOUTH ZONE
Joint Drugs Controller (India) CDSCO, North Zone, CGO Building-I, Kamla Nehru Nagar, Hapur Road, Ghaziabad-201002 Phone : 0120-4750013 E-mail : cdsco@mantraonline.com	Dy. Drugs Controller (India) CDSCO, South Zone, Shastri Bhavan, Annex Building, IInd Floor, Haddows Rd., Chennai-600006 Phone : 8278186 Fax : 8212079
EAST ZONE	WEST ZONE
Dy. Drugs Controller (India) CDSCO East Zone, Nizam Palace, 2nd Floor, CGO Bldg., 234/4, Lower Circular Rd., Kolkata-700020 Phone : 033-2470513/ 2801391 Fax : 033-2813806	Dy. Drugs Controller (India) CDSCO, West Zone CGHS Dispensary No. 8, 1st Floor, Sector-I, Kane Nagar, Antop Hill, Mumbai-400037 Phone : 022-24026353/ 24011091 Fax : 24015125 E-mail : cdsco@vsnl.net

SUB ZONAL OFFICES

Andhra Pradesh	Gujarat
Asstt. Drugs Controller (India) CDSCO Sub Zonal Office, Air Cargo Complex, A-10-1 to 8, Sardar Patel Rd., Begumpet, Hyderabad-500016 Phone : 040-7760141	Drugs Inspector Office of the Asstt. Drugs Controller (India) CDSCO Sub Zonal Office, Air Cargo Complex, Rear Old Terminal Bldg, Airport, Ahmedbad-380016 Phone : 079-2865244

Indian Pharmacopoeia Commission (IPC)

Indian Pharmacopoeial Commission is an Autonomous Institution under the Ministry of Health & Family Welfare, Govt. of India dedicated for setting of standards for drugs, pharmaceuticals and healthcare devices/ technologies etc besides providing Reference Substances and Training. Its functions are :

(a) To develop comprehensive monographs for drugs to be included in the Indian Pharmacopoeia, including active pharmaceutical ingredients, excipients and dosage forms as well as medical devices, and to keep them updated by revision on a regular basis.

(b) To accord priority to monographs of drugs included in the national Essential Drugs List and their dosage forms.

(c) To prepare monographs for products that have normally been in the market for not less than 2 years except for certain special categories of new drugs like antiretrovirals, antituberculosis and anticancer drugs and their formulations introduced more recently, which may be accorded priority attention

(d) To give special attention to the methods of manufacture used by the indigenous industry in selecting the pharmacopoeial tests for monitoring the toxic impurities of the concerned drug.

(e) To take note of the different levels of sophistication in analytical testing/ instrumentation available while framing the monographs.

(f) To accelerate the process of preparation, certification and distribution of IP Reference Substances, including the related substances, impurities and degradation products required.

(g) To collaborate with pharmacopoeias like the Ph Eur, BP, USP, JP and International Pharmacopoeia with a view to harmonizing with global standards.

(h) To organize educational programs and research activities for spreading and establishing awareness on the need and scope of quality standards for drugs and related articles/ materials.

The Indian Pharmacopoeia Commission has been registered as a Society under the provisions of the Societies Registration Act, 1860(Act No. 21 of 1860) for the registration of Literary, Scientific and Charitable Societies, on 09 December 2004.

The Director of Indian Pharmacopoeial Commission is Dr. G. N. Singh, Raj Nagar, Sector-23, Ghaziabad 201002 (U.P) Phone: 95120-2783401(D) 2783337; Fax: 091 -24783311, E-mail : ipclab@vsnl.net.

(**Ref.** : official website of CDSCO: www.cdsco.nic.in)

USP (United States Pharmacopoeia)

The United States Pharmacopeia (USP) is an official public standards-setting authority for all prescription and over the counter medicines and other health care products manufactured or sold in the United States. USP also sets widely recognized standards for food ingredients and dietary supplements. USP sets standards for the quality, purity, strength, and consistency of these products-critical to the public health. USP's standards are recognized and used in more than 130 countries around the globe. These standards have helped to ensure public health throughout the world for close to 200 years.

USP is a non-governmental, not for profit public health organization whose independent, volunteer experts work under strict conflict of interest rules to set its scientific standards. USP's contributions to public health are enriched by the participation and oversight of volunteers representing pharmacy, medicine, and other health care professions as well as academia, government, the pharmaceutical and food industries, health plans and consumer organizations.

Mission

To improve the health of people around the world through public standards and related programs that help ensure the quality, safety, and benefit of medicines and foods.

Functions

Product Quality-Standards and Verification

USP establishes state of the art documentary and reference standards to ensure quality medicines, food ingredients, and other health care products. Developed through a unique process of public involvement, standards setting is a core activity for USP.

USP's documentary standards and reference standards are used by regulatory agencies and manufacturers of pharmaceuticals, over the counter drugs, dietary supplements, and food ingredients to ensure that these products are of the appropriate strength, quality, and purity.

Prescription and over the counter medicines available in the United States must, by federal law, meet USP's public standards, where such standards exist. Many other countries require the use of high quality standards such as USP's to assure the quality of medicines and related products. USP disseminates its standards for medicines to pharmaceutical manufacturers, pharmacists, and other users through its United States Pharmacopeia-National Formulary (USP-NF) and its standards for food ingredients through the Food Chemicals Codex (FCC), as well as through official USP Reference Standards materials and Pharmacopeial Education courses.

USP also conducts verification programs for dietary supplement ingredients and products and pharmaceutical ingredients. These programs involve independent testing and review to verify ingredient and product integrity, purity, and potency for manufacturers who choose to participate.

Healthcare Quality and Safety

USP develops authoritative, unbiased information relating to various aspects of drug use and disseminates this information to practitioners, pharmacists, and others who make decisions about health care around the world. Significant among USP's health care information initiatives is the development of a drug classification system that Medicare Prescription Drug Benefit plans may use to develop their formularies. USP also partners with the U.S. Agency for International Development, the World Health Organization, John Snow International, the Bill and Melinda Gates Foundation, and others in worldwide projects that help to assure drug quality and proper drug use in many developing countries. Learn more about healthcare quality and safety at USP.

Drug Quality and Information

USP's Drug Quality and Information (USP DQI) Program is a cooperative agreement with the United States Agency for International Development (USAID). The USP DQI program has established a presence in USAID-priority countries on four continents advancing strategies to improve drug quality and the appropriate use of drugs.

Four main programs that USP promotes are: ensuring drug quality by imparting its expertise in the field of drug quality by working with local governments, USAID missions, the World Health Organization (WHO), and other partners to evaluate a country's readiness and capacity to provide necessary drug quality assurance, providing continuing education for physicians, pharmacists and nurses in drug information and pharmacovigilance to help improve drug dispensing and ensure competence and accountability, developing and disseminating evidence-based drug and therapeutic information through targeted drug and therapeutic information materials for health care providers based on specific needs, and furnishing technical leadership toward regional and international cooperation through USP's system of open conferences, Internet-based communications, and regular publications.

(**Ref.** : official website of www.usp.org)

Chapter 12...
OVERVIEW OF DRUG AND COSMETIC ACT

Object and Introduction

The Drugs and Cosmetics Act was passed in 1940, (10th April 1940), with main object to regulate the import, manufacture, distribution and sale of Drugs and Cosmetics. The Act regulates the import of drugs into India so that no substandard or spurious drug will find its way in the country. The Act regulates the manufacture by making provisions, and rules, which provide control over manufacture of spurious or sub-standard drug in the country. The Act also provides for the control over the sale and distribution of drugs by only registered pharmacists and competent persons. Act also provides for the control over the manufacturer, sale and distribution of Ayurvedic, Siddha, Unani and Homoeopathic drugs. In last few years, cosmetics are widely used in the country and it is necessary to control their quality. Act therefore amended to make certain provisions related to cosmetics which regulates its import manufacture.

The import of certain drugs and cosmetics permitted under licence. All classes of drugs and cosmetics imported into India, shall comply with the prescribed standards and shall labelled in prescribed manner.

Manufacture of all classes of drugs require prior licence issued by licensing authority and licence is also required for sale of Allopathic and Homoeopathic drugs. Each state requires to appoint licensing authority to issue or grant licences for manufacture or sale of drugs and cosmetics. Control over manufacture and sale exercised by Drug Inspectors. Drug Control Laboratories of the State or Central Drug Laboratory provided for the analysis of drugs and cosmetics. Drug and cosmetic rules provide for conditions of licences for manufacture, sale, distribution etc. of drugs and cosmetics and prescribes manner of labelling and packing of drugs and cosmetics. All drugs manufactured shall be labelled and packed in a manner prescribed. The Act also provides for the establishment of 'Drugs Technical Advisory Board' to advice Government on technical matters arising out of administration of the Act and 'Drugs Consultative Committee' to advice to the Board and Government to secure uniformity in the administration of the Act throughout India.

Successive amendments were made in the Act and rules thereunder from time-to-time to widen its scope, conception and purpose. The problems of adulteration of drugs and also of production of spurious and sub-standard drugs are posing serious threat to the health of the users. It is therefore, considered essential to amend the Act so as to impose more stringent penalties on the antisocial components indulging in the manufacture or sale of adulterated or spurious drugs or drugs not of standard quality. The opportunity also being availed of to incorporate provisions on the aspects of effective control on the manufacture, distribution and sale of drugs and cosmetics.

The Act consists of five chapters each chapter related to particular subject,

Chapter I - Introductory/Definitions.
Chapter II - Drugs Technical Advisory Board, Drugs Consulatative Committee, Central Drugs Laboratory.
Chapter III - Import of Drugs and Cosmetics.
Chapter IV - Manufacture, Sale and Distribution of Drugs and Cosmetics.
Chapter IV A - Provisions relating to Ayurvedic, Siddha and Unani Drugs.
Chapter V - Miscellaneous.

The Rules of the Act are divided in different parts. Each part is related to a particular subject.

Part I - Preliminary/Definitions.
Part II - Central Drugs Laboratory.
III - Omitted vide S.R.Q. 2136 dt. 15-6-1957.
IV - Import/Registration.
V - Government Analysts and Inspectors. Licensing authorities, Licensing and Controlling Authority.
VI - Sale of Drugs (other than Homoeopathic).
VI-A - Sale of Homoeopathic medicines.
VII - Manufacture (other than Homoeopathic) of drugs.
VII-A - Manufacture of Homoeopathic drugs.
VIII - Manufacture for examination, test or analysis.
IX - Labelling and packing of drugs other than Homoeopathic medicines.
IX-A - Labelling and packing of Homoeopathic medicines.
X - Special provisions relating to biological and other special products.
XA - Import and manufacture of new drugs for clinical trials or marketing.
XB - Requirement for the collection; storage and processing of whole Human Blood and Human Blood components, by blood banks and manufacture of blood products.
XI - Exemptions.
XII - Standards.

XIII - Import of Cosmetics.

XIV - Manufacture of Cosmetics.

XV - Labelling, packing and standards of cosmetics.

XV-A - Approval of institutions for carrying out analysis of drugs and cosmetics and raw materials.

XVI - Manufacture of Ayurvedic, Siddha or Unani drugs.

XVIA - Approval of institutions for carrying and test Ayurvedic, Siddha and Unani drugs.

XVII - Labelling and packing and limit of alcohol in Ayurvedic, Siddha or Unani drugs.

XVIII - Government Analysts and Inspectors for Ayurvedic, Siddha or Unani drugs.

XIX - Standards of Ayurvedic, Siddha or Unani drugs.

There are two schedules to the Act and twenty seven schedules to the Rules.

SCHEDULES TO THE ACT

1. **First Schedule :** List of Ayurvedic, Siddha and Unani books.

2. **Second Schedule :** Standards to be complied with by imported drugs and by drugs manufactured for sale, sold, stocked or exhibited for sale or distributed.

Schedules to the Rules

Schedule   Contents

A - List of forms used for making applications for issuing licences, granting licences, sending memorandum.

B - Fees for test or analysis by the Central Drugs Laboratory or Government Analyst.

C - Biological and special products.

C (1) - Other special products (The import, manufacture and sale of schedule C and C (1) drugs governed by special provisions).

D - Class of exempted drugs, which are exempted from a certain provisions applicable to import of drugs.

E - List of poisonous substances omitted (22-6-82).

E (1) - List of Ayurvedic Siddha and Unani poisons.

F - Provisions applicable to Vaccines, Toxins, Antigens Sera etc.

F (I) - Provisions applicable to other biological and special products such as Vaccines, Antigens, Diagnostic Antigens, Tuberculin etc. regarding their production, testing, storage, packing etc.

F (II) - Standard for surgical dressings.

F(III) - Standards for umbilical tapes.

FF - Standards for opthalmic preparations.

G - List of substances required to be taken only under supervision of a Registered Medical Practioner.

H - Prescription drugs which are required to be sold by retail only on prescription of a Registered Medical Practitioner.

I - Calculation of proportion of poisons in certain cases - Omitted (22-6-82).

J - List of diseases and ailments which a drug may not claim to prevent or cure.

K - List of drugs exempted, from certain provisions applicable to manufacture of drugs and sale of drugs.

L - List of drugs to be sold on prescription only. Omitted (22-6-82).

M - Good Manufacturing practices and requirements of factory premises, plant, equipment etc. for the manufacture of drugs.

M(I) - Requirement of factory premises, plant, equipment etc. for manufacture of Homoeopathic drugs.

M(II) - Requirement of factory premises, plant, equipments for the manufacture of cosmetics.

M(III) - Requirement of factory premises for manufacture of Medical Devices.

N - List of minimum equipment for the efficient running of a pharmacy.

O - Standards for disinfectant fluids.

P - Life periods of Drugs.

Q - List of coaltar colours permitted to be used in cosmetics and soaps.

R - Standards for condoms made up of rubber latex intended for single use and other mechanical contraceptives.

S - Standard for cosmetics.

T - Requirements for factory premises and hygienic conditions for manufacture of Ayurvedic (including Siddha) and Unani drugs.

U - Particulars to be shown in manufacturing and analytical records of drugs.

U(I) - Particulars to be shown in manufacturing records of cosmetics.

V - Standards for patent and proprietary medicines and for patent and proprietary medicines containing vitamins.

W - List of drugs which shall be marketed under generic name only.

X - List of habit forming, psychotropic and other such drugs.

Y - Requirements and guidelines for clinical trials, import and manufacture of new drugs.

Definitions

1. **Drug :**

   It includes,
   (i) All medicines for internal or external use of human beings or animals and all substances intended to be used for; or in the diagnosis, treatment, mitigation or prevention of any disease or disorder in human beings or animals, including preparations applied on human body for the purpose of repelling insects like mosquitoes.
   (ii) Such substances (other than food) intended to affect the structure or any function of the human body or intended to be used for the destruction of vermin or insects which cause disease in the human beings or animals.
   (iii) All substances intended for use as components of a drug including empty gelatin capsules.
   (iv) Such devices intended for internal or external use in diagnosis, treatment, mitigation or prevention of disease or disorders in human beings or animals.

2. **Ayurvedic, Siddha or Unani Drug : (Section 3 (a))**

   It includes all medicines intended for internal or external use for, or in the diagnosis, treatment, mitigation or prevention of disease or disorder in human beings or animals and manufactured inaccordance with the formulae described in the authoritative books of Ayurvedic, Siddha or Unani systems of medicine, specified in First Schedule.

3. **Misbranded Drugs : (Section 17)**

   Drugs shall be deemed to be misbranded.
   (a) If it is so coloured, coated, powdered or polished that, damage is concealed or if it is made to appear of better or greater therapeutic value than it really is or
   (b) If it is not labelled in the prescribed manner, or
   (c) If it's label or container or anything accompanying the drugs bears any statement design or device which makes any false claim for the drug or which is false or misleading in any particular.

4. **Adulterated Drugs : (Section 17-A)**

   A drug shall be deemed to be adulterated.

   (a) If it consists, in whole or in part, of any filthy, putrid or decomposed substance, or,

   (b) If it has been prepared, packed or stored under insanitary conditions whereby it may have been contaminated with filth or whereby it may have been injurious to health, or,

   (c) If its container is composed in whole or in part, of any poisonous or deleterious substance which may render the contents injurious to health, or

   (d) If it bears or contains, a colour other than prescribed which may be used for the purpose of colouring only, or

   (e) If it contains any harmful or toxic substance which may render it injurious to health, or

   (f) If any substance mixed with it so as to reduce its quality or strength.

5. **Spurious Drugs : (Section 17-B)**

   A drug shall be deemed to be spurious.

   (i) If it is manufactured under a name which belongs to another drug.

   (ii) If it is an imitation of or is a substitute for another drug or resembles to another drug in a manner to deceive or bear upon its label or container the name of another drug unless plainly or conspicuously marked so as to revel its true character and its lack of identity with such other drugs; or

   (iii) If the label or container of which bears the name of an individual or company purporting to be the manufacturer of drug, which individual or company is fictitious or does not exists; or

   (iv) If it has been substituted wholly or in part by another drug or another substance; or (v) If it purports to be the product of a manufacturer of whom it is not truly a product.

6. **New Drug : (Rule - 122E)**

   (i) A new substance of chemical, biological or biotechnological origin in bulk or prepared dosage form used for prevention, diagnosis, or treatment of disease in man or animals, which except during local clinical trials has not been used in the country to any significant extent and which, except during local clinical trials has not been recognised in the country as effective and safe for the proposed claims.

   (ii) A drug already approved by the licensing authority for certain claims, which is now proposed to be marketed with modified or new claims namely indications, dosage, dosage form (including sustained release dosage form) and route or administration.

(iii) A fixed dose combination of two or more drugs, individually approved earlier for certain claims which are now proposed to be combined for the first time in a ratio or if the ratio of ingredients in an already marketed combinations is proposed to be changed with certain claims viz. indications, dosage, dosage form (including sustained release dosage form) and route of administration.

Explanation :

(i) A new drug shall continue to be considered as a new drug for a period of four years from the date of its first approval or its inclusion in the Indian Pharmacopoeia whichever is earlier.

(ii) All vaccines shall be new drugs unless certified otherwise by the Licencing authority.

7. **Inspector : (Section 3 (e))**

(i) In relation to a Ayurvedic, Siddha or Unani drug, an Inspector appointed by Central or State Government under Section 33-G;

(ii) In relation to any other drugs or cosmetics, an Inspector appointed by Central or State Government under Section 21.

8. **Cosmetic : (Section 3 (aaa))**

It means any article intended to be rubbed, poured, sprinkled or sprayed on or introduced into or applied to any part of the human body, for cleansing, beautifying, promoting attractiveness or altering the appearance and includes any article intended for use as a component of cosmetic.

9. **Misbranded Cosmetic : (Sec. 17 c)**

A cosmetic shall be deemed to be misbranded if :

(a) It contains a colour which is not prescribed; or

(b) It is not labelled in the prescribed manner; or

(c) The label or container or anything accompanying the cosmetic bears any statement which is false or misleading in any particular.

10. **Spurious Cosmetic : (Sec 17-D)**

A cosmetic shall be deemed to be spurious if :

(a) It is manufactured under a name which belongs to another cosmetic; or

(b) It is an immitation of, or is a substitute for another cosmetic, or resembles another cosmetics in a manner likely to deceive or bears upon it or it's label or container the name of another cosmetic, unless it is plainly and conspicuously marked so as to reveal it's true character and it's lack of identity with such other cosmetic; or

(c) The label or container bears the name of an individual or a company purporting to be the manufacturer of the cosmetic which is fictitious or does not exist; or

(d) It purports to be the product of a manufacturer of whom it is not truly a product.

11. Drug Store : (Rules 65 (15 (a)))

A description Drug Store shall be displayed by Licensees who do not require the services of a registered Pharmacist.

12. Chemists and Druggists : (Rule 65 (15 (b)))

A description 'Chemist and Druggist' shall be displayed by licensees who employed services of a 'Registered Pharmacist' but where the drugs are not compounded against prescriptions.

13. Pharmacy : (Rule 65 (15 (C)))

A description 'Pharmacy Pharmacist, Dispensing Chemist shall be displayed by Licensees who employ the services of a 'Registered Pharmacist' and maintain Pharmacy for compounding against prescriptions.

14. Registered Pharmacist : (Rule 15)

It means a person who : Is a registered pharmacist, as defined in clause (i) of Section (2) of the Pharmacy Act 1948.

14A. Qualified Person : (RULE 65 151)

Person who are already approved as qualified persons by licensing authorities on or before 31st Dec. 1969.

15. Government Analyst : (Sec. 3 (c))

In relation to Ayurvedic, Siddha or Unani drugs, a person appointed by Central Government or State Government under section 33 - F, and

16. Manufacture : (Sec. 3 (t))

Manufacture in relation to any drug or cosmetic includes any process or part of a process for making, altering, ornamenting, finishing, packing, labelling, breaking up or otherwise treating or adopting any drug or cosmetic for sale or distribution but does not include compounding or dispending of any drug or the packing of any drug or cosmetic in the ordinary course or retail business and to manufacture shall be construed accordingly.

17. Patent or Proprietary Medicine (Ayurvedic, Siddha or Unani) :

All formulations containing only such ingredients mentioned in the formulae described in the authoritative books of Ayurveda, Siddha or Unani systems of medicine specified in the First Schedule but does not include medicine administered by parenteral route and also a formulation included in the authoritative books listed in the First Schedule.

18. Patent or Proprietary Medicine : (Sec. 3 (h) (ii))

In relation to any other system of medicine.

A drug which is remedy or prescription presented in a form ready for internal or external administration of human beings or animals and which is not included in the edition of the Indian pharmacopoeia for the time being or any other Pharmacopoeia authorised in this behalf by the Central Government after consultation with Drugs Technical Advisory Board constituted under Sec. 5.

19. Homoeopathic Medicines : (Rule 2 (dd))

It includes any drug recorded in Homoeopathic provings or the drugs whose therapeutic efficacy has been established through long clinical experience as recorded in authoritative Homoeopathic literature and which are prepared according to the techniques of homoeopathic pharmacy and covers combination of ingredients of such homoeopathic medicines but does not include medicines which is administered by parenteral route.

20. New Homoeopathic Medicines : (Rule - 30 A)

(i) A homoeopathic medicine, not specified in the Homoeopathic Pharmacopoeia of India, or the U. S. A. or U. K. or the German Homoeopathic Pharmacopoeia; or

(ii) Which is not recognised in authoritative Homoeopathic literature; as efficatious under the conditions recommended; or

(iii) A combination of Homoeopathic medicines of which one or more medicines which are not in any of the above mentioned Homoeopathic Pharmacopoeia and also not recognised in authoritative homoeopathic literature as efficacious under the conditions recommended.

21. Registered Medical Practitioner : (Rule 2 (ee)) Means a person :

(i) Holding a qualification granted by an authority specified in section 3 of Indian Medical Degrees Act, 1916 or specified in the schedules to the Indian Medical Council Act 1956, or

(ii) Registered or eligible for registration in a medical register of the State meant for the registration of persons practising the modern scientific system of medicine excluding the Homoeopathic system of medicine, or

(iii) Registered in a medical register (other than for Homoeopathic practitioners) of a state, who although not failing within sub-clauses (i) or (ii) is declared by a general or special order made by the State GoverDnent to be practicing modern scientific systems of medicine; or

(iv) Registered or eligible for registration in the register of Dentist for a State under Dentists Act, 1948; or

(v) Who is engaged in the practice of veterinary medicine and who possesses qualifications approved by the State Government.

22. Registered Homoeopathic Medical Practitioner : (Rule 2 (ea))

A Person who is registered in the Central or State Register of Homoeopathy.

23. Sale By Way of Wholesale Dealings : (Rule 2 (g))

It means sale to a person for the purpose of selling again and also includes the sale to hospitals, dispensaries, or medical, educational or research institutions.

24. Retail Sale : (Rule 2 (f))

It means a sale weather to a hospital or a dispensary or a medical educational or research institute or to any other person other than a sale by way of wholesale dealings.

25. Repacking of Drugs : (Rule 69 (5))

It means the process of breaking up any drug from a bulk container into small packages and the labelling of each such package with a view to it's sale and distribution, but does not include the compounding or dispensing or the packing of any drug in the ordinary course of retail business.

26. Loan Licence : (Rule 69-A)

It means a licence issued by a licencing authority to a applicant who does not have his own arrangements for manufacture but who intends to avail himself of the manufacturing facilities owned by another license.

27. Import : (Sec. 3 (9))

Means to bring into India.

28. Central Licence Approving Authority : (Rule 2(6))

Means the Drugs Controller India appointed by Central Government.

29. Large Volume Parenterals : (Rule 76)

Large volume parenterals means the sterile solutions intended for parenteral administration with a volume of 100 ml or more (and shall include anticoagulant solutions) in one container of the finished dosage form intended for single use.

30. Blood-Bank : (Rule 122F)

Means a place or organisational unit or an institution for carrying out all or any of the operations of manufacture of human blood components or blood products or whole human blood for its collection storage processing, distribution from selected human donors.

31. Pharmacy : (Rule 64)

Pharmacy include every store or shop or other place -

(i) Where drugs are dispensed, that is measured or weighed or made up and supplied; or

(ii) Where prescriptions are compounded; or

(iii) Where drugs are prepared; or

(iv) Which has upon it or displayed with it or affixed to or used in connection with it, a sign bearing the word or words 'Pharmacy'; 'Pharmacist'; 'Dispensing Chemist' or Pharmaceutical Chemist; or

(v) Which by sign, symbol, or indication within or upon it gives the impression that the operations mentioned at (i), (ii) and (iii) are carried out in the premises; or

(vi) Which is advertised in terms referred to in (iv) above.

ADMINISTRATIVE BODIES

The Central Government and State Government establish or appoint following bodies for efficient running of the Act.

(A) Advisory :
(i) Drugs Technical Advisory Board;
(ii) Drugs Consultative Committee.

(B) Analytical :
(i) The Central Drugs Laboratory.
(ii) Drugs Control Laboratories in States.
(iii) Government analyst.

(C) Executive :
(i) Licensing Authorities (Central and State).
(ii) Drug Inspectors.
(iii) Customs Collectors.

Drugs Technical Advisory Board : (D.T.A.B.)

Under the provisions (Sec. 5) of the Act the Central Government appoints the Drugs Technical Advisory Board to advice the Central and the State Governments on technical matters arising out of the administration of this Act, and to carry out the other functions assigned to it by this Act.

Constitution of D.T.A.B. : The board consists of the following members :

(a) Ex-officio-members :
1. The Director-General of Health Services, who is the Chairman of the Board.
2. The Drugs Controller of India.
3. The Director of the Central Drugs Laboratory, Calcutta.
4. The Director of the Central Research Institute Kasauli.
5. The Director of the Indian Veterinary Research Institute, Izatnagar.
6. Director, Central Drug Research Institute, Lucknow.
7. The President, Pharmacy Council of India.
8. The President, Medical Council of India.

(b) Nominated members :

The following members are nominated by Central Government :
1. Two persons from among persons who are in charge of the drugs control in the States.
2. One person from the pharmaceuticals industry.
3. Two Government Analysts.
4. One teacher in Pharmacy, Pharmaceuticals Chemistry or Pharmacognosy on the staff of an university or affiliated college elected by the executive Committee of Pharmacy Council of India.
5. One teacher in medicine or therapeutics on the staff of an university or affiliated college elected by the Executive Committee of the Medical Council of India.
6. One Pharmacologist, elected by the Governing Body of the Indian Council of Medical Research.
7. One person elected by the Central Council of Indian Medical Association.
8. One person elected by Council of the Indian Pharmaceutical Association.

The nominated and elected members holds office for 3 years and are eligible for renomination and re-election. The Central Government appoints a secretary of the board, and also provides clerical and other staff. The Board may constitute sub-committees and may appoint persons to such subcommittees who are not members of the board for the consideration of particular matters.

There is separate Aurvedic and Unani Drugs Technical Advisory Board constituted under sec. 33 - C of the Act.

Drugs Consultative Committee (DCC)

This is an advisory committee constituted by Central Government to advise the Central and State Governments and the Drugs Technical Advisory Board on any matter to secure uniformity throughout India in the administration of this Act.

Constitution : It consists of :

1. Two representatives of Central Government nominated by Central Government and
2. One representative of each State Government nominated by the concerned Government.

There is separate "The Ayurvedic, Siddha and Unani Drugs Consultative Committee "constituted under sec. 33 D of the Act.

Central Drugs Laboratory (CDL)

The Central government establishes a Central Drugs Laboratory (Calcutta) under the control of Director.

Functions :

1. To analyse or test the samples of drugs or cosmetics sent to it by,
   (a) Customers collectors or any authorised officers (under sub sec. (2) of Sec. (11); or
   (b) Courts [under sub sec. (4) of sec. 25].
2. To carry out such other duties as may be entrusted to it by the Central Government or by the State Government with the permission of Central Government after consultation with the Drugs Technical Advisory Board.
3. (a) In case of the following drugs or classes of drugs, functions of CDL are carried out at Central Research Institute Kasauli and such functions are exercised by the Director of the said institute :
   (i) Sera
   (ii) Vaccines
   (iii) Toxins
   (iv) Antigens
   (v) Antitoxins
   (vi) Solution of serum proteins intended for injection
   (vii) Sterilized surgical ligature and suture
   (viii) Bacteriophages.

The functions regarding Oral Polio Vaccine are exercised by the Deputy Director and Head of the Polio Vaccine Testing Laboratory of Central Research Institute Kasauli.

(a) The functions of Laboratory in respect of Oral Polio Vaccine shall be carried out by the following institutes and the functions of the Director in respect of the said drugs shall be exercised by the Director of the respective institutes.
   (i) Pasteur Institute of India Conoor.
   (ii) Enterovirous Research Centre (Indian Council of Medical Research) Haffkin Institute Compound, Parel Mumbai - 400012.
   (iii) The National Institute of Biologicals, Noida.

(b) In case of the following drugs or classes of drugs functions of CDL are carried out at the Indian Veterinary Research Institute, Izatnagar or Mukteshwar. Such functions are exercised by the Director of either of the Institutions.
   (i) Anti-sera for veterinary use
   (ii) Vaccines for veterinary use
   (iii) Toxoids for veterinary use
   (iv) Diagnostic antigens for veterinary use.

(c) In case of **Condoms** the functions of CDL are carried out at the Central Indian Pharmacopoeia Laboratory, Ghaziabad, and such functions are exercised by the Director of the said laboratory.

(d) In case of **VDRL ANTIGEN** (Veneral Disease Ref. Lab.) the functions of the CDL are carried out at the Laboratory of the Serologist and Chemical Examiner to the Government of India, Calcutta, such functions are exercised by the Serologist and Chemical Examiner of the said laboratory.

(e) The functions of the Laboratory in respect of Intra Uterine Devices and Falope Rings shall be carried out at the Central Drugs Testing Laboratory, Thane, Maharashtra and the functions of the Director in respect of the said devices shall be exercised by the Director of the said Laboratory.

(f) The functions of the Laboratory in respect of human blood and human blood products including components, to test for freedom from HIV antibodies, shall be carried out by the following Institutes/Hospitals and the functions of the Director in respect of the above mentioned products shall be exercised by the head of the respective Institute, namely :
   (i) National Institute of Communicable Disease, Department of Microbiology, Delhi.
   (ii) National Institute of Virology, Pune.
   (iii) Centre for advanced Research in Virology, Christian Medical College, Vellore.

(g) The functions of the laboratory in respect of Homoeopathic medicines shall be carried out at the Homoeopathic Pharmacopoeia Laboratory Gaziabad, and the functions of the Director in respect of the Homoeopathic medicines shall be exercised by the Director of the laboratory.

(h) The function of the Laboratory in respect of Blood Grouping reagents and diagnostic kits for Human Immunodeficiency Virus, Hepatitis-13 surface Antigen and Hepatitis-C Virus shall be carried out at the National Institute of Biologicals, NOIDA and the function of the Director in respect of the said drugs shall be exercised by the Director of the said laboratory.

Despatch of samples for test or analysis :
1. Samples for test or analysis under subsection (4) of Section 25 of the Act shall be sent by registered post in a sealed packet, enclosed, together with a memorandum in Form 1, in an outer cover addressed to the Director.
2. The packet as well as the outer cover, shall be marked with a distinguishing number.
3. A copy of the memorandum in Form 1 and a specimen impression of the seal used to seal the packet shall be sent separately by registered post to the Director.

Recording of condition of seals : On receipt of the packet, it shall be opened by an officer authorised in writing in that behalf by the Director, who shall record the condition of the seal on the packet.

Report or result of test or analysis : After test or analysis, the result, of the test or analysis, together with full protocols of the tests applied, shall be supplied forthwith to the sender in Form 2.

Fees : The fees for test and analysis shall be those specified in Schedule B.

Signature of certificates : Certificates issued under these Rules by the Laboratory shall be signed by the Director or by an officer authorised by the Central Government by notification in the Official Gazette to sign such certificates.

Dispatch of samples for test or analysis to CDL :

Samples for test or analysis under sub-section (4) of section 25 of the act shall be sent by registered post in a sealed packet, marked with a distinguishing number with a memorandum in Form 1, in an outer cover addressed to the director.

A specimen impression of the seal used to seal the packet and a copy of memorandum (in Form 1) are to be sent separately by registered post.

On receipt of the packet, authorised officer on behalf of the director opens the packet and records the conditions of the seals on the packet. After completion of test or analysis, the report is supplied in Form 2, together with full protocols of the test applied. Certificate regarding the report is to be signed by the Director or the authorised officer on his behalf.

Drugs Control Laboratories in the States

Every State has a laboratory for the analysis and testing of the drugs and cosmetics manufactured or sold or to be sold with in the respective areas. Samples sent by the Drug Inspectors are analysed in these laboratories. These laboratories may also test or analyse the samples of drugs sent by purchaser of a drug on payment of specified feed prescribed in schedules B.

GOVERNMENT ANALYST (SECTION 20)

State Government by notifying in the Official Gazette, appoint Government analyst under sub-section (1) of section 20, of the Act, for the analysis and testing of samples of drugs and cosmetics in the Drug Control Laboratories.

Central Government may also appoints Government Analyst for specified categories of the drugs or cosmetics under sub-section (2) of section 20 of the Act.

A person to be appointed as a Government Analyst should have no finanical interest in the import, manufacture or sale of the drugs or cosmetics.

Government Analyst for Ayurvedic, Siddha and Unani drugs is appointed by State and Central Government under section 33-F, of the Act.

Qualifications : (Rule-44)

A person appointed as a Government Analyst should possess the following qualifications :

(i) A graduate in medicine or science or pharmacy or pharmaceutical chemistry of a recognised University, or equivalent qualification recognized and notified by Central Government for such purpose and had not less than 5 years post graduate experience; in the testing of drugs in a laboratory under the control of (i) Government Analyst appointed under the Act or (ii) the head of an institution or testing laboratory approved for the purpose by appointing authority or has completed two years training on testing or drugs including items stated in Schedule C in Central Drugs Laboratory.

(ii) A post graduate degree in medicine or science or pharmacy or pharmaceutical chemistry of a recognised University or has an equivalent qualification recognised and notified by Central Government for such purpose.

Associateship Diploma of the Institution of Chemists (India) with 'Analysis of Drugs and Pharmaceuticals' as one of the subjects and has had not less than 3 years experience in the testing of drugs in a laboratory under the control of,

(a) A government Analyst; or

(b) Head of an Institution or testing laboratory approved for the purpose by the appointing authority or has completed two years training on testing of Drugs, including items stated in Schedule C in Central Drugs Laboratory.

Provided that :
- (a) For the purpose of testing or analysis of drugs specified in schedule C,
  - (i) The persons appointed under clause (i) or (ii) and having degree in medicine, physiology, pharmacology, microbiology, pharmacy should have experience or training in testing of said items in an institution or laboratory approved by the appointing authority for a period of not less than six months.
  - (ii) The person appointed under clause (i) or (ii) but not having degree in the above subject should have experience or training in testing of said schedule C drugs for a period of not less than three years in an institution or laboratory approved by the appointing authority or have completed two years training on testing of drugs including item stated in Schedule C in the Central Drug Laboratory.
- (b) For a period of 4 years from the day on which chapter IV of the Act (Manufacture, Sale and Distribution of Drugs and Cosmetics) takes effect in the States, persons whose training and experience are considered adequate and competence may be appointed as Government Analysts and such persons may be continued in service after 4 years also.
- (c) A person to be appointed as a Government Analyst should not be engaged directly or indirectly in trade or business connected with the manufacturer drugs.
- (d) For the purpose of examination of the veterinary biological products (Antisera, toxoid and Vaccines and Diagnostic antigens) the person appointed as Government Analyst should be graduate in veterinary science or general science or medicine or pharmacy with not less than five years experience in the standardization of biological products or a person having post graduate degree in above faculties with not less than 3 years said experience.
- (e) The persons already appointed as Government Analyst may continue to remain in service if the appointing authority so desires, eventhough he does not fulfill the said qualifications.

Duties of Government Analyst : (Rule-45)
- (i) To analyse or test the samples of drugs and cosmetics sent to him by Drug Inspectors or other persons and to furnish the reports of the results of such analysis or test.
- (ii) To forward to the Government the reports of analytical and research work with a view to their publication at the discretion of the Government.

Procedure on Receipt of Samples : (Rule 46)

On receipt of a package of a sample from Drug Inspector, the Government analyst compares the seals on the package or on portion of sample or container with the specimen impression of the seal received separately and notes the condition of seals on the pack or on the portion of sample or container.

On completion of test or analysis, he supplies to the Inspector a report of analysis in triplicate in Form 13, together with full protocols of the tests applied.

If purchaser wants to analyse or test drug or cosmetic, he has to make an application for test or analysis in Form 14-A accompanied with prescribed fees and the report of test or analysis of such drug or cosmetic is to be supplied in Form 14 B, by Government Analyst.

DRUG INSPECTORS (SECTION 21)

The Central Government or a State Government by notification in the Official Gazette appoints Inspectors having prescribed qualifications under section 21 of the Act, for the specified area.

A person to be appointed as a Drug Inspector should have no financial interest in the import, manufacture or sale of the drugs or cosmetics, Drug Inspector is a 'Public Servant' under sec. 21 of Indian Penal Code.

Qualifications : (Rule-49)

A person appointed as 'Drug Inspector' should possess the following qualifications :

1. Graduate in Pharmacy or Pharmaceuticals Sciences or Medicine with specialization in Clinical Pharmacology or Microbiology of a recognised University;

   Provided that for the purpose of Inspection of manufacture of substances specified in schedule C, a person appointed as a Drug Inspector should have,

   (i) not less than 18 months experience in the manufacture of atleast one of the substances specified in schedule C; or

   (ii) not less than 18 months experience in testing of at least one of the substances specified in a schedule C in a approved laboratory; or

   (iii) not less than 3 years experience in the inspection of firms manufacturing any of the substances specified in schedule C during the course of their services as the Drugs Inspectors.

Provided further that the requirement as to the academic qualification shall not apply to persons appointed as inspectors on or before the 18th day of October 1993.

Powers of Drugs Inspector : (Section-22)

Within the local limits for which the Inspector is appointed, he may,

(i) **Inspect :**
   (a) Any premises wherein any drug or cosmetic is being manufactured. And also he may inspect the means employed for standardising and testing the drug or cosmetic.
   (b) Any premises wherein any drug or cosmetic is being sold or stocked or exhibited or offered for sale, or distributed.

(ii) **Take Samples of any drug or Cosmetic :**
   (a) Which is being manufactured or being sold or is stocked or offered for sale or exhibited or being distributed.
   (b) From any person, conveying, delivering or preparing to deliver any drug or cosmetic to a purchaser or a consignee.

(iii) **Search** any person in connection with the offence under this chapter at all reasonable times.

(iv) **Enter and search** at all reasonable times, any place or premises in which he has reason to believe that an offence is being committed or has been committed.

(v) **Stop and search** any vehicle or other conveyance which he has reason to believe, used for carrying any drug or cosmetic in respect of which offence has been or has being committed.

(vi) **Give order** in writing to the person in possession of drug or cosmetic in respect of which offence has been committed or is being committed, not to dispose stock of such drug or cosmetic for a specified period not exceeding twenty days or unless the defect may be removed by the possessor of the drug or cosmetic, and may sieze the stock of such drug or cosmetic or any substance or article employed for commission of offence.

(vii) **Examine** any record, register, document or any other material object found while exercising above powers and sieze the same if he has reason to believe that it is an evidence of the commission of an offence under the Act.

(viii) Exercise any other powers as may be necessary, for carrying out the purpose of this act and the rules made the thereunder.

Duties of Drug Inspector

The duties of Drug Inspector are conveniently grouped as follows :

(i) Duties in relation to the sale of drugs and cosmetics.
(ii) Duties in relation to the manufacture of drugs and cosmetics.

(i) Duties in relation to the sale of drugs and cosmetics : (Rule-51)

Subject to the instructions of the Controlling Authority, it shall be the duty of Inspector,

(a) To inspect at least once a year all establisments licensed for sale of drugs in the area assigned to him and to satisfy himself whether the conditions of the licences are observed or not.

(b) If he thinks necessary, to obtain and send the samples of imported drugs and cosmetics for test or analysis, which are being sold, or stocked in contravention of the provisions of the Act.

(c) To investigate any complaint in writing made to him.

(d) To institute prosecutions in case of breach of the Act and Rules.

(e) To maintain the records relating to all inspections and actions taken by him and to submit copies of such records to the controlling authority.

(f) To make inquires and inspections regarding the sale of drugs in contravention of the act.

(g) To detain the imported packages, if he suspects to contain drugs, the import of which is prohibited.

(ii) Duties in relation to the manufacture of drugs and cosmetics : (Rule-52)

Subject to the instructions by the controlling authority it shall be the duty of Drug Inspector authorised for this purpose.

(a) To inspect at least once a year, all premises licensed for manufacture of drugs within the area alloted to him and to satisfy whether the conditions of the licence and the provisions of the Act and Rules thereunder being observed or not.

(b) To inspect premises licensed for manufacture of drugs specified in Schedule C and C(1) and to observe process of manufacture, means employed, for standardization and testing of drugs, storage conditions, qualifications of technical staff employed, and all other details of location, construction, administration of establishment which may likley to affect potency or purity of the product.

(c) To send after each inspection, a detailed report of inspection to the controlling authority with which condition of licence and provisions of the Act and the Rules thereunder being observed and which being not observed.

(d) To take samples of drugs manufactured on the premises and send them for test or analysis.

(e) To check all records and registers required to be maintained under the Rules.

(f) To institute prosecutions in respect of the breaches of the Act and Rules thereunder.

Procedure of Inspections (Section 23, 25 rules 57)

(A) For taking samples of drugs for analysis and their despatch to the Government Analyst :

Where an Inspector takes any sample of drug or cosmetic, he shall,

(i) Intimate the purpose to a person from whom, he takes sample, in writing in a prescribed form (Form - 17).

(ii) Tender fair price of the sample and obtain acknowledgement thereof. If price is refused, by such person, he has to tender receipt thereof in prescribed form (Form - 17-A).

(iii) Divide the sample in the presence of such person in four parts unless the willfully absents himself and efffectively seals and mark the portions so sealed.

If sample is taken from manufacturing premises, it should be divided in only three parts. Further if drug is packed in small volume containers or gets damaged or deteriorate on exposure, three or four container to be taken as the case may be and sealed and marked.

(iv) (a) Restore one portion or container with a person from whom sample is taken.

(b) Send one portion/container to the Government analyst for test or analysis. By register post or by hand in a scaled packet enclose together with memorandum in Form 18. The copy of memorandum in Form 18 and specimen impression of seal used to seal the packet shall be send to government analyst separately by register post or by hand.

(c) Reserve one portion/container for production before the court if proceeding are instituted in case of such sample.

(d) Send remaining portion to a person (whose name address and other particulars have been disclosed under Section 18A). Every person not being manufacturer or his agent if so required disclose to the inspector the name and address and other particulars of the person from whom he acquired the drug or cosmetic.

(B) For Seizure of Stocks :

Whenever Inspector suspects that any drug or cosmetics contravences any of the provision of the Act, he may seize any stock of such drug or records, registers, documents etc. which are believed to be evidence of the commission of an offence and he should inform to a judicial magistrate as soon as possible and take his order for the custody of the same.

If the alleged contravention by such that, defect may be remedied by the possessor and if Inspector on being satisfied, he can revoke his order and may return the material to possessor.

Penalty for obstructing Inspector : (Section 22 (3))

If any person willfully obstructs an Inspector in the exercise of the powers conferred upon him or refuses to produce any record, register or any document when required, he shall be punishable with imprisonment upto 3 years or with fine or with both.

Reports of the Government Analyst : (Section 25)

On receipt of sample from Inspector, and on completion of analysis or tests, Government Analyst sends a signed report in triplicate in prescribed form. The Inspector on receipt of reports from Government Analyst delivers one copy of the report to the person from whom the sample was taken and another copy to a warrantor if any, and reserves the third copy for use in any prosecution in respect of the sample.

The report signed by the Government Analyst, taken to be the evidence of the facts therein and is considered conclusive unless, challenged within 28 days of receipt of the report by a person from whom sample is taken or by a person whose name is disclosed under Sec. 18 A. If such report is challenged, then sample of such drug or cosmetic is sent to CDL by court and the report signed by the Director CDL is considered final.

Licensing Authorities

Central Government appoints an authority called "Licensing authority" to issue licence for import of drugs. Each State Government appoints licensing authorities to issue licence for manufacture, distribution and sale of drugs or cosmetics, for a specified area. The licensing authorities have the power to issue or refuse licence, depending upon whether the applicant satisfy the conditions prescribed or not. The licensing authorities is also empowered to cancel or suspend the licences issued by them, if licensees fail to observe any of the conditions of licence, after giving reasonable opportunity to explain their case. The decision of licensing authority may be appealed before the state or central government as the case may be.

Central Licence Approving Authority

The Central Government may appoint Central licence approving authority, from the commencement of the Drug and Cosmetics Amendment Rule 1992, to issue licence for the manufacture or sale or distribution of drugs as specified from time to time by notification in the official gazette, for grant or renewal of licence as the case may be. Following categories of drugs presently notified for this purpose.

   (i) Large volume, Parenterals and Sera and Vaccines.
   (ii) Operation of Blood Bank/Processing of whole Human bood for components and manufacture of blood products.

Drug Controller India is appointed as a central approving authority for this purpose.

Delegation of Powers by the Central Licence Authority

The CLAA may with the approval of central government by notification delegate his powers of signing licences and any other power under the rule to any person under his control having same qualifications as prescribed for controlling authority.

Qualifications of Licensing Authority : (Rule 49A)

No person shall be qualified to be a Licensing Authority under the Act unless,

(i) He is a graduate in pharmacy or pharmaceutical chemistry or in medicine with specification in clinical pharmacology or microbiology from a university established in India by laws; and

(ii) He has experience in the manufacture or testing of drugs or enforcement of the provisions of the Act for a minimum period of five years.

Provided that the requirement as to the academic qualification shall not apply to Inspectors and the Government Analysts appointed under this Act and who are holding those positions on the 12th April 1989.

Controlling Authority : (Rule 50A)

The Central or State Government may appoint controlling authority having prescribed qualifications.

(i) All Inspectors appointed by the Central Government shall be under the control of an officer appointed in this behalf by the Central Government.

(ii) All Inspectors appointed by the State Government shall be under the control of an officer appointed in this behalf by the State Government.

Qualifications of Controlling Authority : (Rule 50A)

No person shall be qualified to be a controlling Authority under the Act unless :

(i) He is a graduate in pharmacy or pharmaceutical chemistry or in medicine with specification in clinical pharmacology or microbiology from a university established in India by laws; and

(ii) He has experience in the manufacture or testing of drugs or enforcement of the provisions of the Act for a minimum period of five years.

Provided that the requirement as to the academic qualification shall not apply to Inspectors and the Government Analysts appointed under this Act and who are holding position on the 12th April 1989.

(C) Customers Collectors

The laws relating to the sea customs and goods, import to which is prohibited under the Sec. 18 of Sea Customs Act. 1878 is time being applicable for the drugs and cosmetics, the import of which prohibited under Sec. 13 of this Act. The customs collector or any officer authorised in his behalf, may detain any imported package which he suspects to contain, any drug or cosmetics import of which is prohibited any reports such detention to Drug Controller, India, and if required forwards sample of such drug or cosmetic to CDL.

SCHEDULE G
Rule 97

Drugs to be given under supervision of RMP (Registered Medical Practitioner)

Aminopterin

L-Asparaginase

Bleomycin

Busulphan ; its salts

Carbutamide

Chlorambucil ; its salts

Chlorothiazide and other derivatives of 1, 2, 4 benzothiadrazine

Chlorpropamide ; its salts

Chlorthalidone and other derivatives of Chlorobenzene compound

[Cis-Platin]

Cyclophosphomide ; its salts

[Cytarabine]

Daunorubicin

Di-Isopropyl Eluorophosphate

Disodium Stilboestrol Diphosphate

Doxorubicin Hydrochloride

Ethacrynic Acid ; its salts

Ethosuximide

Glibenclamide

Hydanatoin ; its salts, its derivatives, their salts

Hydroxyurea

Insulin, all types

Lomustine Hydrochloride

Mannomustine ; its salts

Mercaptopurine ; its salts

Metformin ; its salts

Methsuximide Mustine ; its salts

Paramethadione
Phenacemide
Phenformin ; its salts
5-Phenylhydantoin, its alkyl and aryl derivatives; its salts
Primadone
[Procarpazine Hydrochloride]
Quinthazone
Sarcolysine
[Sodium 2 Mercaptoethanesul fonate]
Tamoxiten Citrate
Testolactone
Thiotepa
Tolbutamide
Tretamine ; its salts
Troxidone
Antihistaminic substances, their salts, their derivatives, salts of their derivatives.
Antazoline
Bromodiphenhydramine
Buclizine
Chlorcyclizine
Chlorpheniramine
Clemizole
Cyproheptadine
Diphenhydramine
Diphenyl pyraline
Doxylamine Succinate
Isothipendyl
Mebhydrolin Napadisylate
Meclozine
Phenindomine
Pheniramine
Promethazine
Thenalidine
Triprolidine
Substance being tetra-N-substituted derivatives of Ethylene Diamine or Prophylenediamine

Note : Preparations containing the above substances excluding those intended for topical or external use are also covered by this Schedule.

SCHEDULE H

Rules 65 and 97
Prescription Drugs

Acebutol of Hydrochloride	Astemizole
Aclarubicin Inj.	Atenolol
Actilyse	Atracurim Besylate Injection
Acyclovir	Auranofin
Adrenocorticotrophic hormone (ACTH)	Azathioprine
	Bacampicillin
Alclometasone Dipropionate	Barbituric acid, its salts, derivative of Barbituric acid, their salts
Allopurinol	
Alphachymotrypsin	Benserazide Hydrochloride
Alprazolam	Betahistine Dihydrochloride
Amantadine Hydrochloride	Bethanidine Sulphate
Amikacin	Bezafibrate
Amiloride Hydrochloride	Biclotymol
Amineptine	Biperiden Hydrochloride
Aminoglutethimide Tab.	Bitoscanate
Aminosalicylic Acid	Bleomycin Oil Suspension
Amiodarone Hydrochloride	Bromhexine Hydrochloride
Amitriptyline, it salts	Bromocriptine Mesylate
Amoscanate Amoxapine	Budesonide
Amrinone Lactate	Bupivacaine Hydrochloride
Analgin	Buspirone
Androgenic, Anabolic, Oestrogenic and Progestational Substances	Captopril
	Carbidopa
Antibiotics	Carbocisteine
Aprotinin	Carboplatin Injection
Arsenic for injection	Carboquone
Articaine Hydrochloride	Carisoprodol

Carnitine
Cefadroxyl
Cefatoxime Sodium
Cefazolin Sodium
Ceftazidine Pentahydrate
Ceftizoxime Sodium Sterile
Cefuroxime
Cefuroxime Axetil
Centbutindole
Centchromani
Chlordiazepoxide, its salts
Chlormezanone
Chlorpromazine, its salts
Chlorzoxazone
Ciclopirox Olamine
Cimetidine Cinnarizine
Ciprofloxacin HCL monohydrate/lactate
Clavulanic Acid
Clidinium Bromide
Clindamycin
Clobetasol Propenate
Clobetasone 17-Butyrate
Clofazimine
Clofibrate
Clonidine Hydrochloride
Clopamide
Clostebol Acetate
Clotrimazole
Codeine, its salts and derivatives
Colchicine
Corticosteroids, their esters their derivatives and their dosage forms
Cotrimoxazole
Cyclandelate
Cyclosporin Oral Solution
Danazol
Dapsone, its salts and derivatives
Decanoate
Desogestrol
Dextranomer
Dextropropoxyphene, its salts
Diazepam
Diazoxide
Diclofenac Sodium
Digoxine
Dilazep Hydrochloride
Diltiazem
Diphenoxylate, its salts
Disopyramide
Domperidone
Dopamine Hydrochloride
Dothiepin Hydrochloride
Doxapram Hydrochloride
Doxepin Hydrochloride
D-Penicillamine
Enalapril Malenate
Epinephrine, its salts
Epirubicine Injection

Ergot, alkaloids of whether hydrogenated or not their homologous any salt of any substance falling within this item

Estradiol Succinate

Estramustine Phosphate Capsule

Ethacridine Lactate

Ethambutol Hydrochloride

Ethamsylate

Ethinyloestradiol

Ethionamide

Etoposide Cap. & Injection

Famotidine

Flavoxate Hydrochloride

Flufenamic acid, its salts, its esters their salts

Flunaritine Hydrochloride

Fluoxetine Hydrochloride

Flupenthixol

Fluphenazine Enanthate and Decanoate

Fluraxepam

Flurbiprofen

Flutamide

Galanthamine Hydrobromide.

Gallamine, its salts, its quaternary compound

Gemfibrozil

Genodeoxycholic Acid

Gliclazide

Glycopyrrolate

Glydiazinamide

Guanethidine

Gugulipid

Halogenated

Haloperidol

Heparin

Hepatitis B. Vaccine

Hyaluronidase

Hydrocortisone 17-Butyrate

Hydrotalcite

Hydroxyquinolines

Hydroxyzine, its salts

Ibuprofen

Imipramine, its salts

Indomethacin, its salts

Insulin Human

Interferon Alpha Injection

Intralipid (intravenous Fat Emulsion)

Iohexol Sterile Solution

Iopamidol Sterile Solution

Iopromide

Iron Preparation for parenteral use

Isoflurane

Isonicotinic acid hydrazine and other hydrazine derivatives of isonicotinic acid, their derivatives, their salts

Isorcarboxazid

Isosorbide Dinitrate

Isosorbide Mononitrate

Isoxsuprine
Ketamine Hydrochloride
Ketoconazole Acetate
Ketoprofen
Labetalol Hydrochloride
Lavarternol, its salts
Levodopa
Lidoflazine
lindapamide
Lithium Carbonate
Lofepramine Decanoate
Lopermide
Lorazepam
Loxapine
Mebendazole
Mebeverine Hydrochloride
Medroxy Progesterone Acetate tablets
Mefenamic Acid, its salts, its ester, their salts
Megestrol Acetate
Meglumine Iocarmate
Melagenina Lotion
Mephenesin, its esters
Mephentermine
Mesterolone
Methicillin Sodium
Methocarbomal
Met-oclopramide
Metoprolol tartarate
Metrizamide
Metronidazole
Mexiletine Hydrochloride

Mianserin Hydrochloride
Miconazole
Minocycline
Minoxidil
Mitoxantrone Hydrochloride
Momentasone Furoate
Morphazinamide Hydrochloride
Nadolol
Nalidixic Acid
Naproxen
Narcotic Drugs listed in the Narcotic Drugs and Psychotropic Substances Act, 1985
Natamycin
Netilmicin Sulphate
Nicergoline
Nifedipine
Nimustine Hydrochloride
Nitrazepam
Nitroglycerin Injection
Norethisterone Enathate Injection
Norfloxacin
Ofloxacin
Organic compound of
Orphenadrine, its salts
Orthoclone Sterile
Oxazepam
Oxazolidine, its salts
Oxethazaine Hydrochloride
Oxolinic Acid
Oxprenolol Hydrochloride
Oxyfedrine
Oxymetazoline

- Oxyphenbutazone
- Oxytocin
- Ozothine
- Pancuronium Bromide
- Paraamino benzene sulphonamide, its salts and derivatives
- Paraamino salicylic acid, its salts, its derivatives
- Pentazocine
- Pentoxifylline
- Pepleomcyin Injection
- Phenelzine, its salts
- Phenothiazine, derivatives of and salts of its derivatives
- Phenobarbital
- Phenylbutazine, its salts
- Pimozide
- Pindolol
- Piracetam
- Piroxicam
- Pituitary gland, the active principles of, not otherwise specified in this schedule and their salts
- Polidocanol Injection
- Polyestradiol Phosphate Injection
- Praziquantel
- Prednimustine Tablets
- Prednisolone Stearoylglycolate
- Prenoxdiazin Hydrochloride
- Promazine Hydrochloride
- Propafenon Hydrochloride
- Propranolol Hydrochloride
- Protristyline Hydrochloride
- Pyrazinamide
- Pyrvinium, its salts
- Quinidine Sulphate
- Ranitidine
- Rauwolfia alkaloids of their salts derivatives of the alkalids or rauwolfia their salts
- Reproterol Hydrochloride
- Rosoxacin
- Salbutamol Sulphate
- Salicylazosulphapyridine
- Satranidazole
- Septopal Beads and Chains
- Serratio Peptidase
- Sisomicin Sulphate
- Sodium and Meglumine Iothalamates
- Sodium Cromoglycate
- Sodium Hyaluronate Solution
- Sodium Valproate
- Sotalol
- Spectinomycin Hydrochloride
- Spironolactone
- Sucralfate
- Sulphadoxine
- Sulphamethoxine
- Sulphamethoxypyridazine
- Sulphaphenazole
- Sulprostone Injection
- Teratolol Hydrochloride
- Terbutaline Sulphate
- Terfenadine
- Terizidone
- Testosterone Undecoanoate
- Thiacetazone

Thiopropazate, its salts
Thomidate
Tiaprofenic Acid
Timolol Maleate
Tinazoline
Tinldazole
Tobramycin
Tranylcypromine, its salts
Trazodone
Tretinoin
Triflueperidol Hydrochloride

Trifluperazine
Trimetazidine Dihydrochloride
Trimipramine
Tripotassium Dicitrate Bismuthate
Urokinase
Vasopression
Vecuronium Bromide Inj.
Verapamil Hydrochloride
Xipamide
Zidovudine Cap.

Note :
1. Preparations exempted under provision to para 2 of Note to Schedule X shall also be covered by this schedule.
2. Preparations containing the above substances excluding those intended for topical or external use are also covered by this Schedule. The inclusion of a substance in Schedule H does not imply or convey that substance is exempted from the provisions of Rule 122-A of the Drugs and Cosmetics Rules, 1945.

SCHEDULE J

Rule 106

Diseases and Ailments (By Whatever Name Described) which a Drug may not Purport to Prevent or Cure or Make Claims to Prevent or Cure

1. AIDS
2. Angina Pectoris
3. Appendicitis
4. Arteriosclerosis
5. Baldness
6. Blindness
7. Bronchial Asthma
8. Cancer and Benign Tumour
9. Cataract
10. Change in colour of the hair and growth of new hair
11. Change of foetal sex by drugs.
12. Congenital malformations
13. Deafness
14. Diabetes
15. Diseases and disorders of uterus

16. Epileptic-fits and psychiatric disorders
17. Encephalitis
18. Fairness of the skin
19. Form, structure of breast
20. Gangrene
21. Genetic disorders
22. Glaucoma
23. Goitre
24. Hernia
25. High/Low Blood Pressure
26. Hydrocele
27. Insanity
28. Increase in brain capacity and improvement of memory
29. Improvement in height of children/adults
30. Improvement in size and shape of the sexual organ and in duration of sexual performance
31. Improvement in the strength of the natural teeth
32. Improvement in vision
33. Jaundice/Hepatitis/Liver disorders
34. Leukaemia
35. Leucoderma
36. Maintenance or improvement of the capacity of the human being for sexual pleasure
37. Mental retardation, subnormalities and growth
38. Myocardial infarction
39. Obesity
40. Paralysis
41. Parkinsonism
42. Piles and Fistulae
43. Power to rejuvinate
44. Premature ageing
45. Premature greying of hair
46. Rheumatic Heart Diseases
47. Sexual Impotence, Premature ejaculation and spermatorrhoea
48. Spondylitis
49. Stammering
50. Stones in gall-bladder, kidney, bladder
51. Varicose Vein.

Chapter 13...

REGULATORY GUIDELINES

Revised SCHEDULE M
(See rule 71, 74, 76 and 78)
**Good manufacturing practices and requirements of premises,
Plant and equipment for pharmaceutical products**

Note :

To achieve the objectives listed below, each licensee shall evolve appropriate methodology, systems and procedures which shall be documented and maintained for inspection and reference; and the manufacturing premises shall be used exclusively for production of drugs and no other manufacturing activity shall be undertaken therein.

PART I
GOOD MANUFACTURING PRACTICES FOR PREMISES AND MATERIALS

(I) General Requirements

1. Location and Surroundings

The factory building(s) for manufacture of drugs shall be so situated and shall have such measures as to avoid risk of contamination from external environment including open sewage, drain, public lavatory or any factory which produces disagreeable or obnoxious, odour, fumes, excessive soot, dust, smoke, chemical or biological emissions.

2. Buildings and Premises

The building(s) used for the factory shall be designed, constructed, adapted and maintained to suit the manufacturing operations so as to permit production of drugs under hygienic conditions. They shall conform to the conditions laid down in the Factories Act, 1948 (63 of 1948).

The premises used for manufacturing, processing, warehousing, packaging, labeling and testing purposes shall be :

(i) Compatible with other drug manufacturing operations that may be carried out in the same or adjacent area/section;

(ii) Adequately provided with working space to allow orderly and logical placement of equipment, materials and movement of personnel so as to :

    (a) Avoid the risk of mix-up between different categories of drugs or with raw materials, intermediates and in-process material;

    (b) Avoid the possibilities of contamination and cross-contamination by providing suitable mechanism;

(iii) Designed/constructed/maintained to prevent entry of insects, pests, birds, vermins and rodents. Interior surface (walls, floors, and ceilings) shall be smooth and free from cracks, and permit easy cleaning, painting and disinfection;

(iv) Air conditioned, where prescribed for the operations and dosage forms under production. The production and dispensing areas shall be well lighted, effectively ventilated, with air control facilities and may have proper Air Handling Units (wherever applicable) to maintain conditions including temperature and, wherever necessary, humidity, as defined for the relevant product. These conditions shall be appropriate to the category of drugs and nature of the operation. These shall also be suitable to the comforts of the personnel working with protective clothing, products handled, operations undertaken within them in relation to the external environment. These areas shall be regularly monitored for compliance with required specifications;

(v) Provided with drainage system, as specified for the various categories of products, which shall be of adequate size and so designed as to prevent back-flow and/or to prevent insects and rodents entering the premises. Open Channels shall be avoided in manufacturing areas and, where provided, these shall be shallow to facilitate cleaning and disinfection;

(vi) The walls and floors of the areas where manufacture of drugs is carried out shall be free from cracks and open joints to avoid accumulation of dust. These shall be smooth, washable, coved and shall permit easy and effective cleaning and disinfection. The interior surfaces shall not shed particles. A periodical record of cleaning and painting of the premises shall be maintained.

3. Water System

There shall be validated system for treatment of water drawn from own or any other source to render it potable in accordance with standards specified by the Bureau of Indian Standards or Local Municipality, as the case may be, so as to produce Purified Water conforming to Pharmacopoeial specification. Purified Water so produced shall only be used for all the operations except washing and cleaning operations where potable water may be used. Water shall be stored in tanks, which do not adversely affect quality of water and ensure freedom from microbiological growth. The tank shall be cleaned periodically and records maintained by the licensee in this behalf.

4. Disposal of Waste

(i) The disposal of sewage and effluents (solid, liquid and gas) from the manufactory shall be in conformity with the requirements of Environment Pollution Control Board.

(ii) All biomedical waste shall be destroyed as per the provisions of the Bio-Medical Waste (Management and Handling) Rules, 1996.

(iii) Additional precautions shall be taken for the storage and disposal of rejected drugs. Records shall be maintained for all disposal of waste.

(iv) Provisions shall be made for the proper and safe storage of waste materials awaiting disposal. Hazardous, toxic substances and flammable materials shall be stored in suitably designed and segregated, enclosed areas in conformity with Central and State Legislations.

(II) Warehousing Area

1. Adequate areas shall be designed to allow sufficient and orderly warehousing of various categories of materials and products like starting and packaging materials, intermediates, bulk and finished products, products in quarantine, released, rejected, returned or recalled, machine and equipment spare parts and change items.

2. Warehousing areas shall be designed and adapted to ensure good storage conditions. They shall be clean, dry and maintained within acceptable temperature limits. Where special storage conditions are required (e.g., temperature, humidity), these shall be provided, monitored and recorded. Storage areas shall have appropriate house-keeping and rodent, pests and vermin control procedures and records maintained. Proper racks, bins and platforms shall be provided for the storage of materials.

3. Receiving and dispatch bays shall protect materials and products from adverse weather conditions.

4. Where quarantine status is ensured by warehousing in separate earmarked areas in the same warehouse or store, these areas shall be clearly demarcated. Any system replacing the physical quarantine, shall give equivalent assurance of segregation. Access to these areas shall be restricted to authorized persons.

5. There shall be a separate sampling area in the warehousing area for active raw materials and excipients. If sampling is performed in any other area, it shall be conducted in such a way as to prevent contamination, cross contamination and mix-up.

6. Segregation shall be provided for the storage of rejected, recalled or returned materials or products. Such areas, materials or products shall be suitably marked and secured. Access to these areas and materials shall be restricted.

7. Highly hazardous, poisonous and explosive materials such as narcotics, psychotropic drugs and substances presents potential risks of abuse, fire or explosion shall be stored in safe and secure areas. Adequate fire protection measures shall be provided in conformity with the rules of the concerned civic authority.

8. Printed packaging materials shall be stored in safe, separate and secure areas.
9. Separate dispensing areas for β (Beta) lactum, Sex hormones and Cytotoxic substances or any such special categories of products shall be provided with proper supply of filtered air and suitable measures for dust control to avoid contamination. Such areas shall be under differential pressure.
10. Sampling and dispensing of sterile materials shall be conducted under aseptic conditions conforming to Grade A, which can also be performed in a dedicated area within the manufacturing facility.
11. Regular checks shall be made to ensure adequate steps are taken against spillage, breakage and leakage of containers.
12. Rodent treatments (pest control) should be done regularly and at least once in a year and record maintained.

(III) Production Area

1. The production area shall be designed to allow the production preferably in uni-flow and with logical sequence of operations.
2. In order to avoid the risk of cross-contamination, separate dedicated and self-contained facilities shall be made available for the production of sensitive pharmaceutical products like penicillin or biological preparations with the live micro-organisms. Separate dedicated facilities shall be provided for the manufacture of contamination causing and potent products such as Beta lactum, Sex hormones and Cytotoxic substances.
3. Working and in-process space shall be adequate to permit orderly and logical positioning of equipment and materials and movement of personnel to avoid cross contamination and to minimize risk of omission or wrong application of any of manufacturing and control measures.
4. Pipe-work, electrical fittings, ventilation openings and similar service lines shall be designed, fixed and constructed to avoid creation of recesses. Service lines shall preferably be identified by colours and the nature of the supply and direction of the flow shall be marked/indicated.

(IV) Ancillary Areas

1. Rest and refreshment rooms shall be separate from other areas. These areas shall not lead directly to the manufacturing and storage areas.
2. Facilities for changing, storing clothes and for washing and toilet purposes shall be easily accessible and adequate for the number of users. Toilets, separate for males and females, shall not be directly connected with production or storage areas. There shall be written instructions for cleaning and disinfection for such areas.

3. Maintenance workshops shall be separate and away from production areas. Whenever spares, changed parts and tools are stored in the production area, these shall be kept in dedicated rooms or lockers. Tools and spare parts for use in sterile areas shall be disinfected before these are carried inside the production areas.

4. Areas housing animals shall be isolated from other areas. The other requirements regarding animal houses shall be those as prescribed in rule 150-C(3) of the Drugs and Cosmetics Rules, 1945 which shall be adopted for production purposes.

(V) Quality Control Area

1. Quality Control Laboratories shall be independent of the production areas. Separate areas shall be provided each for physico-chemical, biological, microbiological or radio-isotope analysis. Separate instrument room with adequate area shall be provided for sensitive and sophisticated instruments employed for analysis.

2. Quality Control Laboratories shall be designed appropriately for the operations to be carried out in them. Adequate space shall be provided to avoid mix-ups and cross contamination. Sufficient and suitable storage space shall be provided for test samples, retained samples, reference standards, reagents and records.

3. The design of the laboratory shall take into account the suitability of construction materials and ventilation. Separate air handling units and other requirements shall be provided for biological, microbiological and radio isotopes testing areas. The laboratory shall be provided with regular supply of water of appropriate quality for cleaning and testing purposes.

4. Quality Control Laboratory shall be divided into separate sections i.e. for chemical, microbiological and wherever required, biological testing. These shall have adequate area for basic installation and for ancillary purposes. The microbiology section shall have arrangements such as airlocks and laminar air flow work station, wherever considered necessary.

(VI) Personnel

1. The manufacture shall be conducted under the direct supervision of competent technical staff with prescribed qualifications and practical experience in the relevant dosage form and/or active pharmaceutical products.

2. The head of the Quality Control Laboratory shall be independent of the manufacturing unit. The testing shall be conducted under the direct supervision of competent technical staff who shall be whole time employees of the licensee.

3. Personnel for Quality Assurance and Quality Control operations shall be suitably qualified and experienced.
4. Written duties of technical and Quality Control personnel shall be laid and followed strictly.
5. Number of personnel employed shall be adequate and in direct proportion to the workload.
6. The licensee shall ensure in accordance with a written instruction that all personnel in production area or into Quality Control Laboratories shall receive training appropriate to the duties and responsibility assigned to them. They shall be provided with regular in-service training.

(VII) Health, Clothing and Sanitation of Workers
1. The personnel handling Beta-lactum antibiotics shall be tested for Penicillin sensitivity before employment and those handling sex hormones, cytotoxic substances and other potent drugs shall be periodically examined for adverse effects. These personnel should be moved out of these sections (except in dedicated facilities), by rotation, as a health safeguard.
2. Prior to employment, all personnel, shall undergo medical examination including eye examination, and shall be free from Tuberculosis, skin and other communicable or contagious diseases. Thereafter, they should be medically examined periodically, at least once a year. Records shall be maintained thereof. The licensee shall provide the services of a qualified physician for assessing the health status of personnel involved in different activities.
3. All persons, prior to and during employment, shall be trained in practices which ensure personnel hygiene. A high level of personal hygiene shall be observed by all those engaged in the manufacturing processes. Instructions to this effect shall be displayed in change-rooms and other strategic locations.
4. No person showing, at any time, apparent illness or open lesions which may adversely affect the quality of products, shall be allowed to handle starting materials, packaging materials, in-process materials, and drug products until his condition is no longer judged to be a risk.
5. All employees shall be instructed to report about their illness or abnormal health condition to their immediate supervisor so that appropriate action can be taken.
6. Direct contact shall be avoided between the unprotected hands of personnel and raw materials, intermediate or finished, unpacked products.
7. All personnel shall wear clean body coverings appropriate to their duties. Before entry into the manufacturing area, there shall be separate change rooms for each

sex with adequate facilities for personal cleanliness such as wash basin with running water, clean towels, hand dryers, soaps, disinfectants etc. The change rooms shall be provided with cabinets for the storage of personal belongings of the personnel.

8. Smoking, eating, drinking, chewing, keeping plants, food, drink and personal medicines shall not be permitted in production, laboratory, storage and other areas where they might adversely influence the product quality.

(VIII) Manufacturing Operations and Controls

1. All manufacturing operations shall be carried out under the supervision of technical staff approved by the Licensing Authority. Each critical step in the process relating to the selection, weighing and measuring of raw material addition during various stages shall be performed by trained personnel under the direct personal supervision of approved technical staff.

    The contents of all vessels and container used in manufacture and storage during the various manufacturing stages shall be conspicuously labelled with the name of the product, batch no., batch size and stage of manufacture. Each label should be initialed and dated by the authorized technical staff.

    Products not prepared under aseptic conditions are required to be free from pathogens like Salmonella, Escherichia coli, Pyocyanea etc.

2. Precautions against mix-up and cross-contamination :

    (a) The licensee shall prevent mix-up and cross-contamination of drug material and drug product (from environmental dust) by proper air-handling system, pressure differential, segregation, status labelling and cleaning. Proper records and Standard Operating Procedures thereof shall be maintained.

    (b) The licensee shall ensure processing of sensitive drugs like Beta-Lactum antibiotics, sex hormones and cycotoxic substances in segregated areas or isolated production areas within the building with independent air-handling unit and proper pressure differentials. The effective segregation of these areas shall be demonstrated with adequate records of maintenance and services.

    (c) To prevent mix-ups during production stages, material under-process shall be conspicuously labelled to demonstrate their status. All equipment used for production shall be labelled with their current status.

    (d) Packaging lines shall be independent and adequately segregated. It shall be ensured that all left-overs of the previous packaging operations, including labels, cartons and caps are cleared before the closing hour.

(e) Before packaging operations are begun, steps shall be taken to ensure that the work area, packaging lines, printing machines, and other equipment are clean and free from any products, materials, and spillages. The line clearance shall be performed according to an appropriate checklist and recorded.

(f) The correct details of any printing (for example of batch numbers or expiry dates) done separately or in the course of the packaging shall be re-checked at regular intervals. All printing and over-printing shall be authorised in writing.

(g) The manufacturing environment shall be maintained at the required levels of temperature, humidity and cleanliness.

(h) Authorised persons shall ensure change-over into specific uniforms before undertaking any manufacturing operations including packaging.

(i) There shall be segregated enclosed areas, secured for recalled or rejected material and for such material which are to be reprocessed or recovered.

(IX) Sanitation in the Manufacturing Premises

1. The manufacturing premises shall be cleaned and maintained in an orderly manner, so that it is free from accumulated waste, dust, debris and other similar material. A validated cleaning procedure shall be maintained.

2. The manufacturing areas should not be used for storage of materials, except for the material being processed. It should not be used as a general thoroughfare.

3. A routine sanitation program shall be drawn up and observed, which shall be properly recorded and which shall indicate :
   (a) specific areas to be cleaned and cleaning intervals;
   (b) cleaning procedure to be followed, including equipment and materials to be used for cleaning; and
   (c) personnel assigned to and responsible for the cleaning operation.

4. The adequacy of the working and in-process storage space shall permit the orderly and logical positioning of equipment and materials so as to minimise the risk of mix-up between different pharmaceutical products or their components to avoid cross-contamination, and to minimise the risk of omission or wrong application of any of the manufacturing or control steps.

5. Production areas shall be well lit, particularly where visual on-line controls are carried out.

(X) Raw Materials

1. The licensee shall keep an inventory of all raw-materials to be used at any stage of manufacture of drugs and maintain records as per Schedule U.

2. All incoming materials shall be quarantined immediately after receipt or processing. All materials shall be stored under appropriate conditions and in an orderly fashion to permit batch segregation and stock rotation by a 'first in/first expiry' 'first-out' principle. All incoming materials shall be checked to ensure that the consignment corresponds to the order placed.

3. All incoming materials shall be purchased from approved sources under valid purchase vouchers. Wherever possible, raw materials should be purchased directly from the producers.

4. Authorised staff appointed by the licensee in this behalf, which may include personnel from the quality control department, shall examine each consignment on receipt and shall check each container for integrity of package and seal. Damaged containers shall be identified, recorded and segregated.

5. If a single delivery of material is made up of different batches, each batch shall be considered as a separate batch for sampling, testing and release.

6. Raw materials in the storage area shall be appropriately labelled. Labels shall be clearly marked with the following information :
   (a) Designated name of the product and the internal code reference, where applicable, and analytical reference number;
   (b) Manufacturer's name, address and batch number;
   (c) The status of the contents (e.g. quarantine, under test, released, approved, rejected);
   (d) The manufacturing date, expiry date and re-test date.

7. There shall be adequate separate areas for materials "under test", "approved", and "rejected" with arrangements and equipment to allow dry, clean and orderly placement of stored materials and products, wherever necessary, under controlled temperature and humidity.

8. Containers from which samples have been drawn shall be identified.

9. Only raw materials which have been released by the Quality Control Department and which are within their shelf-life shall be used. It shall be ensured that shelf-life of formulation product shall not exceed with that of active raw materials used.

10. It shall be ensured that all the containers of raw materials are placed on the raised platforms/racks and not placed directly on the floor.

(XI) Equipment

1. Equipment shall be located, designed, constructed, adapted and maintained to suit the operations to be carried out. The layout and design of life equipment shall aim to minimise the risk of errors and permit effective cleaning and

maintenance in order to avoid cross-contamination, build-up of dust or dirt and, in general, any adverse effect on the quality of products. Each equipment shall be provided with a log book, wherever necessary.

2. Balances and other measuring equipment of an appropriate range, accuracy and precision shall be available in the raw material stores, production and in-process control operations and these shall be calibrated and checked on a scheduled basis in accordance with Standard Operating Procedures and records maintained.

3. The parts of the production equipment that come into contact with the product shall not be reactive, additive or adsorptive to an extent that would affect the quality of the product.

4. To avoid accidental contamination, wherever possible, non-toxic/edible grade lubricants shall be used and the equipment shall be maintained in a way that lubricants do not contaminate the products being produced.

5. Defective equipment shall be removed from production and Quality Control areas or appropriately labelled.

(XII) Documentation and Records

Documentation is an essential part of the Quality assurance system and, as such, shall be related to all aspects of Good Manufacturing Practices (GMPs). Its aim is to define the specifications for all materials, method of manufacture and control, to ensure that all personnel concerned with manufacture know the information necessary to decide whether or not to release a batch of a drug for sale and to provide an audit trail that shall permit investigation of the history of any suspected defective batch.

1. Documents designed, prepared, reviewed and controlled, wherever applicable, shall comply with these rules.

2. Documents shall be approved, signed and dated by appropriate and authorized persons.

3. Documents shall specify the title, nature and purpose. They shall be laid out in an orderly fashion and be easy to check. Reproduced documents shall be clear and legible. Documents shall be regularly reviewed and kept upto date. Any alteration made in the entry of a document shall be signed and dated.

4. The records shall be made or completed at the time of each operation in such a way that all significant activities concerning the manufacture of pharmaceutical products are traceable. Records and associated Standard Operating Procedures (SOP) shall be retained for at least one year after the expiry date of the finished product.

5. Data may be recorded by electronic data processing systems or other reliable means, but Master Formulae and detailed operating procedures relating to the system in use shall also be available in a hard copy to facilitate checking of the accuracy of the records. Wherever documentation is handled by electronic data processing methods, authorized persons shall enter or modify data in the computer. There shall be record of changes and deletions. Access shall be restricted by "passwords" or other means and the result of entry of critical data shall be independently checked. Batch records electronically stored shall be protected by a suitable back-up. During the period of retention, all relevant data shall be readily available.

(XIII) Labels and other Printed Materials

Labels are absolutely necessary for identification of the drugs and their uses. The printing shall be done in bright colours and in a legible manner. The label shall carry all the prescribed details about the product.

1. All containers and equipment shall bear appropriate labels. Different colour coded labels shall be used to indicate the status of a product (for example : under test, approved, passed, rejected).
2. To avoid chance of mix-up of printed packaging materials, product leaflets, relating to different products, shall be stored separately.
3. Prior to release, all labels for containers, cartons and boxes and all circulars, inserts and leaflets and shall be examined by the Quality Control Department of the licensee.
4. Prior to packaging and labelling of a given batch of a drug, it shall be ensured by the licensee that samples are drawn from the bulk and duly tested, approved and released by the quality control personnel.
5. Records of receipt of all labelling and packaging materials shall be maintained for each shipment received indicating receipt, control reference numbers and whether accepted or rejected. Unused coded and damaged labels and packaging materials shall be destroyed and recorded.
6. The label or accompanying document of reference standards and reference culture shall indicate concentration, lot number, potency, date on which container was first opened and storage conditions, where appropriate.

(XIV) Quality Assurance

This is a wide ranging concept concerning all matters that individually or collectively influence the quality of a product. It is the totality of the arrangements made with the object of ensuring that products are of the quality required for their intended use.

1. The system of quality assurance appropriate to the manufacture of pharmaceutical products shall ensure that :
   (a) The pharmaceutical products are designed and developed in a way that takes account of the requirements of Good Manufacturing Practices (GMP) and other associated codes such as those of Good Laboratory Practices (GLP) and Good Clinical Practices (GCP);
   (b) Adequate arrangements are made for manufacture, supply, and use of the correct starting and packaging materials;
   (c) Adequate controls on starting materials, intermediate products and bulk products and other in-process controls, calibrations and validations are carried out;
   (d) The finished product is correctly processed and checked in accordance with established procedures.
   (e) The pharmaceutical products are not released for sale or supplied before authorised persons have certified that each production batch has been produced and controlled in accordance with the requirements of the label claim and any other provisions relevant to production, control and release of pharmaceutical products.

(XV) Self Inspection and Quality Audit

It may be useful to constitute a self inspection team supplemented with a quality audit procedure for assessment of all or part of a system with the specific purpose of improving it.

1. To evaluate the manufacturer's compliance with GMP in all aspects of production and quality control, concept of self-inspection shall be followed. The manufacturer shall constitute a team of independent, experienced, qualified persons from within or outside the company, who can audit objectively the implementation of methodology and procedures evolved. The procedure for self-inspection shall be documented indicating self-inspection results, evaluation, conclusions and recommended corrective actions with effective follow up program. The recommendations for corrective action shall be adopted.

2. The program shall be designed to detect shortcomings in the implementation of Good Manufacturing Practice and to recommend the necessary corrective actions. Self-inspections shall be performed routinely and on specific occasions, like when product recalls or repeated rejections occur or when an inspection by the licensing authorities is announced.

The team responsible for self-inspection shall consist of personnel who can evaluate the implementation of Good Manufacturing Practice objectively; all recommendations for corrective action shall be implemented.

3. Written instructions for self-inspection shall be drawn up which shall include the following :

   (a) Personnel.
   (b) Premises including personnel facilities.
   (c) Maintenance of buildings and equipment.
   (d) Storage of starting materials and finished products.
   (e) Equipment.
   (f) Production and in-process controls.
   (g) Quality control.
   (h) Documentation.
   (i) Sanitation and hygiene.
   (j) Validation and revalidation programmes
   (k) Calibration of instruments or measurement systems.
   (l) Recall procedures.
   (m) Complaints management.
   (n) Labels control.
   (o) Results of previous self-instructions and any corrective steps taken.

(XVI) Quality Control System

Quality control shall be concerned with sampling, specifications, testing, documentation, release procedures which ensure that the necessary and relevant tests are actually carried and that the materials are not released for use, nor products released for sale or supply until their quality has been judged to be satisfactory. It is not confined to laboratory operations but shall be involved in all decisions concerning the quality of the product It shall be ensured that all quality control arrangements are effectively and reliably carried out. The department as a whole shall have other duties such as to establish evaluate, validate and implement all Quality Control Procedures and methods.

1. Every manufacturing establishment shall establish its own quality control laboratory manned by qualified and experienced staff.

2. The area of the quality control laboratory may be divided into Chemical, Instrumentation, Microbiological and Biological testing.

3. Adequate area having the required storage conditions shall be provided for keeping reference samples. The quality control department shall evaluate, maintain and store reference samples.

4. Standard operating procedures shall be available for sampling, inspecting, and testing of raw materials, intermediate, bulk finished products and packing materials and, wherever necessary, for monitoring environmental conditions.

5. There shall be authorized and dated specifications for all materials, products, reagents and solvents including test of identity, content, purity and quality. These shall include specifications for water, solvents and reagents used in analysis.

6. No batch of the product shall be released for sale or supply until it has been certified by the authorised person(s) that it is in accordance with the requirements of the standards laid down.

7. Reference/retained samples from each batch of the products manufactured shall be maintained in a quantity which is at least twice the quantity of the drug required to conduct all the tests, except sterility and pyrogen/Bacterial Endotoxin Test performed on the active material and the product manufactured. The retained product shall be kept in its final pack or a simulated pack for a period of three months after the date of expiry.

8. Assessment of records pertaining to finished products shall include all relevant factors, including the production conditions, the results of in-process testing, the manufacturing (including packaging) documentation, compliance with the specification for the finished product, and an examination of the finished pack. Assessment records should be signed by the in-charge of production and counter signed by the authorised quality control personnel before a product is released for sale or distribution.

9. Quality control personnel shall have access to production areas for sampling and investigation, as appropriate.

10. The quality control department shall conduct stability studies of the products to ensure and assign their shelf life at the prescribed conditions of storage. All records of such studies shall be maintained.

11. The in-charge of Quality Assurance shall investigate all product complaints and records thereof shall be maintained.

12. All instruments shall be calibrated and testing procedures validated before these are adopted for routine testing. Periodical calibration of instrument and validation of procedures shall be carried out.

13. Each specifications for raw materials, intermediates, final products, and packing materials shall be approved and maintained by the Quality Control Department. Periodic revisions of the specifications shall be carried out whenever changes are necessary.

14. Pharmacopoeiae, reference standards, working standards, reference spectra, other reference materials and technical books, as required, shall be available in the Quality Control Laboratory of the licensee.

(XVII) Specification

1. For Raw materials and Packaging materials :

   They shall include,

   (a) The designated name and internal code reference;

   (b) Reference, if any, to a pharmacopoeial monograph;

   (c) Qualitative and quantitative requirements with acceptance limits;

   (d) Name and address of manufacturer or supplier and original manufacturer of the material;

   (e) Specimen of printed material;

   (f) Directions for sampling and testing or reference to procedures;

   (g) Storage conditions; and

   (h) Maximum period of storage before re-testing.

2. For Product Containers and Closures :

   (a) All containers and closures intended for use shall comply with the pharmacopoeial requirements. Suitable validated test methods, sample sizes, specifications, cleaning procedure and sterilization procedure, wherever indicated, shall be strictly followed to ensure that these are not reactive, additive, adsorptive, or leach to an extent that significantly affects the quality or purity of the drug. No second hand or used containers and closures shall be used.

   (b) Whenever bottles are being used, the written schedule of cleaning shall be laid down and followed. Where bottles are not dried after washing, they should be rinsed with deionised water or distilled water, as the case may be.

3. For in-process and bulk products - Specifications for in-process material, intermediate and bulk products shall be available. The specifications should be authenticated.

4. For Finished Products-Appropriate specifications for finished products shall include :

   (a) The designated name of the product and the code reference;

   (b) The formula or a reference to the formula and the pharmacopoeial reference;

   (c) Directions for sampling and testing or a reference to procedures;

(d) A description of the dosage form and package details;

(e) The qualitative and quantitative requirements, with the acceptance limits for release;

(f) The storage conditions and precautions, where applicable, and

(g) The shelf-life.

5. For preparation of containers and closures : The requirements mentioned in the Schedule do not include requirements of machinery, equipments and premises required for preparation of containers and closures for different dosage forms and categories of drugs. The suitability and adequacy of the machinery, equipment and premises shall be examined taking into consideration the requirements of each licensee in this respect.

(XVIII) Master Formula Records

There shall be Master Formula records relating to all manufacturing procedures for each product and batch size to be manufactured. These shall be prepared and endorsed by the competent technical staff i.e. head of production and quality control. The Master Formula shall include :

(a) The name of the product together with product reference code relating to its specifications;

(b) The patent or proprietary name of the product along with the generic name, a description of the dosage form, strength, composition of the product and batch size;

(c) Name, quantity and reference number of all the starting materials to be used. Mention shall be made of any substance that may 'disappear' in the course of processing;

(d) A statement of the expected final yield with the acceptable limits, and of relevant intermediate yields, where applicable;

(e) A statement of the processing location and the principal equipment to be used;

(f) The methods, or reference to the methods, to be used for preparing the critical equipment including cleaning, assembling, calibrating, sterilizing;

(g) Detailed stepwise processing instructions and the time taken for each step;

(h) The instructions for in-process controls with their limits;

(i) The requirements for storage conditions of the products, including the container, labelling and special storage conditions where applicable;

(j) Any special precautions to be observed;

(k) Packing details and specimen labels.

(XIX) Packaging Records

There shall be authorised packaging instructions for each product, pack size and type. These shall include or have a reference to the following :

(a) Name of the product;

(b) Description of the dosage form, strength and composition;

(c) The pack size expressed in terms of the number of doses, weight or volume of the product in the final container;

(d) Complete list of all the packaging materials required for a standard batch size, including quantities, sizes and types, with the code or reference number relating to the specifications of each packaging material;

(e) Reproduction of the relevant printed packaging materials and specimens indicating where the batch number and expiry date of the product have been applied;

(f) Special precautions to be observed, including a careful examination of the area and equipment in order to ascertain the line clearance before the operations begin;

(g) Description of the packaging operation, including any significant subsidiary operations and equipment to be used;

(h) Details of in-process controls with instructions for sampling and acceptance;

(i) Upon completion of the packing and labelling operation, a reconciliation shall be made between number of labelling and packaging units issued, number of units labelled, packed and excess returned or destroyed. Any significant or unusual discrepancy in the numbers shall be carefully investigated before releasing the final batch.

(XX) Batch Packaging Records

1. A batch packaging record shall be kept for each batch or part batch processed. It shall be based on the relevant parts of the packaging instructions, and the method of preparation of such records shall be designed to avoid transcription errors.

2. Before any packaging operation begins, checks shall be made and recorded that the equipment and the work stations are clear of the previous products, documents or materials not required for the planned packaging operations, and that the equipment is clean and suitable for use.

(XXI) Batch Processing Records

1. There shall be Batch Processing Record for each product. It shall be based on the relevant parts of the currently approved Master Formula. The method of preparation of such records included in the Master Formula shall be designed to avoid transcription errors;

2. Before any processing begins, check shall be performed and recorded to ensure that the equipment and work station are clear of previous products, documents or materials not required for the planned process are removed and that equipment is clean and suitable for use.

3. During processing, the following information shall be recorded at the time each action is taken and the record shall be dated and signed by the person responsible for the processing operations :

   (a) The name of the product,
   (b) The number of the batch being manufactured,
   (c) Dates and time of commencement, of significant intermediate stages and of completion of production,
   (d) Initials of the operator of different significant steps of production and where appropriate, of the person who checked each of these operations,
   (e) The batch number and/or analytical control number as well as the quantities of each starting material actually weighed,
   (f) Any relevant processing operation or event and major equipment used,
   (g) A record of the in-process controls and the initials of the person(s) carrying them out, and the results obtained,
   (h) The amount of product obtained after different and critical stages of manufacture (yield),
   (i) Comments or explanations for significant deviations from the expected yield limits shall be given,
   (j) Notes on special problems including details, with signed authorization, for any deviation from the master formula,
   (k) Addition of any recovered or reprocessed material with reference to recovery or reprocessing stages.

(XXII) Standard Operating Procedures (SOPs) and Records

1. **Receipt of Materials :**

   (i) There shall be written Standard Operating Procedures and records for the receipt of each delivery of raw, primary and printed packaging material.

   (ii) The records of the receipts shall include;

   (a) the name of the material on the delivery note and the number of containers;
   (b) the date of receipt;
   (c) the manufacturer's and/or supplier's name;

(d) the manufacturer's batch or reference number;

(e) the total quantity and number of containers, quantity in each container received;

(f) the control reference number assigned after receipt;

(g) any other relevant comment or information.

(iii) There shall be written standard operating procedures for the internal labelling, quarantine and storage or starting materials, packaging materials and other materials, as appropriate.

(iv) There shall be Standard Operating Procedures available for each instrument and equipment and these shall be placed in close proximity to the related instrument and equipment.

2. Sampling

(i) There shall be written Standard Operating Procedures for sampling, which include the person(s) authorized to take the samples.

(ii) The sampling instructions shall include :

(a) the method of sampling and the sampling plan,

(b) the equipment to be used,

(c) any precautions to be observed to avoid contamination of the material or any deterioration in its quality,

(d) the quantity of samples to be taken,

(e) instructions for any required sub-division or pooling of the samples,

(f) the type of sample container to be used,

(g) any specific precautions to be observed, especially in regard to sampling of sterile or hazardous material.

3. Batch Numbering

(a) There shall be Standard Operating Procedures describing the details of the batch (lot) numbering set up with the objective of ensuring that each batch of intermediate, bulk or finished product is identified with a specific batch number.

(b) Batch numbering standard operating procedures applied to a processing stage and to the respective packaging stage shall be same or traceable to demonstrate that they belong to one homogeneous mix.

(c) Batch number allocation shall be immediately recorded in a logbook or by electronic data processing system. The record shall include date of allocation, product identity and size of batch.

4. **Testing**

   There shall be written procedures for testing materials and products at different stages of manufacture, describing the methods and equipment to be used. The tests performed shall be recorded.

5. **Records of analysis**

   1. The records shall include the following data :
      - (a) name of the materials or product and the dosage form;
      - (b) batch number and, where appropriate the manufacturer and/or supplier;
      - (c) references to the relevant specifications and testing procedures;
      - (d) test results, including observations and calculations, and reference to any specifications (limits);
      - (e) dates of testing;
      - (f) initials of the persons who performed the testing;
      - (g) initials of the persons who verified the testing and the detailed calculations;
      - (h) a statement of release or rejection; and
      - (i) signature and date of the designated responsible person.
   2. There shall be written standard operating procedures and the associated records of actions taken for :
      - (a) equipment assembly and validation;
      - (b) analytical apparatus and calibration;
      - (c) maintenance, cleaning and sanitation;
      - (d) personnel matters including qualification, training, clothing, hygiene;
      - (e) environmental monitoring;
      - (f) pest control;
      - (g) complaints;
      - (h) recalls made;
      - (i) returns received.

(XXIII) Reference samples

(a) Each lot of every active ingredient, in a quantity sufficient to carry out all the tests, except sterility and pyrogens/Bacterial Endotoxin Test, shall be retained for a period of 3 months after the date of expiry of the last batch produced from the that active ingredient.

(b) Samples of finished formulations shall be stored in the same or simulated containers in which the drug has been actually marketed.

(XXIV) Reprocessing and Recoveries

1. Where reprocessing is necessary, written procedures shall be established and approved by the Quality Assurance Department that shall specify the conditions and limitations of repeating chemical reactions. Such reprocessing shall be validated.
2. If the product batch has to be reprocessed, the procedure shall be authorized and recorded. An investigation shall be carried out into the causes necessitating reprocessing and appropriate corrective measures shall be taken for prevention of recurrence. Re-processed batch shall be subjected to stability evaluation.
3. Recovery of product residue may be carried out, if permitted, in the master production and control records by incorporating it in subsequent batches of the product.

(XXV) Distribution records

1. Prior to distribution or dispatch of given batch of a drug, it shall be ensured that the batch has been duly tested, approved and released by the quality control personnel. Pre-dispatch inspection shall be performed on each consignment on a random basis to ensure that only the correct goods are dispatched. Details instructions for warehousing and stocking of Large Volume Parenterals, if stocked, shall be in existence and shall be complied with after the batch is released for distribution. Periodic audits of warehousing practices followed at distribution centres shall be carried out and records thereof shall be maintained. Standard Operating Procedures shall be developed for warehousing of products.
2. Records for distribution shall be maintained in a manner such that finished batch of a drug can be traced to the retail level to facilitate prompt and complete recall of the batch, if and when necessary.

26. Validation and Process Validation

1. Validation studies shall be an essential part of Good Manufacturing Practices and shall be conducted as per the pre-defined protocols. These shall include validation of processing, testing and cleaning procedures.
2. A written report summarizing recorded results and conclusions shall be prepared, documented and maintained.
3. Processes and procedures shall be established on the basis of validation study and undergo periodic revalidation to ensure that they remain capable of achieving the intended results. Critical processes shall be validated, prospectively or retrospectively.

4. When any new master formula or method of preparation is adopted, steps shall be taken to demonstrate its suitability for routine processing. The defined process, using the materials and equipment specified shall be demonstrated to yield a product consistently of the required quality.

5. Significant changes to the manufacturing process, including any change in equipment or materials that may affect product quality and/or the reproducibility of the process, shall be validated.

(XXVII) Product Recalls

1. A prompt and effective product recall system of defective products shall be devised for timely information of all concerned stockists, wholesalers, suppliers, up to the retail level within the shortest period. The licensee may make use of both print and electronic media in this regard.

2. There shall be an established written procedure in the form of Standard Operating Procedures for effective recall of products distributed by the licensee. Recall operations shall be capable of being initiated promptly so as to effectively reach at the level of each distribution channel.

3. The distribution records shall be readily made available to the persons designated for recalls.

4. The designated person shall record a final report issued, including a reconciliation between the delivered and the recovered quantities of the products.

5. The effectiveness of the arrangements for recalls shall be evaluated from time to time.

6. The recalled products shall be stored separately in a secured segregated area pending final decision on them.

(XXVIII) Complaints and Adverse Reactions

1. All complaints thereof concerning product quality shall be carefully reviewed and recorded according to written procedures. Each complaint shall be investigated/evaluated by the designated personnel of the company and records of investigation and remedial action taken thereof shall be maintained.

2. Reports of serious adverse drug reactions resulting from the use of a drug along with comments and documents shall be forthwith reported to the concerned Licensing Authority.

3. There shall be written procedures describing the action to be taken, recall to be made of the defective product.

(XXIX) Site Master File

The licensee shall prepare a succinct document in the form of 'Site Master File' containing specific and factual Good Manufacturing Practices about the production and/or control of pharmaceutical manufacturing preparations carried out at the licensed premises. It shall contain the following :

1. **General information**
   (a) Brief information of the firm;
   (b) Pharmaceutical manufacturing activities as permitted by the licensing authority;
   (c) Other manufacturing activities, if any, carried out on the premises;
   (d) Type of products licensed for manufacture with flowcharts mentioning procedures and process flow;
   (e) Number of employees engaged in the production, quality control, storage and distribution;
   (f) Use of outside scientific, analytical or other technical assistance in relation to manufacture and analysis;
   (g) Short description of the Quality Management system of the firm;
   (h) Products details registered with foreign countries.

2. **Personnel**
   (a) Organizational chart showing the arrangement for quality assurance including production and quality control;
   (b) Qualification, experience and responsibilities of key personnel;
   (c) Outline for arrangements of basic and in-service training and how the records are maintained;
   (d) Health requirements for personnel engaged in production;
   (e) Personnel hygiene requirements, includings clothing.

3. **Premises**
   (a) Simple plan or description of manufacturing areas drawn to scale;
   (b) Nature of construction and fixtures/fittings;
   (c) Brief description of ventilation systems. More details should be given for critical areas with potential risk of airborne contamination (schematic drawing of systems). Classification of the room used for the manufacture of sterile products should be mentioned;
   (d) Special areas for the handling of the highly toxic, hazardous and sensitizing materials;

(e) Brief description of water systems (schematic drawings of systems), including sanitation;

(f) Description of planned preventive maintenance programs for premises and of the recording system.

4. **Equipment**

(a) Brief description of major equipment used in production and quality control laboratories (a list of equipment required);

(b) Description of planned preventive maintenance programs for equipment and of the recording system;

(c) Qualification and calibration, including the recording systems and arrangements for computerised systems validation.

5. **Sanitation**

Availability of written specifications and procedures for cleaning manufacturing areas and equipment.

6. **Documentation**

(a) Arrangements for the preparation, revision and distribution

(b) Necessary documentation for the manufacture;

(c) Any other documentation related to product quality that is not mentioned elsewhere (e.g. microbiological controls about air and water)

7. **Production**

(a) Brief description of production operations using, wherever possible, flow sheets and charts specifying important parameters;

(b) Arrangements for the handling of starting materials, packaging materials, bulk and finished products, including sampling, quarantine, release and storage;

(c) Arrangements for the handling of rejected materials and products;

(d) Brief description of general policy for process validation.

8. **Quality Control**

Description of the quality control system and of the activities of the quality control department. Procedures for the release of the finished products.

9. **Loan Licence manufacture and Licensee**

(a) Description of the way in which compliance of Good Manufacturing Practices by the loan licensee shall be assessed.

10. **Distribution, Complaints and Product Recall**
    (a) Arrangements and recording system for distribution;
    (b) Arrangements for the handling of complaints and product recalls.

11. **Self Inspection**
    Short description of the self-inspection system indicating whether an outside, independent and experienced external expert was involved in evaluating the manufacturer's compliance with Good Manufacturing Practices in all aspects of production.

12. **Export of Drugs**
    (a) Products exported to different countries;
    (b) Complaints and product recall, if any.

PART IA
SPECIFIC REQUIREMENTS FOR MANUFACTURE OF STERILE PRODUCTS, PARENTERAL PREPARATIONS AND STERILE OPHTHALMIC PREPARATIONS

Note : The general requirements as given in Part I of this Schedule relating to Requirements of Good Manufacturing Practices for Premises and Materials for pharmaceutical products shall be complied with, *mutatis mutandis,* for the manufacture of Sterile Products, Parenteral preparations (Small Volume Injectables and Large Volume Parenterals) and Sterile Opthalmic Preparations. In addition to these requirements, the following specific requirements shall also be followed, namely :

1. **General**

   Sterile products, being very critical and sensitive in nature, a very high degree of precautions, prevention and preparations are needed. Dampness, dirt and darkness are to be avoided to ensure aseptic conditions in all areas. There shall be strict compliance in the prescribed standards especially in the matter of supply of water, air, active materials and in the maintenance of hygienic environment.

2. **Buildings and Civil Works**

   (i) The building shall be built on proper foundation with standardized materials to avoid cracks in critical areas like aseptic solution preparation, filling and sealing rooms.

   (ii) Location of services like water, steam, gases etc. shall be such that their servicing or repair shall not pose any threat to the integrity of the facility. Water lines shall not pose any threat of leakage of aseptic area.

   (iii) The manufacturing areas shall be clearly separated into support areas (e.g. washing and component preparation areas, storage areas etc.), preparation areas (e.g. bulk manufacturing area, non-aseptic blending areas etc.) change areas and aseptic areas. Operations like removal of outer cardboard wrappings of primary packaging materials shall be done in the de-cartoning areas which are segregated from the washing areas. Wooden pallets, fiber boards drums, cardboard and other particle shedding materials shall not be taken inside the preparation areas.

(iv) In aseptic areas :

    (a) Walls, floors and ceiling should be impervious, non-shedding, non-flaking and non-cracking. Flooring should be unbroken and provided with a cove both at the junction between the wall and the floor as well as the wall and the ceiling;

    (b) Walls shall be flat, and ledges and recesses shall be avoided. Wherever other surfaces join the wall (e.g. sterilisers, electric sockets, gas points etc.) these shall flush the walls. Walls shall be provided with a cove at the joint between the ceiling and floor;

    (c) Ceiling shall be solid and joints shall be sealed. Light-fittings and air-grills shall be flush with walls and not hanging from the ceiling, so as to prevent contamination;

    (d) There shall be no sinks and drains in Grade A and Grade B areas;

    (e) Doors shall be made of non-shedding material. These may be made preferably of Aluminium or Steel material. Wooden doors shall not be used. Doors shall open towards the higher-pressure area so that they close automatically due to air pressure.

    (f) Windows shall be made of similar material as the doors, preferably with double panel and shall be flush with the walls. If fire escapes are to be provided, these shall be suitably fastened of the walls without any gaps;

    (g) The furniture used shall be smooth, washable and made of stainless steel or any other appropriate material other than wood.

(v) The manufacturing and the support areas shall have the same quality of civil structure described above for aseptic areas, except the environment standards which may vary in the critical areas.

(vi) Change rooms with entrance in the form of air-locks shall be provided before entry into the sterile product manufacturing areas and then to the aseptic area. Separate exit space from the aseptic areas is advisable. Change rooms to the aseptic areas shall be clearly demarcated into 'black', 'gray' and white rooms' with different levels of activity and air cleanliness. The 'black' change room shall be provided with a handwashing sink. The sink and its drain in the un-classified (first) change rooms may be kept clean all the time. The specially designed drain shall be periodically monitored to avoid presence of pathogenic micro-organisms. Change room doors shall not be opened simultaneously. An appropriate inter-locking system and a visual and/or audible warning system may be installed to prevent the opening of more than one door at a time.

(vii) For communication between aseptic areas and non-aseptic areas, intercom telephones or speak-phones shall be used. These shall be minimum in number.

(viii) Material transfer between aseptic areas and outside shall be through suitable airlocks or pass-boxes. Doors of such air-locks and pass-boxes shall have suitable interlocking arrangements.

(ix) Personal welfare areas like rest rooms, tea room, canteen and toilets shall be outside and separated from the sterile product manufacturing area.

(x) Animal houses shall be away from the sterile product manufacturing area and shall not share a common entrance or air handling system with the manufacturing area.

3. **Air Handling System (Central Air-Conditioning)**

(a) Air Handling Units for sterile product manufacturing areas shall be different from those for other areas. Critical areas, such as the aseptic filling area, sterilized components unloading area and change rooms conforming to Grades B, C and D respectively shall have separate Air Handling Units. The filter configuration in the air handling system shall be suitably designed to achieve the Grade of air as given in Table 13.1. Typical operational activities for clean areas are highlighted in Table 13.2 and Table 13.3.

(b) For products which are filled aseptically, the filling room shall meet Grade B conditions at rest unmanned. This condition shall also be obtained within a period of about 30 minutes of the personnel leaving the room after completion of operations.

(c) The filling operations shall take place under Grade A conditions which shall be demonstrated under working of simulated conditions which shall be achieved by providing Laminar Air flow work stations with suitable HEPA filters or isolator technology.

(d) For products, which are terminally sterilized, the filling room shall meet Grade C conditions at rest. This condition shall be obtainable within a period of about 30 minutes of the personnel leaving the room after completion of operations.

(e) Manufacturing and component preparation areas shall meet Grade C conditions.

(f) After completion of preparation, washed components and vessels shall be protected with Grade C background and if necessary, under Laminar Air Flow work station.

(g) The minimum air changes for Grade B and Grade C areas shall not be less than 20 air changes per hour in a room with good air flow pattern and appropriate HEPA filters. For Grade A Laminar Air Flow work stations, the air flow rates shall be 0.3 meter persecond ± 20% (for vertical flows) and 0.45 meter per second ± 20% (for horizontal flows).

(h) Differential pressures between areas of different environmental standards shall be at least 15 Pascal (0.06 inches or 1.5 mm water gauge). Suitable manometers or gauges shall be installed to measure and verify pressure differential.

(i) The final change rooms shall have the same class of air as specified for the aseptic area. The pressure, differentials in the change room shall be in the descending order from 'white to 'black'.

(j) Unless there are product specific requirements, temperature and humidity in the aseptic areas shall not exceed 27 degree centigrade and relative humidity 55%, respectively.

Table 13.1 : Air Borne Particulate Classification for Manufacture of Sterile Products

Grade	At rest (b)		In Operation (a)	
	Maximum number of permitted particles per cubic metre equal to or above			
	0.5 µm	5 µm	0.5 µm	5 µm
A	3520	29	350,0	29
B(a)	35,200	293	3,52,000	2,930
C(a)	3,52,000	2,930	35,20,000	29,300
D(a)	35,20,000	29,300	Not defined(c)	Not defined(c)

Notes :

(a) In order to reach the B, C and D air grades, the number of air changes shall be related to the size of the room and the equipment and personnel present in the room. The air system shall be provided with the appropriate filters such as HEPA for Grades A, B and C. The maximum permitted number of particles in the "at rest" condition shall approximately be as under :

Grade A corresponds with Class 100 or M 3.5 or ISO class 5; Grade B with class 1000 or M 4.5 or ISO Class 6; Grade C with Class 10000 or M 5.5 or ISO Class 7; Grade D with Class 100,000 or 6.5 or ISO Class 8.

(b) The requirement and limit for the area shall depend on the nature of the operation carried out.

(c) Type of operations to be carried out in the various grades are given in Table 13.2 and Table 13.3 as under :

Table 13.2 : Types of Operations to be Carried out in the Various Grades for Aseptic Preparations

Grade	Types of operations for aseptic preparations
A	Aseptic preparation and filling
B	Background room conditions for activities requiring Grade A
C	Preparation of solution to be filtered
D	Handling of components after washing

Table 13.3 : Types of Operations to be Carried out in the Various Grades for Terminally Sterilized Products

Grade	Types of operations for terminally sterilized products
A	Filling of products, which are usually at risk.
C	Placement of filling and sealing machines, preparation of solutions, when usually, at risk. Filling of product when unusually at risk.
D	Moulding, blowing (pre-forming) operations of plastic containers, Preparations of solutions and components for subsequent filling.

4. **Environment Monitoring**

(i) All environmental parameters listed under point 3 shall be verified and established at the time of installation and thereafter monitored at periodic intervals. The recommended frequencies of periodic monitoring shall be as follows :

(a) Particulate monitoring in air-6 Monthly

(b) HEPA filter integrity testing (smoke testing)-Yearly

(c) Air change rates-6 Monthly

(d) Air pressure differentials-Daily

(e) Temperature and humidity-Daily

(f) Microbiological monitoring by settle plates and/or swabs in aseptic areas-Daily, and at decreased frequency in other areas.

Note : The above frequencies of monitoring shall be changed as per the requirements and load in individual cases.

(ii) There shall be a written environmental monitoring program and microbiological results shall be recorded. Recommended limits for microbiological monitoring of clean areas "in operation" are as given in the Table 13.4 :

Table 13.4 : Recommended Limits for Microbiological Monitoring of Clean Areas "in operation"

Grade	Air sample Cfu/m^3	Settle plates (dia. 90 mm Cfu/2 hrs.)	Contact plates (dia. 55 mm) cfu per plate	Glove points (five fingers Cfu per glove)
A	<1	<1	<1	<1
B	10	5	5	5
C	100	50	25	–
D	500	100	50	–

Notes :
 (a) These are average values.
 (b) Individual settle plates may be exposed for not less than two hours in Grade B. C and D areas and for not less than thirty minutes in Grade A area.
(iii) Appropriate action shall be taken immediately if the result of particulate and microbiological monitoring indicates that the counts exceed the limits. The Standard Operating Procedures shall contain corrective action. After major engineering modification to the HVAC system of any area, all monitoring shall be re-performed before production commences.

5. **Garments**
   (a) This section covers garments required for use by personnel working only in aseptic areas. Outdoor clothing shall not be brought into the sterile areas.
   (b) The garments shall be made of non-shedding and tight weave material. Cotton garments shall not be used. The garments shall shed virtually no fibers or particulate matter.
   (c) The clothing and its quality shall be adopted to the process and the work place and worn in such a way as to protect the product from contamination. Garments shall be single piece with fastenings at cuffs, neck and at legs to ensure close fit. Trouser legs shall be tucked inside the cover boots. Suitable design of garments shall either include a hood (headcover) or a separate hood which can be tucked inside the over-all. Pockets, pleats and belts shall be avoided in garments. Zips (if any) shall be of Plastic material. Garments with damaged zips shall not be used.

(d) Only clean, sterilized and protective garments shall be used at each work session where aseptic filtration and filling operations are undertaken and at each work shift of products intended to be sterilized, post-filling. The mask and gloves shall be changed at every work session in both instances.

(e) Gloves shall be made of latex or other suitable plastic materials and shall be powder free. These shall be long enough to cover wrists completely and allow the over-all cuff to be tucked in.

(f) The footwear shall be of suitable plastic or rubber material and shall be daily cleaned with a bactericide.

(g) Safety goggles or numbered glasses with side extensions shall be used inside aseptic areas. These shall be sanitised by a suitable method.

(h) Garment changing procedure shall be documented and operators trained in this aspect. A full size mirror shall be provided in the final change room for the operator to verify that he is appropriately attired in the garments. Periodic inspection of the garments shall be done by responsible staff.

6. Sanitation

(a) There shall be written procedures for the sanitation of sterile processing facilities. Employees carrying out sanitation of aseptic areas shall be trained specifically for this purpose.

(b) Different sanitizing agents shall be used in rotation and the concentrations of the same shall be as per the recommendations of the manufacturer. Records of rotational use of sanitizing agents shall be maintained.

(c) Distilled water freshly collected directly from the distilled water plant or water maintained above 70 degree centigrade from the re-circulation loop shall be used for dilution of disinfectants. Alternately, distilled water sterilised by autoclaving or membrane filtration shall be used. The dilution shall be carried out in the 'white' change room.

(d) Where alcohol or Isopropyl alcohol is used for dilution of disinfectants for use as hand sprays, the preparation of the same shall be done in the bulk preparation area and the diluted solution membrane-filtered into suitable sterile containers held in aseptic area.

(e) Diluted disinfectants shall bear the label 'use before', based on microbiological establishment to their germicidal properties. The solutions shall be adequately labelled and documents maintained.

(f) Formaldehyde or any other equally effective fumigant is recommended for the fumigation of aseptic areas or after major civil modifications. There shall be

Standard Operating Procedures for this purpose. Its use for routine purposes shall be discouraged and an equally effective surface cleaning regime shall be followed.

(g) Cleaning of sterile processing facilities shall be undertaken with air suction devices or with non-linting sponges or clothes.

(h) Air particulate quality shall be evaluated on a regular basis and records maintained.

7. **Equipment**

(a) The special equipment required for manufacturing sterile products includes component washing machines, steam sterilizers, by dry heat sterilizers, membrane filter assemblies, manufacturing vessels, blenders, liquid filling machines, powder filling machines, sealing and labelling machines, vacuum testing chambers, inspection machines, lyophilisers, pressure vessels etc. Suitable and fully integrated washing-sterilizing-filling lines may be provided, depending upon the type and volume of activity.

(b) Unit-sterilizers shall be double-ended with suitable inter-locking arrangements between the doors. The effectiveness of the sterilization process shall be established initially by biological inactivation studies using microbial spore indicators and then at least once a year by carrying out thermal mapping of the chamber. Various sterilization parameters shall be established based on these studies and documented. For membrane filters used for filtration, appropriate filter integrity tests that ensure sterilization shall be carried out before and after filtration.

(c) Filling machines shall be challenged initially and then at periodic intervals by simulation trials including sterile media fill. Standard Operating Procedures and acceptance criteria for media fills shall be established, justified and documented. Special simulation trial procedures shall be developed, validated and documented for special products like ophthalmic ointments.

(d) The construction material used for the parts which are in direct contact with products and the manufacturing vessels may be stainless steel 316 or Boro-silicate glass (if glass containers) and the tubing shall be capable of being washed and autoclaved.

(e) On procurement, installation qualification of each of the equipment shall be done by engineers with the support of production and quality assurance personnel. Equipment for critical processes like aseptic filling and sterilizers shall be suitably validated according to a written program before putting them to use.

(f) Standard Operating Procedures shall be available for each equipment for its calibration and operation and cleaning. Gauges and other measuring devices attached to equipment shall be calibrated at suitable intervals against a written program. Calibration status of equipment and gauges shall be adequately documented and displayed.

8. Water and Steam Systems

(i) Potable water meeting microbiological specification of not more than 500 cfu/ml and indicating absence of individual pathogenic micro-organisms. Escherichia coli, Salmonella, Staphylococcus aureus and Pseudomonas aeruginosa per 100 ml sample shall be used for the preparation of purified water.

(ii) Purified water prepared by de-mineralization shall meet the microbiological specification of not more than 100 cfu per ml and indicate absence of pathogenic microorganisms in 100 ml. Purified water shall also meet IP specifications for chemical quality. Purified water shall be used for hand washing in change rooms. Containers, closures and machine parts may be washed with potable water followed by suitably filtered purified water. Purified water shall be stored in stainless steel tanks or plastic tanks.

(iii) Water for Injection (hereinafter referred as WFI) shall be prepared from potable water or purified water meeting the above specifications by distillation. Water for Injection shall meet microbiological specification of not more than 10 cfu per 100 ml. WFI shall also meet IP specification for Water for Injection and shall have an endotoxin level of not more than 0.25 EU/ml. Bulk solutions of liquid parenterals shall be made in WFI. Final rinse of product containers and machine parts shall be done with WFI. Disinfectant solutions for use in aseptic areas shall be prepared in WFI.

(iv) Water for Injection for the manufacture of liquid injectables shall be freshly collected from the distillation plant or from a storage or circulation loop where the water has been at above 70 degree centigrade. At the point of collection, water may be cooled using suitable heat exchanger.

(v) Water for non-injectable sterile products like eye drops shall meet IP specifications for purified water. In addition, microbiological specification of not more than 10 cfu per 100 ml and absence of Pseudomonas aeruginosa and Enterobacter coli in 100 ml shall also be met.

(vi) Water for Injection shall be stored in steam jacketted stainless steel tanks of suitable size and the tanks shall have hydrophobic bacterial retention with 0.22 µ vent filters. The filers shall be suitably sterilized at periodic intervals. The distribution lines for purified water and distilled water shall be of stainless steel 316 construction and shall not shed particles.

(vii) There shall be a written procedure and program for the sanitation of different water systems including storage tanks, distribution lines, pumps and other related equipment. Records of sanitation shall be maintained.

(viii) There shall be written microbiological monitoring program for different types of water. The results shall justify the frequency of sampling and testing. Investigation shall be carried out and corrective action taken in case of deviation from prescribed limits.

(ix) Steam coming in contact with the product, primary containers and other product contract surfaces shall be sterile and pyrogen free. The steam condensate shall meet microbiological specification of not more than 10 cfu per 100 ml. The condensate shall also meet IP specification for Water for Injection and shall have an endotoxin levels of not more than 0.25 EU/ml. There shall be a suitable schedule for the monitoring to steam quality.

9. **Manufacturing Process**

(i) Manufacture of sterile products shall be carried out only in areas under defined conditions.

(ii) Bulk raw materials shall be monitored for bio-burden periodically. Bio-burden of bulk solution prior to membrane filtration shall be monitored periodically and a limit of not more than 100 cfu per ml is recommended.

(iii) The time between the start of the preparation of the solution and its sterilization for filtration through a micro-organism retaining filter shall be minimised. There shall be a set maximum permissible time for each product that takes into account its composition and method of storage mentioned in the Master formula record.

(iv) Gases coming in contact with the sterile product shall be filtered through two 0.22 µ hydrophobic filters connected in-series. These filters shall be tested for integrity. Gas cylinders shall not be taken inside aseptic areas.

(v) Washed containers shall be sterilized immediately before use. Sterilized containers, if not used within an established time, shall be rinsed with distilled or filtered purified water and re-sterilized.

(vi) Each lot of finished product shall be filled in one continuous operation. In each case, where one batch is filled in using more than one operation, each lot shall be tested separately for sterility and held separately till sterility test results are known.

(vii) Special care shall be exercised while filling products in powder form so as not to contaminate the environment during transfer of powder to filling machine-hopper.

10. Form-Fill-Seal Technology or Blow, Fill-Seal Technology

(a) Form-Fill-Seal units are specially built automated machines in which through one continuous operation, containers are formed from thermoplastic granules, filled and then sealed. Blow, fill-seal units are machines in which containers are moulded /blown (preformed) in separate clean rooms, by non-continuous operations.

(b) Form-Fill-Seal/Blow, Fill-Seal machines used for the manufacture of products for terminal sterilization shall be installed in at least Grade C environment and the filling zone within the machine shall fulfill Grade A requirements.

(c) Terminally Sterilized Products

  (i) Preparation of primary packaging material such as glass bottles, ampoules and rubber stoppers shall be done in at least Grade D environment. Where there is unusual risk to the product from microbial contamination, the above operation shall be done in Grade C environment. All the processes used for component preparation shall be validated.

  (ii) Filling of products requiring terminal sterilization shall be done under Grade A environment with a Grade C background.

(d) Preparation of solutions, which are to be sterilized by filtration, shall be done in Grade C environment and if not to be filtered, the preparation of materials and products shall be in a Grade A environment with Grade B in background.

(e) Filtration (Membrane)

  (i) Solutions for Large Volume Parenterals shall be filtered through a non-fiber releasing, sterilizing grade cartridge/membrane filter of nominal pore size of 0.22 μ for aseptic filling whereas 0.45 μ porosity shall be used for terminally sterilized products.

  (ii) A second filtration using another 0.22 flu sterilizing grade cartridge/ membrane filter shall be performed immediately prior to filling. Process specifications shall indicate the maximum time during which a filtration system may be used with a view to precluding microbial build-up to levels that may affect the microbiological quality of the Large Volume Parenterals.

  (iii) The integrity of the sterilized filter shall be verified and confirmed immediately after use by an appropriate method such as Bubble Point, Diffusive Flow or Pressure Hold Test.

(f) Sterilization (Autoclaving)
  (i) Before any sterilization process is adopted, its suitability for the product and its efficacy in achieving the desired sterilizing conditions in all parts of each type of load pattern to be processed, shall be demonstrated by physical measurements and by biological indicators, where appropriate.
  (ii) All the sterilization processes shall be appropriately validated. The validity of the process shall be verified at regular intervals, but at least annually. Whenever significant modifications have been made to the equipment and product, records shall be maintained thereof.
  (iii) The sterilizer shall be double ended to prevent mix-ups.
  (iv) Periodic bio-burden monitoring of products before terminal sterilization shall be carried out and controlled to limits specified for the product in the Master Formula.
  (v) The use of biological indicators shall be considered as an additional method for monitoring the sterilization. These shall be stored and used according to the manufacturer's instructions. Their quality shall be checked by positive controls. If biological indicators are used, strict precautions shall be taken to avoid transferring microbial contamination from them.
  (vi) There shall be clear means of differentiating 'sterilized' and 'unsterilized' products. Each basket, tray or other carrier of products or components shall be clearly labelled with the name of the material, its batch number, and sterilization status. Indicators shall be used, where appropriate, to indicate whether a batch (or sub-batch) has passed through the sterilization process.
  (vii) Sterilization records shall be available for each sterilization-run and may also include thermographs and sterilization monitoring strips. They shall be maintained as part of the batch release procedure.

(g) Sterilization (by Dry Heat)
  (i) Each heat sterilization cycle shall be recorded on a time/temperature chart of a suitable size by appropriate equipment of the required accuracy and precision. The position of temperature probes used for controlling and/or recording shall be determined during the validation and, where applicable, shall also be checked against a second independent temperature probe located in the same position. The chart shall form a part of the batch record. Container mapping may also be carried out in the case of Large Volume Parenterals.

(ii) Chemical or biological indicators may also be used, but shall not take the place of physical validation.

(iii) Sufficient time shall be allowed for the load to reach the required temperature before measurement of sterilization time commences. This time shall be separately determined for each type of load to be processed.

(iv) After the high temperature phase of a heat sterilization cycle, precautions shall be taken against contamination of sterilized load during cooling. Any cooling fluid or gas in contact with the product shall be sterilized unless it can be shown that any leaking container would not be approved for use. Air inlet and outlets shall be provided with bacteria retaining filters.

(v) The process used for sterilization by dry heat shall include air-circulation within the chamber and the maintenance of a positive pressure to prevent the entry of non-sterile air. Air inlets and outlets should be provided with microorganism retaining filters. Where this process of sterilization by dry heat is also intended to remove pyrogens, challenge tests using endotoxins would be required as part of the validation process.

(h) Sterilization (By Moist Heat)

(i) Both the temperature and pressure shall be used to monitor the process. Control instrumentation shall normally be independent of monitoring instrumentation and recording charts. Where automated control and monitoring systems are used for these applications, these shall be validated to ensure that critical process requirements are met. System and cycle faults shall be registered by the system and observed by the operator. The reading of the independent temperature indicator shall be routinely checked against the chart-recorder during the sterilization period. For sterilizers fitted with a drain at the bottom of the chamber, it may also be necessary to record the temperature at this position throughout the sterilization period. There shall be frequent leak tests done on the chamber during the vacuum phase of the cycle.

(ii) The items to be sterilized, other than products in sealed containers, shall be wrapped in a material which allows removal of air and penetration of steam but which prevents re-contamination after sterilization. All parts of the load shall be in contact with the sterilizing agent at the required temperature for the required time.

(iii) No Large Volume Parenteral shall be subjected to steam sterilization cycle until it has been filled and sealed.

(iv) Care shall be taken to ensure that the steam used for sterilization is of a suitable quality and does not contain additives at a level which could cause contamination of the product or equipment.

(i) Completion / Finalisation of Sterile Products

    (i) All unit operations and processes in the manufacture of a batch shall have a minimum time specified and the shortest validated time shall be used from the start of a batch to its ultimate release for distribution.

    (ii) Containers shall be closed by appropriately validated methods. Containers closed by fusion, e.g. glass or plastic ampoules shall be subjected to 100% integrity testing. Samples of other containers shall be checked for integrity according to appropriate procedures.

    (iii) Containers sealed under vacuum shall be tested for required vacuum conditions.

    (iv) Filled containers of parenteral products shall be inspected individually for extraneous contamination or other defects. When inspection is done visually, it shall be done under suitably controlled conditions of illumination and background. Operators doing the inspection shall pass regular eye-sight checks with spectacles, if worn, and be allowed frequent rest from inspection. Where other methods of inspection are used, the process shall be validated and the performance of the equipment checked at suitable intervals. Results shall be recorded.

11. Product Containers and Closures

(a) All containers and closures intended for use shall comply with the pharmacopoeial and other specified requirements. Suitable sample sizes, specifications, test methods, cleaning procedures and sterilization procedures, shall be used to assure that containers, closures and other component parts of drug packages are suitable and are not reactive, additive, adsorptive or leachable or presents the risk of toxicity to an extent that significantly affects the quality or purity of the drug. No second hand or used containers and closures shall be used.

(b) Plastic granules shall also comply with the Pharmacopoeial requirements including physiochemical and biological tests.

(c) All containers and closures shall be rinsed prior to sterilization with water for injection according to written procedure.

(d) The design of closures, containers and stoppers shall be such as to make cleaning, easy and also to make an airtight seal when fitted to the bottles.

(e) It shall be ensured that containers and closures chosen for a particular product are such that when coming into contact they are not absorbed into the product and they do not affect the product adversely. The closures and stoppers should be of such quality substances as not to affect the quality of the product and avoid the risk of toxicity.

(f) Whenever glass bottles are used, the written schedule of cleaning shall be laid down and followed. Where bottles are not dried after washing, these shall be finally rinsed with distilled water or pyrogen free water, as the case may be, according to written procedure.

(g) Individual containers of parenteral preparations, ophthalmic preparations shall be examined against black/while background fitted with diffused light after filling so as to ensure freedom from foreign matters.

(h) Glass bottles

Shape and design of the glass bottle shall be rational and standardized. Glass bottles made of USP Type-I and USP Type-II glass shall only be used. Glass bottles shall not be reused. Before use, USP Type-II bottles shall be validated for the absence of particulate matter generated over a period of the shelf-life of the product and shall be regularly monitored after production, following statistical sampling methods. USP Type-III glass containers may be used for non-parenteral sterile products such as Otic Solutions.

(i) Plastic Containers

   (i) Pre-formed plastic containers intended to be used for the packing of Large Volume Parenteral shall be moulded in-house by one-continuous operation through an automatic machine.

   (ii) Blowing, filling and sealing (plugging) operations shall be conducted in room(s) conforming to requirements as mentioned in Table 13.3. Entry to the area where such operations are undertaken, shall be through a series of air locks. Blowers shall have an air supply which is filtered though 0.22 u filters. Removal of runners and plugging operations shall be conducted under a laminar airflow work station.

(j) Rubber Stoppers

The rubber stoppers used for Large Volume Parenterals shall comply with specifications prescribed in the current edition of the Indian Pharmacopoeia.

12. Documentation

(a) The manufacturing records relating to manufacture of sterile products shall indicate the following details :

   (1) Serial number of the Batch Manufacturing Record.

(2) Name of the product.
(3) Reference to Master Formula Record.
(4) Batch/Lot number.
(5) Batch/Lot size.
(6) Date of commencement of manufacture and date of completion of manufacture.
(7) Date of manufacture and assigned date of expiry.
(8) Date of each step in manufacturing.
(9) Names of all ingredients with the grade given by the quality control department.
(10) Quantity of all ingredients.
(11) Control reference numbers for all ingredients.
(12) Time and duration of blending, mixing etc. whenever applicable.
(13) pH of solution whenever applicable.
(14) Filter integrity testing records.
(15) Temperature and humidity records whenever applicable.
(16) Records of plate-counts whenever applicable.
(17) Results of pyrogen and/or bacterial endotoxin & toxicity.
(18) Records of weight or volume of drug filled in containers.
(19) Bulk sterility in case of aseptically filled products.
(20) Leak test records.
(21) Inspection records.
(22) Sterilization records including autoclave leakage test records, load details, date, duration, temperature, pressure etc.
(23) Container washing records.
(24) Total number of containers filled.
(25) Total numbers of containers rejected at each stage.
(26) Theoretical yield, permissible yield, actual yield and variation thereof.
(27) Clarification for variation in yield beyond permissible yield.
(28) Reference numbers of relevant analytical reports.
(29) Details of reprocessing, if any.
(30) Name of all operators carrying out different activities.
(31) Environmental monitoring records.
(32) Specimens of printed packaging material.

(33) Records of destruction of rejected containers and printed packaging materials.

(34) Signature of the competent technical staff responsible for manufacture and testing.

Notes :

(1) Products shall be released only after complete filling and testing.

(2) Result of the tests relating to sterility, pyrogens, and bacterial endotoxins shall be maintained in the analytical records.

(3) Validation details and simulation trial records shall be maintained separately.

(4) Records of environmental monitoring like temperature, humidity, microbiological data etc. shall be maintained. Records of periodic servicing of HEPA filters, sterilizers and other periodic maintenance of facilities and equipment carried out shall also be maintained.

(5) Separate facilities shall be provided for filling-cum-sealing of Small Volume Injectables and Large Volume Parenterals.

(6) It is advisable to provide separate facilities for manufacture of Large Volume parenterals in glass containers and/or plastic containers.

(7) For manufacture of Large volume parenterals in plastic containers, it is advisable to install automatic (with all operations). Form-Fill-Seal machines having one continuous operation.

PART IB
SPECIFIC REQUIREMENTS FOR MANUFACTURE OF ORAL SOLID DOSAGE FORMS

Note :

The general requirements as given in Part I of this Schedule relating to requirements of Good Manufacturing Practices for Premises and materials for pharmaceutical products shall be complied with, mutatis mutandis, for the manufacture of oral Solid Dosage Forms (Tablets and capsules). In addition to these requirements, the following Specific Requirements shall also be followed, namely :

1. **General**

    (a) The processing of dry materials and products creates problems of dust control and cross-contamination. Special attention is, therefore, needed in the design, maintenance and use of premises and equipment in order to overcome these problems. Wherever required, enclosed dust control manufacturing systems shall be employed.

(b) Suitable environmental conditions for the products handled shall be maintained by installation of air-conditioning where necessary. Effective air-extraction systems, with discharge points situated to avoid contamination of other products and processes shall be provided. Filters shall be installed to retain dust and to protect the factory and local environment.

(c) Special care shall be taken to protect against subsequent contamination of the product and particles of metal or wood. The use of metal detector is recommended. Wooden equipment should be avoided. Screens, sieves, punches and dies shall be examined for wear and tear or for breakage before and after each use.

(d) All ingredients for a dry product shall be sifted before use unless the quality of the input material can be assured. Such sifting shall normally be carried out at dedicated areas.

(e) Where the facilities are designed to provide special environmental conditions of pressure differentials between rooms, these conditions shall be regularly monitored and any specification results brought to the immediate attention of the Production and Quality assurance departments which shall be immediately attended.

(f) Care shall be taken to guard against any material lodging and remaining undetected in any processing or packaging equipment. Particular care shall be taken to ensure that any vacuum, compressed air or air extraction nozzles are kept clean and that there is no evidence of lubricants leaking into the product from any part of the equipments.

2. **Sifting, Mixing and Granulation**
    (a) Unless operated as a closed system, mixing, sifting and blending equipments shall be fitted with dust extractors.
    (b) Residues from sieving operations shall be examined periodically for evidence of the presence of unwanted materials.
    (c) Critical operating parameters like time and temperature for each mixing, blending and drying operation shall be specified in a Master Formula, monitored during processing, and recorded in the batch records.
    (d) Filter bags fitted to fluid-bed-drier shall not be used for different products, without being washed in-between use. With certain highly potent or sensitizing products, bags specific to one product only shall be used. Air entering the drier shall be filtered. Steps shall be taken to prevent contamination of the site and local environment by dust in the air leaving the drier due to close positioning of the air-inlets and exhaust.
    (e) Granulation and coating solutions shall be made, stored and used in a manner which minimises the risk of contamination or microbial growth.

3. **Compression (Tablets)**
   (a) Each tablet compressing machine shall be provided with effective dust control facilities to avoid cross contamination. Unless the same product is being made on each machine, or unless the compression machine itself provides its own enclosed air controlled environment, the machine shall be installed in separate cubicles.
   (b) Suitable physical, procedural and labelling arrangements shall be made to prevent mix-up of materials, granules and tablets on compression machinery.
   (c) Accurate and calibrated weighing equipment shall be readily available and used for in-process monitoring of tablet weight variation. Procedures used shall be capable of detecting out-of-limits tablets.
   (d) At the commencement of each compression run and in case of multiple compression points in a compression machine, sufficient individual tablets shall be examined at fixed intervals to ensure that a tablet from each compression station or from each compression point has been inspected for suitable pharmacopoeias parameters like 'appearance', 'weight variation', 'disintegration', 'hardness', 'friability' and 'thickness'. The results shall be recorded as part of the batch documentation.
   (e) Tablets shall be de-dusted, preferably by automatic device and shall be monitored for the presence of foreign materials besides any other defects.
   (f) Tablets shall be collected into clean, labelled containers.
   (g) Rejected or discarded tablets shall be isolated in identified containers and their quantity recorded in the Batch Manufacturing Record.
   (h) In process control shall be employed to ensure that the products remain within specification. During compression, samples of tablets shall be taken at regular intervals of not greater than 30 minutes to ensure that they are being produced in compliance with specified in-process specification. The tablets shall also be periodically checked for additional parameters such as 'appearance', 'weight variation', 'disintegration', 'hardness', 'friability' and 'thickness'. The results shall be recorded as part of the batch documentation.

4. **Coating (Tablets)**
   (a) Air supplied to coating pans for drying purposes shall be filtered air and of suitable quality. The area shall be provided with suitable exhaust system and environmental control (temperature, humidity) measures.
   (b) Coating solutions and suspensions shall be made afresh and used in a manner, which shall minimise the risk of microbial growth. Their preparation and use shall be documented and recorded.

5. **Filling of Hard Gelatin Capsule**

Empty capsule shells shall be regarded as 'drug component' and treated accordingly. They shall be stored under conditions which shall ensure their safety from the effects of excessive heat and moisture.

6. **Printing (Tablets And Capsules)**

   (a) Special care shall be taken to avoid product mix-up during any printing of tablets and capsules. Where different products, or different batches of the same products, are printed simultaneously, the operations shall be adequately be segregated. Edible grade colours and suitable printing ink shall be used for such printing.

   (b) After printing, tablets and capsules shall be approved by Quality Control before release for packaging or sale.

7. **Packaging (Strip and Blister)**

   (a) Care shall be taken when using automatic tablet and capsule counting, strip and blister packaging equipment to ensure that all 'rogue' tablets, capsules or foils from packaging operation are removed before a new packaging operation is commenced. There shall be an independent recorded check of the equipment before a new batch of tablets or capsules is handled.

   (b) Uncoated tablets shall be packed on equipment designed to minimise the risk of cross-contamination. Such packaging shall be carried out in an isolated area when potent tablets or Beta-lactum containing tablets are being packed.

   (c) The strips coming out of the machine shall be inspected for defects such as misprint, cuts on the foil, missing tablets and improper sealing.

   (d) Integrity of individual packaging strips and blisters shall be subjected to vacuum test periodically to ensure leak proofness of each pocket strip and blister and records maintained.

PART IC

SPECIFIC REQUIREMENTS FOR MANUFACTURE OF ORAL LIQUIDS

Note :

The general requirements as given in Part I of this Schedule relating to Requirements of Good Manufacturing Practices for Premises and Materials for pharmaceutical products shall be complied with, mutatis mutandis, for the manufacture of (Syrups, Elixirs, Emulsions and Suspensions).

In addition to these requirements, the following Specific Requirements shall also be followed, namely :

1. **Building and Equipment**
   (a) The premises and equipment shall be designed, constructed and maintained to suit the manufacturing of Oral Liquids. The layout and design of the manufacturing area shall strive to minimize the risk of cross-contamination and mix-ups.
   (b) Manufacturing area shall have entry through double door air-lock facility. It shall be made fly proof by use of 'fly catcher' and/or `air curtain'.
   (c) Drainage shall be of adequate size and have adequate traps, without open channels and the design shall be such as to prevent back flow. Drains shall be shallow to facilitate cleaning and disinfecting.
   (d) The production area shall be cleaned and sanitized at the end of every production process.
   (e) Tanks, containers, pipe work and pumps shall be designated and installed so that they can be easily cleaned and sanitized. Equipment design shall be such as to prevent accumulation of residual microbial growth or cross-contamination.
   (f) Stainless steel or any other appropriate material shall be used for parts of equipments coming in direct contact with the products. The use of glass apparatus shall be minimum.
   (g) Arrangements for cleaning of containers, closures and droppers shall be made with the help of suitable machines/devices equipped with high pressure air, water and steam jets.
   (h) The furniture used shall be smooth, washable and made of stainless steel.

2. **Purified Water**
   (a) The chemical and microbiological quality of purified water used shall be specified and monitored routinely. The microbiological evaluation shall include testing for absence of pathogens and shall not exceed 100 cfu/ml (as per Appendix 12.5 of IP 1996).
   (b) There shall be a written procedure for operation and maintenance of the purified water systems. Care shall be taken to avoid the risk of microbial proliferation with appropriate methods like recalculation, use of UV treatment, treatment with heat and sanitizing agent. After any chemical sanitisation of the water system, a flushing shall be done to ensure that the sanitizing agent has been effectively removed.

3. **Manufacturing**
   (a) Manufacturing personnel shall wear non-fiber shedding clothing to prevent contamination of the product.
   (b) Materials likely to shed fiber like gunny bags, or wooden pallets shall not be carried into the area where products and cleaned-containers are exposed.

(c) Care shall be taken to maintain the homogeneity of emulsion by the use of appropriate emulsifier and suspensions by use of appropriate stirrer during filling. Mixing and filling processes shall be specified and monitored. Special care shall be taken at the beginning of the filling process, after stoppage due to any interruption and at the end of the process to ensure that the product is uniformly homogeneous during the filling process.

(d) The primary packaging area shall have an air supply which is filtered through 5 micron filters. The temperature of the area shall not exceed 30 degrees centigrade.

(e) When the bulk product is not immediately packed, the maximum period of storage and storage conditions shall be specified in the Master Formula. The maximum period of storage time of a product in the bulk stage shall be validated.

PART ID
SPECIFIC REQUIREMENTS FOR MANUFACTURE OR TOPICAL PRODUCTS I.E. EXTERNAL PREPARATIONS

The general requirements as given in Part I of this Schedule relating to Requirements of Good Manufacturing Practices for Premises and Materials for pharmaceutical products shall be complied with, mutatis mutandis, for the manufacture of Topical Products i.e. External Preparations (Creams, Ointments, Pastes, Emulsions, Lotions, Solutions, Dusting powders and identical products used for external applications). In addition to these requirements, the following Specific Requirements shall also be followed, namely :

1. The entrance to the area where topical products are manufactured shall be through a suitable airlock. Outside the airlock, insectocutors shall be installed.
2. The air to this manufacturing area shall be filtered through at least 20 μ air filters and shall be air-conditioned. The area shall be ventilated.
3. The area shall be fitted with an exhaust system of suitable capacity to effectively remove vapours, fumes, smoke, floating dust particles.
4. The equipment used shall be designed and maintained to prevent the product from being accidentally contaminated with any foreign matter or lubricant.
5. No rags or dusters shall be used in the process of cleaning or drying the process equipment or accessories used.
6. Water used in compounding shall be Purified Water IP.
7. Powders, whenever used, shall be suitably sieved before use.
8. Heating vehicles and a base like petroleum jelly shall be done in separate mixing area in suitable stainless steel vessels, using steam, gas, electricity, solar energy etc.
9. A separate packing section may be provided for primary packaging of the products.

PART IE
SPECIFIC REQUIREMENTS FOR MANUFACTURE OF METERED-DOSE INHALERS (MDI)

Note :

The general requirements as given in Part I of this schedule relating to requirements of Good Manufacturing Practices for Premises and Materials for pharmaceutical products shall be complied with, mutatis mutandis, for the manufacture of Metered-Dose Inhalers (MDI). In addition to these requirements, the following Specific Requirements shall also be followed, namely :

1. **General**

   Manufacture of Metered-Dose-Inhaler shall be done under conditions which shall ensure minimum microbial and particulate contamination. Assurance of the quality of components and the bulk product is very important. Where medicaments are in suspended state, uniformity of suspension shall be established.

2. **Building and Civil Works**

   (a) The building shall be located on a solid foundation to reduce risk of cracking walls and floor due to the movement of equipment and machinery.

   (b) All building surfaces shall be impervious, smooth and non-shedding. Flooring shall be continuous and provided with a cove between the floor and the wall as well the wall to the ceiling. Ceiling shall be solid, continuous and covered to walls. Light fittings and air-grills shall be flush with the ceiling. All service lines requiring maintenance shall be erected in such a manner that these are accessible from outside the production area.

   (c) The manufacturing area shall be segregated into change rooms for personnel, container preparation area, bulk preparation and filling area, quarantine area and spray testing and packing areas.

   (d) Secondary change rooms shall be provided for operators to change from factory clothing to special departmental clothing before entering the manufacturing and filling area.

   (e) Separate area shall be provided for de-cartoning of components before they are air washed.

   (f) The propellants used for manufacture shall be delivered to the manufacturing area distribution system by filtering them through 2 F filters. The bulk containers of propellants shall be stored, suitably identified, away from the manufacturing facilities.

3. **Environmental Conditions**
   (a) Where products or clean components are exposed, the area shall be supplied with filtered air of Grade C.
   (b) The requirements of temperature and humidity in the manufacturing area shall be decided depending on the type of product and propellants handled in the facility. Other support areas shall have comfort levels of temperature and humidity.
   (c) There shall be a difference in room pressure between the manufacturing area and the support areas and the differential pressure shall be not be less than 15 Pascals, (0.06 inches or 1.5 mm Water gauge).
   (d) There shall be a written schedule for the monitoring of environmental conditions. Temperature and humidity shall be monitored daily.

4. **Garments**
   (a) Personnel in the manufacturing and filling section shall wear suitable single piece garment made out of non-shedding, tight weave material. Personnel in support areas shall wear clean factory uniforms.
   (b) Gloves made of suitable material having no interaction with the propellants shall be used by the operators in the manufacturing and filling areas. Preferably, disposable gloves shall be used.
   (c) Suitable department-specific personnel protective equipment like footwear and safety glasses shall be used wherever hazard exists.

5. **Sanitation**
   (a) There shall be written procedures for the sanitation of the MDI manufacturing facility. Special care should be taken to handle residues and rinses of propellants.
   (b) Use of water for cleaning shall be restricted and controlled. Routinely used disinfectants are suitable for sanitising the different areas. Records of sanitation shall be maintained.

6. **Equipment**
   (a) Manufacturing equipment shall be of closed system. The vessels and supply lines shall be of stainless steel.
   (b) Suitable check weights, spray testing machines and labelling machines shall be provided in the department.
   (c) All the equipment shall be suitably calibrated and their performance validated on receipt and thereafter periodically.

7. Manufacture

(a) There shall be an approved Master Formula Records for the manufacture of metered dose inhalers. All propellants, liquids and gasses shall be filtered through 2p filters to remove particles.

(b) The primary packing material shall be appropriately cleaned by compressed air suitably filtered through 0.2 F filter. The humidity of the compressed air shall be controlled as applicable.

(c) The valves shall be carefully handled and after de-cartoning, these shall be kept in clean, closed containers in the filling room.

(d) For suspensions, the bulk shall be kept stirred continuously.

(e) In-process controls shall include periodical checking of weight of bulk formulation filled in the containers. In a two-shot-filling process (liquid filling followed by gaseous filling), it shall be ensured that 100% check on weight is carried out.

(f) Filled containers shall be quarantined for a suitable period established by the manufacturer to detect leaking containers prior to testing, labelling and packing.

8. Documentation

In addition to the routine goods manufacturing practices documentation manufacturing records shall show the following additional information :

(1) Temperature and humidity in the manufacturing area.

(2) Periodic filled weights of the formulation.

(3) Records of rejections during on line check weighing.

(4) Records of rejection during spray testing.

PART IF
SPECIFIC REQUIREMENTS OF PREMISES, PLANT AND MATERIALS FOR MANUFACTHRE OF ACTIVE PHARMACEUTICAL INGREDIENTS (BULK DRUGS)

Note :

The General Requirements as given in Part I of this schedule relating to requirements of Good Manufacturing Practices for Premises Materials for pharmaceutical products shall be complied with, mutatis mutarldis for the manufacture of active pharmaceutical ingredients (Bulk Drugs). In addition to these requirements, the following Specific Requirements shall also be followed, namely :

1. Buildings and Civil Works

(a) Apart from the building requirements contained in Part-I, General ante, the active pharmaceutical ingredients facilities for manufacture of hazardous reactions, Beta-Lactum antibiotics, Steroids and Steroidal Harmones/Cytotoxic substances shall be provided in confined areas to prevent contamination of the other drugs manufactured.

(b) The final stage of preparation of a drug, like isolation/filtration/drying/milling/sieving and packing operations shall be provided with air filtration systems including pre-filters and finally with a 5 micron filter. Air handling suitable systems with adequate number of air charges per hour or any other suitable system to control the air borne contamination shall be provided. Humidity/Temperature shall also be controlled for all the operations wherever required.

(c) Air filtration systems including pre-filters and particulate matter retention air filters shall be used, where appropriate, for air supplies to production areas. If air is re-circulated to production areas, measures shall be taken to control re-circulation of floating dust particles from production. In areas where air contamination occurs during production, there shall be adequate exhaust system to control contaminants.

(d) Ancillary area shall be provided for Boiler-house. Utility areas like heat exchangers, chilling workshop, store and supply of gases shall also be provided.

(e) For specified preparation like manufacture of sterile products and for certain antibiotics, sex hormones, cytotoxic and oncology products, separate enclosed areas shall be designed. The requirements for the sterile active pharmaceutical ingredient shall be in line with the facilities required for formulations to be filled aseptically.

Sterile Products : Sterile active pharmaceutical ingredient filled aseptically shall be treated as formulation from the stage wherever the process demands like crystallization, lyophilisation, filtration etc. All conditions applicable to formulations that are required to be filled aseptically shall apply mutatis mutandis for the manufacture of sterile active pharmaceutical ingredients involving stages like filtration, crystallization and lyophilisation.

Utilities /Services : Equipment like chilling plant, boiler, heat exchangers, vacuum and gas storage vessels shall be serviced, cteamed, sanstised and maintained at applopriaFte intervals to prevent mal-functions or contamination that may interfere with safety, identity, strength, quality or purity of the drug product.

2. **Equipment Design, Size and Location**
   (i) Equipment used in the manufacture, processing, packing or holding of an active pharmaceutical ingredient shall be of appropriate design, adequate size and suitably located to facilitate operations for its intended use and for its cleaning and maintenance.

(ii) If equipment is used for different intermediates and active pharmaceutical ingredients, proper cleaning before switching from one product to another becomes particularly important. If cleaning of a specific type of equipment is difficult, the equipment may need to be dedicated to a particular intermediate or active pharmaceutical ingredient.

(iii) The choice of cleaning methods, detergents and levels of cleaning shall be defined and justified. Selection of cleaning agents (e.g. solvents) should depend on;

   (a) The suitability of the cleaning agent to remove residues of raw materials, intermediates, precursors, degradation products and isomers, as appropriate;

   (b) Whether the cleaning agent leaves a residue itself;

   (c) Compatibility with equipment construction materials like centrifuge/filtration, dryer/fluid bed dryer, rotocone proton dryer, vacuum dryer, frit mill, multi-mill/jet, mills/sewetters cut sizing;

   (d) Test for absence of intermediate or active pharmaceutical ingredient in the final rinse.

(iv) A written procedures shall be established and allowed for cleaning and maintenance of equipment, including utensils used in the manufacture, processing, packing or holding of active pharmaceutical ingredients. These procedures shall include but should not be limited to the following :

   (a) Assignment of responsibility for cleaning and maintaining equipment;

   (b) Maintenance and cleaning program schedules, including where appropriate, sanitizing schedules;

   (c) A complete description of the methods and materials used to clean and maintain equipment, including instructions for dis-assembling and re-assembling each article of equipment to ensure proper cleaning and maintenance;

   (d) Removal or obliteration of previous batch identification;

   (e) Protection of clean equipment from contamination prior to use;

   (f) Inspection of equipment for cleanliness immediately before use;

   (g) Establishing the maximum time that may elapse between completion of processing and equipment cleaning as well as between cleaning and equipment reuse.

(v) Equipment shall be cleaned between successive batches to prevent contamination and carry-over of degraded material or contaminants unless otherwise established by validation.

(vi) As processing approaches the final purified active pharmaceutical ingredient, it is important to ensure that incidental carry over between batches does not have adverse impact on the established impurity profile. However, this does not generally hold good for any biological, active pharmaceutical ingredient where many of the processing steps are accomplished aseptically and where it is necessary to clean and sterilize equipment between batches.

3. **In-process Controls**
   (i) In-process controls for chemical reactions may include the following :
      (a) reaction time or reaction completion;
      (b) reaction mass appearance, clarity, completeness or pH solutions
      (c) reaction temperature,
      (d) concentration of a reactant;
      (e) assay or purity of the product;
      (f) process completion check by TLC/any other means.
   (ii) In-process controls for physical operations may include the following :
      (a) appearance and colour;
      (b) uniformity of the blend;
      (c) temperature of a process;
      (d) concentration of a solution;
      (e) processing rate or time;
      (f) particle size analysis;
      (g) bulk/tap density;
      (h) pH determination;
      (i) moisture content.

4. **Product Containers and Closures**
   (i) All containers and closures shall comply with the pharmacopoeial or any other requirement, suitable sampling methods, sample sizes, specification, test methods, cleaning procedures and sterilization procedures, when indicated, shall be used to assure that containers, closures and other component parts of drug packages are suitable and are not reactive, additive, adsorptive or leachable to an extent that significantly affects the quality or purity of the drug.
   (ii) The drug product container shall be re-tested or re-examined as appropriate and approved or rejected and shall be identified and controlled under a quarantine system designed to prevent their use in manufacturing or processing operations for which these are unsuitable.

(iii) Container closure system shall provide adequate protection against foreseeable external factors in storage/transportation and use that may cause deterioration or contamination of the active pharmaceutical ingredient.

(iv) Bulk containers and closures shall be cleaned and, where indicated by the nature of the active pharmaceutical ingredient, sterilized to ensure that they are suitable for their intended use.

(v) The container shall be conspicuously marked with the name of the product and the following additional information concerning :

   (a) quality and standards, if specified;

   (b) manufacturing licence number/drug master file number (whichever applicable), batch number;

   (c) date of manufacture and date of expiry;

   (d) method for container disposal (label shall give the methodology, if required);

   (e) storage conditions, if specified and name and address of the manufacturer, if available.

(vi) Areas for different operation of active pharmaceutical ingredients (Bulk drugs) section shall have appropriate areas which may be suitably partitioned for different operations.

PART II
REQUIREMENTS FOR PLANT AND EQUIPMENT

1. **External Preparations**

The following equipment is recommended for the manufacture of External preparations i.e. Ointments, Emulsions, Lotions, Solutions, Pastes, Creams, Dusting Powders and such identical products used for external applications whichever is applicable, namely :

(1) Mixing and storage tanks (Stainless steel).

(2) Jacketted Kettle (steam, gas or electrically heated).

(3) Mixer (Electrically operated).

(4) Planetary mixer.

(5) A colloid mill or a suitable emulsifier.

(6) A triple roller mill or an ointment mill.

(7) Liquid filling equipment (Electrically operated).

(8) Jar or tube filling equipment (Electrically operated).

Area :

(1) A minimum area of 30 m² for basic installation and 10 m² for Ancillary area is recommended.

(2) Areas for formulations meant for external use and internal use shall be separately provided to avoid mix up.

2. **Oral Liquid Preparations**

The following equipment is recommended for the manufacture of oral/internal use preparations i.e. Syrups, Elixirs, Emulsions and Suspensions, whichever is applicable, namely :

(1) Mixing and storage tanks (Stainless steel).
(2) Jacketted Kettle/Stainless steel tank (steam, gas or electrically heated).
(3) Portable stirrer (Electrically operated).
(4) A colloid mill or suitable emulsifier (Electrically operated).
(5) Suitable filtration equipment (Electrically operated).
(6) Semi-automatic/automatic bottle filling machine.
(7) Pilfer proof cap sealing machine.
(8) Water distillation unit deioniser.
(9) Clarity testing inspection units.

Area : A minimum area of 30 m² for basic installation and 10 m² for Ancillary area is recommended.

3. **Tablets**

The Tableting section shall be free from dust and floating particles and may be air-conditioned. For this purpose, each tablet machine shall be isolated into cubicles and connected to a vacuum dust collector or an exhaust system. For effective operations, the tablet production department shall be divided into four distinct and separate sections as follows :

(a) Mixing, Granulation and Drying section.
(b) Tablet compression section.
(c) Packaging section (strip/blister machine wherever required)
(d) Coating section (wherever required)

(i) The following electrically operated equipment are recommended for the manufacture of compressed tablets and hypodermic tablets, in each of the above sections, namely :

    (a) Granulation-cum-Drying section.
        (1) Disintegrator and sifter.
        (2) Powder mixer.

(3) Mass mixer/Planetary mixer/Rapid mixer granulator.

(4) Granulator.

(5) Thermostatically controlled hot air oven with trays (preferably mounted on a trolley) / Fluid bed dryer.

(6) Weighing machines.

(b) Compression section.

(1) Tablet compression machine, single/multi punch/rotatory.

(2) Punch and dies storage cabinets.

(3) Tablet de-duster.

(4) Tablet Inspection unit/belt.

(5) Dissolution test apparatus.

(6) In-process testing equipment like single pan electronic balance, hardness tester, friability and disintegration test apparatus.

(7) Air-conditioning and dehumidification arrangement (wherever necessary).

(c) Packaging section.

(1) Strip/blister packaging machine

(2) Leak test apparatus (vacuum system)

(3) Tablet counters (wherever applicable)

(4) Air-conditioning and dehumidification arrangement (wherever applicable).

Area : A minimum area of 60 m^2 for basic installation and 20 m^2 for Ancillary area is recommended for un-coated tablets.

(d) Coating section.

(1) Jacketted kettle (steam, gas, or electrically heated for preparing coating suspension).

(2) Coating pan (Stainless steel).

(3) Polishing pan (where applicable).

(4) Exhaust system (including vacuum dust collector).

(5) Air conditioning and Dehumidification Arrangement.

(6) Weighing balance.

(ii) The coating section shall be made dust free with suitable exhaust system to remove excess powder and fumes resulting from solvent evaporation. It shall be air-conditioned and dehumidified wherever considered necessary.

Area : A minimum additional area of 30 m^2 for coating section for basic installation and 10 m^2 for Ancillary area is recommended.

Separate area and equipment for mixing, granulation, drying, tablet compression, coating and packing shall be provided for Penicillin group of drugs on the lines indicated above. In case of operations involving dust and floating particles, care shall be exercised to avoid cross-contamination.

(iii) The manufacture of Hypodermic tablets shall be conducted under aseptic conditions in a separate air-conditioned room, the walls of which shall be smooth and washable. The granulation, tableting and packing shall be done in this room.

(iv) The manufacture of effervescent and soluble/dispersible tablets shall be carried out in air-conditioned and dehumidified areas.

4. Powders

The following equipment is recommended for the manufacture of powders, namely :

(1) Disintegrator.
(2) Mixer (electrically operated).
(3) Sifter.
(4) Stainless steel vessels and scoops of suitable sizes.
(5) Filling equipment (electrically operated).
(6) Weighing balance.

In the case of operation involving floating particles of fine powder, a suitable exhaust system shall be provided. Workers should be provided with suitable masks during operation.

Area : A minimum area of 30 m^2 is recommended to allow for the basic installations. Where the actual blending is to be done on the premises, an additional room shall be provided for the purpose.

5. Capsules

For the manufacture of capsules, separate enclosed area suitably air-conditioned and dehumidified with an airlock arrangement shall be provided. The following equipment is recommended for filling Hard Gelatin Capsules, namely:

(1) Mixing and blending equipment (electrically or power driven).
(2) Capsule filling units (preferably semi automatic or automatic filling machines).
(3) Capsules counters (wherever applicable).
(4) Weighing balance.
(5) Disintegration test apparatus.
(6) Capsule polishing equipment.

Separate equipment and, filling and packaging areas shall be provided in penicillin and non-penicillin sections. In case of operations involving floating particles of fine powder, a suitable exhaust system shall be provided. Manufacture and filling shall be carried out in air-conditioned areas. The room shall be dehumidified.

Area : A minimum area of 25 m^2 for basic installation and 10 m^2 for Ancillary area each for penicillin and non-penicillin sections is recommended.

6. Surgical Dressing

The following equipment is recommended for the manufacture of surgical dressings other than Absorbent Cotton Wool, namely :

(1) Rolling machine.
(2) Trimming machine.
(3) Cutting equipment.
(4) Folding and pressing machine for gauze.
(5) Mixing tanks for processing medicated dressing.
(6) Hot air dry oven.
(7) Steam sterilizer or dry heat sterilizer or other suitable equipment.
(8) Work tables/benches for different operations.

Area : A minimum area of 30 m^2 is recommended to allow for the basic installations. In case medicated dressings are to be manufactured, another room with a minimum area of 30 m^2 shall be provided.

7. Ophthalmic Preparations

For the manufacture of Ophthalmic preparations, separate enclosed areas with air lock arrangement shall be provided. The following equipment is recommended for manufacture under aseptic conditions of Eye-ointment, Eye-lotions and other preparations for external use, namely :

(1) Thermostatically controlled hot air ovens (preferably double ended).
(2) Jacketted kettle/Stainless stell tanks (steam, gas or electrically heated).
(3) Mixing and storage tanks of stainless steel/Planetary mixer.
(4) Collcoid mill or ointment mill.
(5) Tube filling and crimping equipment (semi-automatic or automatic filling machines).
(6) Tube cleaning equipment (air jet type).
(7) Tube washing and drying equipment, if required.
(8) Automatic vial washing machine.
(9) Vial drying oven.

(10) Rubber bung washing machine.

(11) Sintered glass funnel, seitz filter or filter candle (preferably cartridge and membrane filters).

(12) Liquid filling equipment (semi-automatic or automatic filling machines).

(13) Autoclave (preferably ventilator autoclave).

(14) Air-conditioning and dehumidification arrangement (preferably centrally air-conditioned and dehumidification system).

(15) Laminar air flow units.

Area :

(1) A minimum area of 25 m^2 for basic installation and 10 m^2 for Ancillary area is recommended. Manufacture and filling shall be carried out in air-conditioned areas under aseptic conditions. The rooms shall be further dehumidified as considered necessary if preparations containing antibiotics are manufactured.

(2) Areas for formulations meant for external use and internal use shall be separately provided to avoid mix up.

8. Pessaries and Suppositories

The following equipment is recommended for manufacture of Pessaries and Suppositories, namely :

(1) Mixing and pouring equipment.

(2) Moulding equipment.

(3) Weighing devices.

Area :

(i) A minimum area of 20 m^2 is recommended to allow for the basic installation.

(ii) In the case of pessaries manufactured by granulation and compression, the requirements as indicated under "item 3 of Tablet", shall be provided.

9. Inhalers and Vitrallae

The following equipment is recommended for manufacture of inhalers and vitrallae, namely :

(1) Mixing equipment.

(2) Graduated delivery equipment for measurement of the medicament during filling.

(3) Sealing equipment.

Area :

An area of minimum 20 m^2 is recommended for the basic installations.

10. Repacking of Drugs and Pharmaceutical Chemicals

The following equipment is recommended for repacking of drugs and pharmaceuticals, chemicals, namely :

(1) Powder disintegrator.

(2) Powder sifter (Electrically operated).

(3) Stainless steel scoops and vessels of suitable sizes.

(4) Weighing and measuring equipment.

(5) Filling equipment (semi-automatic/automatic machine).

(6) Electric sealing machine.

Area :

An area of minimum 30 m^2 is recommended for the basic installation. In case of operations involving floating particles of the fine powder, a suitable exhaust system shall be provided.

11. Parenteral Preparations

The whole operation of manufacture of parenteral preparations (small volume injectables and large volume parenterals) in glass and plastic containers may be divided into the following separate areas/rooms, namely:

(i) Parenteral preparations in glass containers,

   (1) Water management area : This includes water treatment and storage.

   (2) Containers and closures preparation area : This includes washing and drying of ampoules, vials, bottles and closures.

   (3) Solution preparation area : This includes preparation and filtration of solution.

   (4) Filling capping and sealing area : This includes filling and sealing of ampoules and/or filling, capping and sealing of vials and bottles.

   (5) Sterilization area.

   (6) Quarantine area.

   (7) Visual inspection area.

   (8) Packaging area.

   The following equipment is recommended for different above mentioned areas, namely :

   (a) Water management area,

      (1) De-ionised water treatment unit.

      (2) Distillation (multi column with heat exchangers) unit

      (3) Thermostatically controlled water storage tank.

      (4) Transfer pumps (teel service lines for carrying water into user areas.

(b) Containers and closures preparation area,
   (1) Automatic rotary ampoule/vial/bottle washing machine having separate air, water, distilled water jets.
   (2) Automatic closures washing machine.
   (3) Storage equipment for ampoules, vials, bottles and closures.
   (4) Dryer/sterilizer (double ended).
   (5) Dust proof storage cabinets.
   (6) Stainless steel benches/stools.
(c) Solution preparation area,
   (1) Solution preparation and mixing Stainless steel tanks and other containers.
   (2) Portable stirrer.
   (3) Filtration equipment with cartridge and membrane filters/bacteriological filters.
   (4) Transfer pumps.
   (5) Stainless steel benches.
(d) Filling, capping and sealing area,
   (1) Automatic ampoule/vial/bottle filling, sealing and capping machine under laminar air flow work station.
   (2) Gas lines (Nitrogen, Oxygen, Carbon dioxide) wherever required.
   (3) Stainless steel benches/stools.
(e) Sterilization area
   (1) Steam sterilizer (preferably with computer control for sterilization cycle along with trolley sets for loading/unloading containers before and after sterilization)
   (2) Hot air sterilizer (preferably double ended)
   (3) Pressure leak test apparatus.
(f) Quarantine area,
   (1) Storage cabinets
   (2) Raised platforms/steel racks
(g) Visual inspection area,
   (1) Visual inspection units (preferably conveyor belt type and composite white and black assembly supported with illumination).
   (2) Stainless steel benches/stools.

(h) Packaging area,
   (1) Batch coding machine (preferably automatic)
   (2) Labelling unit (preferably conveyor belt type)
   (3) Benches/stools.

Area :

(1) A minimum area of 150 m^2 for the basic installation and an Ancillary area of 100 m^2 for Small Volume Injectables is recommended. For Large Volume Parenterals, an area of 150 m^2 each for the basic installation and for Ancillary area is recommended. These areas shall be partitioned into suitable enclosures with airlock arrangements.

(2) Areas for formulations meant for external use and internal use shall be separately provided to avoid mix up.

(3) Packaging materials for large volume Parenteral shall have a minimum area for 100 m^2.

(ii) Parenteral preparations in plastic containers by Form-Fill-Seal /Blow, Fill-Seal technology.

The whole operation of manufacture of large volume parenteral preparations in plastic containers including plastic pouches by automatic (all operations in one station).

Form-Fill-Seal machine or by semi-automatic blow moulding, filling-cum-sealing machine may be divided into the following separate areas/rooms, namely :

(1) Water management area.
(2) Solution preparation area.
(3) Container moulding-cum-filling and sealing area.
(4) Sterilization area.
(5) Quarantine area.
(6) Visual inspection area.
(7) Packaging area.

Following equipment is recommended for different above mentioned areas :

(a) Water management area :
   (1) De-ionised water treatment unit.
   (2) Distillation unit (multi column with heat exchangers).
   (3) Thermostatically controlled water storage tank.
   (4) Transfer pumps.
   (5) Stainless steel service lines for carrying water into user areas.

(b) Solution preparation area,
   (1) Solution preparation area,
   (2) Transfer pumps.
   (3) Cartridge and membrane filters.
(c) Container moulding-cum-filling and sealing area :
   (1) Sterile Form-Fill-Seal machine (all operations in one station with built-in laminar air flow work station having integrated container output conveyor belt through box).
   (2) Arrangement for feeding plastic granules through feeding-cum-filling tank into the machine.
(d) Sterilization area, Super heated steam sterilizer (with computer control for sterilization cycle along with trolley sets for loading/unloading containers for sterilization).
(e) Quarantine area, Adequate number of platforms/racks with storage system.
(f) Visual inspection area, Visual inspection unit (with conveyor belt and composite white and black assembly supported with illumination).
(g) Packaging area,
   (1) Pressure leak test apparatus (pressure belt or rotating disc type).
   (2) Batch coding machine (preferably automatic).
   (3) Labelling unit (preferably conveyor belt type).

Area :
(1) A minimum area of 250 m^2 for the basic installation and an Ancillary area of 150 m^2 for large volume parenteral preparations in plastic containers by Form-Fill-Seal technology is recommended. These areas shall be partitioned into suitable enclosures with air-lock arrangements.
(2) Areas for formulations meant for external use and internal use shall be separately provided to avoid mix up.
(3) Packaging materials for large volume Parenteral shall have a minimum area of 100 m^2.

SCHEDULE M-I
Rule 85-E(2)

1. **Requirements of Factory Premises for Manufacture of Homoeopathic Preparations**

    (a) **Location and surroundings :** The factory shall be situated in a place which shall not be adjacent to an open sewage drain, public laboatory or any factory which produces a disagreeable or obxnoxious odour or fumes or large quantities of soot, dust or smoke. The factory shall be located in a sanitary place, remote and filthy surroundings.

    (b) **Buildings :** The part of the building used for manufacturing shall not be used as a sleeping place and no sleeping place adjoining to it shall communicate therewith except through open air or through an intervening open space. The walls of the room in which manufacturing operations are carried out shall, upto a height of six feet from the floor, be smooth, water-proof and shall be capable of being kept clean. The flooring shall be smooth, even and washable and shall be such as not to permit retention or accumulation of dust. There shall be no chinks or crevices in the walls of floor.

    (c) The building used for the factory shall be constructed so as to permit production under hygienic conditions laid down in the Factories Act, 1948 (63 of 1948).

    (d) **Water supply :** The water used in manufacture shall be pure and of drinkable quality, free from pathogenic micro-organisms.

    (e) **Disposal of waste :** There should be adequate arrangement for disposal of waste water and other residues from the laboratory.

    (f) The rooms should be airy and clean and the temperature of the room should be moderately comfortable.

    (g) **Health, clothing and sanitary requirement of the staff :** All workers shall be free from contagious or obnoxious disease. Their clothing shall consist of a white or coloured uniform suitable to the nature of the work and the climate, and shall be clean. Adequate facilities for personal cleanliness, such as clean towels, soap and hand scrubbing brushes, shall be provided separately for each sex. The workers shall be required to wash and change into clean footwear before entering the rooms where the manufacturing operations are carried on. Workers shall be required to wear either a clean cap or a suitable headgear so as to avoid any possibility of contamination by hair or perspiration.

    (h) **Medical services :** The manufacturer shall provide adequate facilities for First Aid, Medical inspection of workers at the time of employment and periodically check-up thereafter at least once a year.

(i) **Working benches :** Working benches shall be provided for carrying out operations such as filling, labelling, packing etc. Such benches shall be fitted with smooth, impervious tops capable of being washed.

(j) **Container management :** Where operations involving use of containers such as bottles, phials and jars are conducted, there shall be adequate arrangements separated from potentisation chamber for washing, cleaning and drying such containers, with suitable equipment for the purpose. Wherever these are attached manually adequate precaution of perfection in respect of cleanliness and avoidance of pollutants shall be taken.

2. **Requirements of Plants and Equipments**

   (a) **Mother tinctures, External tinctures and Mother solution section :** The following plant and equipment shall be provided, namely :

   (i) Disintegrator.

   (ii) Seived separator.

   (iii) Balances and fluid measures.

   (iv) Chopping boards and knives.

   (v) Macerators with lids.

   (vi) Precolators with lids and regulated discharge.

   (vii) Moisture determination apparatus or other suitable arrangement.

   (viii) Filtering arrangement.

   (ix) Mixing vessels and suitable non-metallic storage containers.

   (x) Portable stirrers.

   (xi) Water still.

   Notes :

   (1) As far as possible metal contacts may be avoided once the drug is processed.

   (2) An area of 55 m^2 is recommended for basic installations.

   (3) Adequate separate storage facility should be provided for raw material quarantine, storage and bonded room for alcohol where applicable.

   (4) Separate and suitable storage facility should be provided for fresh herbs and odorous raw materials.

   (5) Adequate laboratory facility shall be provided for testing of raw materials and finished products.

   (b) **Potentisation Section :**

   1. The following arrangements are recommended for container, for closure preparation section namely :

      (i) Washing tanks with suitable brushing arrangement manual or mechanical.

(ii) Purified Water rinsing tank.
(iii) Closure macerating or washing tanks.
(iv) Drying chambers.

An area of 20 m² is recommended for basic installations.

2. The following arrangements are recommended for potency preparation section, namely :
   (i) Working tables with washable top.
   (ii) Facilities for separate storage of different grades of back potencies.
   (iii) Suitable measuring devices for discharge of drug and diluent in potentisation vial.
   (iv) Potentiser with counter or suitable manual arrangement.

   An area of 20 m² is recommended for basic installations.

   Notes :
   (a) Different droppers shall be used for different drugs potencies.
   (b) All measuring devices shall be metric system and be made of glass and shall be free from metallic contents.
   (c) It is desired that glass droppers etc. intended for re-use after cleaning should be sterilized by autoclave or by heating in a hot air oven.
   (d) Plastics, rubber tubes, bulks etc. coming in contact with tinctures or back potencies should not be re-used for other tincture and potencies.
   (e) Method of potentisation will be adopted as specifed in Homoeopathic Pharmacopoeia of India volume I.

3. Triturating Tableting and Pill / Globules Section :
   The following arrangements are recommended :
   (i)   Triturating machine of suitable device
   (ii) Disintegrator
   (iii) Mass Mixer
   (iv) Granulator
   (v)   Oven
   (vi) Tableting purches or machines
   (vii) Kettle (Steam/gas/electricity heated) for preparation solution
   (viii) Dryers
   (ix) Seived separator, tablet counters and balances.

   Note :
   Tablet section shall be free from dust and floating particles. An area of 55 m² is recommended for basic installations.

4. Ointments and lotion section :

   The following arrangements are recommended namely :
   (i) Mixing tank.
   (ii) Kettle (Steam, gas or electrically heated).
   (iii) Suitable powder mixer.
   (iv) Ointment mill.
   (v) Filling equipment or arrangement.

   An area or 20 m^2 is recommended for basic installations.

5. Syrups and tonics :

   The following arrangements are recommended namely :
   (i) Mixing and storage tank.
   (ii) Portable mixer.
   (iii) Filtering equipment.
   (iv) Water still/Deioniser.
   (v) Filling and sealing equipment.

   An area or 20 m^2 is recommended for basic installations.

6. Opthalmic Preparations : The following equipment is recommended for manufacture under a septic conditions of Eye-ointments, Eye-drops, Eye lotions and other preparations. For external use namely :
   (i) Hot air even electrically heated with thermostatic control.
   (ii) Colloid mill or ointment mill.
   (iii) Kettle (gas or electrically heated) with suitable mixing arrangement.
   (iv) Tube filling equipment.
   (v) Mixing and storage tanks of stainless steel or of other suitable material.
   (vi) Sintered glass funnel, Seitz filter or filter candle.
   (vii) Liquid filling equipment.
   (viii) Autoclaves.

   Adequate precaution should be taken to ensure that the finished product is sterile. An area of 20 m^2 is recommended for basic installations.

7. Adequate arrangements for space and equipment should be made for labelling and packing.

SCHEDULE M-II
Rule 139
REQUIREMENTS OF FACTORY PREMISES FOR MANUFACTURE OF COSMETICS

I. General Requirements

(A) **Location and surroundings :** The factory shall be located in sanitary place and hygienic conditions shall be maintained in the premises. Premises shall not be used for residence or be interconnected with residential areas. It shall be well ventilated and clean.

(B) **Buildings :** The buildings used for the factory shall be constructed so as to permit production under hygienic conditions and not to permit entry of insects, rodents, flies etc. The walls of the room in which manufacturing operations are carried out, shall be upto a height of six feet form the floor, be smooth waterproof and capable of being kept clean. The flooring shall be smooth, washable and shall be such as to permit retention or accumulation of dust.

(C) **Water supply :** The water used in manufacture shall be of potable quality.

(D) **Disposal of water :** Suitable arrangements shall be made for disposal of waste water.

(E) **Health, clothing and sanitary requirements of the staff :** All workers shall be free from contagious or infectious diseases. They shall be provided with clean uniforms, masks, headgears and gloves wherever required. Washing facilities shall also be provided.

(F) **Medical Services :** Adequate facilities for first-aid shall be provided.

(G) Work - benches shall be provided for carrying out operations such as filling, labelling, packing etc. Smooth benches shall be fitted with smooth, impervious tops capable of being washed.

(H) Adequate facilities shall be provided for washing and drying of glass containers if the same are to be used for packing the product.

II. Requirements of Plant and Equipment

The following equipment, area and other requirements are recommended for the manufacture of :

(A) **Powders : Face-powder, Cake makeup, Compacts, Face-packs, Masks and Rouges etc.**

Equipment :

(a) Powder mixer of suitable type provided with a dust collector.

(b) Perfume and colour blender.

(c) Sifter with sieves of suitable mesh size.

(d) Ball mill or suitable grinder.

(e) Trays and scoops (stainless steel).

(f) Filling and sealing equipment provided with dust extractor.

(g) For compacts :
- (i) a separate mixer,
- (ii) compact pressing machine.

(h) Weighing and measuring devices.

(i) Storage tanks.

An area of 15 m^2 is recommended. The section is to be provided with adequate exhaust fans.

(B) Creams, Lotions, Emulsions, Pastes, Cleansing Milks, Shampoos, Pomade, Brilliantine, Shaving-creams and Hair oils etc.

(a) Mixing and storage tanks of suitable materials.

(b) Heating kettle - steam, gas or electrically heated.

(c) Suitable agitator.

(d) Colloidal mill or homogeniser (wherever necessary).

(e) Triple roller mill (wherever necessary).

(f) Filling and sealing equipment.

(g) Weighing and measuring devices.

An area of 25 m^2 is recommended.

(C) Nail Polishes and Nail Lacquers

1. **Equipment :**
   - (a) A suitable mixer
   - (b) Storage tanks
   - (c) Filling machine - hand operated or power driven
   - (d) Weighing and measuring devices.

   An area of 15 m^2 is recommended. The section shall be provided with flame proof of exhaust system.

2. **Premises :** The following are the special requirements related to Nail Polishes and Nail Lacquers.
   - (a) It shall be situated in an industrial area.
   - (b) It shall be separated from other cosmetic-manufacturing areas by metal/brick partition upto ceiling.
   - (c) Floors, walls, ceilings and doors shall be fire proof.

(d) Smoking, cooking and dwelling shall not be permitted and no naked flame shall be brought in the premises.

(e) All electrical wiring and connections shall be concealed and main electric switch shall be outside the manufacturing area.

(f) All equipment, furniture and light fittings in the section shall be flame proof.

(g) Fire extinguisher like foam and dry powder and sufficient number of buckets containing sand shall be provided.

3. **Storage :** All explosive solvents and ingredients shall be stored in metal cupboards or in a separate enclosed area.

4. **Manufacture :**

   (a) Manufacture of lacquer shall not be undertaken unless the above conditions are complied with.

   (b) Workers shall be asked to wear shoes with rubber soles in the section.

5. **Other requirements :** No objection certificate from the Local Fire Brigade Authorities shall be furnished.

(D) **Lipsticks and Lipgloss etc.**

Equipment :

(a) Vertical mixer

(b) Jacketted kettle - steam, gas or electrically heated.

(c) Mixing vessel (stainless steel).

(d) Triple roller mill/Ball mill.

(e) Moulds with refrigeration facility.

(f) Weighing and measuring devices.

An area of 15 m^2 is recommended.

(E) **Depilatories**

Equipment :

(a) Mixing tanks.

(b) Mixer.

(c) Triple roller mill or homogeniser (where necessary)

(d) Filling and sealing equipment.

(e) Weighing and measuring devices.

(f) Moulds (where necessary).

An area of 10 m^2 is recommended.

(F) Preparations used for Eyes

Such preparations shall be manufactured under strict hygienic conditions to ensure that these are safe for use.

1. **Eyebrows, Eyelashes, Eyeliners etc.**

   Equipment :
   (a) Mixing tanks.
   (b) A suitable mixer.
   (c) Homogeniser (where necessary)
   (d) Filling and sealing equipment.
   (e) Weighing and measuring devices.

   An area of 10 m² is recommended.

2. **Kajal and Surma.**

   Equipment :
   (a) Base sterilizer.
   (b) Powder sterilizer (dry heat oven).
   (c) Stainless steel tanks.
   (d) A suitable mixer.
   (e) Stainless steel sieves.
   (f) Filling and sealing arrangements.
   (g) Weighing and measuring devices.
   (h) Homogeniser (where necessary)
   (i) Pestle and Mortar (for Surma).

   An area of 10 m² with a separate area of 5 m² for base sterilization is recommended.

Other requirements for 1 and 2 :
(a) False ceiling shall be made provided wherever required.
(b) Manufacturing area shall be made flyproof. An airlock or an air curtain shall be provided.
(c) Base used for Kajal shall be sterilized by heating the base at 150°C for required time in a separate enclosed area.
(d) The vegetable carbon black powder shall be sterilized in a drying oven at 120 °C for required time.
(e) All utensils used for manufacture shall be of stainless steel and shall be washed with detergent water, antiseptic liquid and again with distilled water.
(f) Containers employed for 'Kajal' shall be cleaned properly with bactericidal solution and dried.
(g) Workers shall put on clean overalls and use handgloves wherever necessary.

(G) Aerosol

1. **Equipment :**
   (a) Air-compressor (wherever necessary).
   (b) Mixing tanks.
   (c) Suitable propellant filling and crimping equipments.
   (d) Liquid filling unit.
   (e) Leak testing equipment.
   (f) Fire extinguisher (wherever necessary).
   (g) Suitable filtration equipment.
   (h) Weighing and measuring devices.

   An area of 15 m^2 is recommended.

2. **Other requirements :** No objection certificate from the Local Fire Brigade Authorities shall be furnished.

(H) Alcoholic Fragrance Solutions Equipment
   (a) Mixing tanks with stirrer.
   (b) Filtering equipment.
   (c) Filling and sealing equipment.
   (d) Weighing and measuring devices.

   An area of 15 m^2 is recommended.

(I) Hair Dyes

Equipment :
   (a) Stainless steel tanks.
   (b) Mixer.
   (c) Filling unit.
   (d) Weighing and measuring devices.
   (e) Masks, gloves and goggles.

   An area of 15 m^2 with proper exhaust is recommended.

(J) Tooth-powders and Toothpastes, etc.

1. **Tooth powder in General :**
   (a) Weighing and measuring devices.
   (b) Dry mixer (powder blender).
   (c) Stainless steel sieves.
   (d) Powder filling and sealing equipments.

   An area of 15 m^2 with proper exhaust is recommended.

2. **Toothpastes :**

   Equipment :
   - (a) Weighing and measuring devices.
   - (b) Kettle - steam, gas or electrically heated (where necessary).
   - (c) Planetory mixer with deaerator system.
   - (d) Stainless steel tanks.
   - (e) Tube filling equipment.
   - (f) Crimping machine.

   An additional area of 15 m^2 with proper exhaust is recommended.

3. **Tooth-powder (Black) :**

   Equipment :
   - (a) Weighing and measuring devices.
   - (b) Dry mixer powder blender.
   - (c) Stainless steel sieves.
   - (d) Powder filling arrangements.

   An area of 15 m^2 with proper exhaust is recommended. Areas for manufacturing 'Black' and 'White' tooth-powders should be separate.

(K) Toilet Soaps :

Equipment :
- (a) Kettle/pans for saponification.
- (b) Boiler or any other suitable heating arrangements.
- (c) Suitable stirring arrangements.
- (d) Storage tanks or trays.
- (e) Driers.
- (f) Amalgamator / chipping machine.
- (g) Mixer.
- (h) Triple roller mill.
- (i) Granulator.
- (j) Plodder.
- (k) Cutter.
- (l) Pressing, stamping and embossing machine.
- (m) Weighing and measuring devices.

A minimum area of 100 m^2 is recommended for the small scale manufacture of toilet soaps.

The areas recommended above are for basic manufacturing of different categories of cosmetics. In addition to that separate adequate space for storage of raw materials, finished products, packing materials shall be provided in factory premises.

Notes :
1. The above requirements of the Schedule are made subject to the modification at the discretion of the Licensing Authority, if he is of the opinion that having regard to the nature and extent of the manufacturing operations it is necessary to relax or alter them in the circumstances of a particular case.
2. The above requirements do not include requirements of machinery, equipments and premises required for preparation of containers and closers of different categories of cosmetics. The Licensing Authority shall have the discretion to examine the suitability and adequacy of the machinery, equipments and premises for the purpose taking into consideration the requirement of the Licensee.
3. Schedule M-II specifics equipments and space required for certain categories of cosmetics only. There are other cosmetics items, viz. Attars, perfumes etc., which are not covered in the above categories. The Licensing Authority shall, in respect of such items or categories of cosmetics, have the discretion to examine the adequacy of factory premises, space, plant and machinery and other requisites having regard to the nature and extent of the manufacturing operations involved and direct the licensee to carry on necessary modification in them.

(SCHEDULE M-III)
REQUIREMENTS OF FACTORY PREMISES FOR MANUFACTURE OF MEDICAL DEVICES

General Requirements
(a) **Location and surroundings :** The factory building(s) shall be located in a sanitary place and hygienic conditions shall be maintained in the premises. Premises shall not be used for residence or be interconnected with residence. It shall be well ventilated and clean.

(b) **Buildings :** The buildings used for the factory shall be constructed so as to permit production under hygienic conditions and not to permit entry of insects, rodents, flies, etc.

The walls of the rooms in which manufacturing operations are carried out, shall be up to a height of six feet from the floor, be smooth, water proof and capable of being kept clean. The floor shall be smooth, even and washable and shall be such as not to permit retention or accumulation of dust.

(c) **Water-supply :** The water used in manufacture shall be of potable quality.

(d) **Disposal of waste :** Suitable arrangements shall be made for disposal of waste water.

(e) **Health, clothing and sanitation of workers :** All workers shall be free from contagious or infectious diseases. They shall be provided with clean uniforms, maska, headgears and gloves wherever required. Washing facilities shall also be provided.

(f) **Medical Services :** Adequate facilities for first-aid shall be provided.

(g) Work-benches shall be provided for carrying out operations such as moulding, assembling, labelling, packing etc. Such benches shall be fitted with smooth impervious capable of being washed.

(h) Adequate facilities shall be provided wherever required for cleaning, washing, drying of different containers of devices.

(i) The premises shall be kept under controlled conditions of temperature and humidity so as to prevent any deterioration in the properties of materials and products due to storage and process conditions.

Requirements for Manufacture of Medical Devices :

The process of manufacture of medical devices shall be conducted at the licensed premises, wherever required, and shall be divided into the following separate operations/sections :

1. Moulding (wherever manufacture of medical devices is to start from granules).
2. Assembling (includes cutting, washing and drying, sealing, packing, labelling, etc).
3. Raw materials.
4. Storage area.
5. Washing, drying and sealing area (wherever required).
6. Sterilization.
7. Testing facilities.

The following equipments and space are recommended for the basic manufacture of different categories of medical devices :

(A) Sterile and Disposable Perfusion and Blood Collection Sets

   (1) Moulding :

      (a) Injection Moulding Machine.

      (b) Extruder Machine.

      (c) PVC Resin Compounding Machine.

(2) Assembling :

    (a) Hand Pressing Machine for filter fixing a Drip Chamber.

    (b) Bag Sealing Machine.

    (c) Compressor Machine.

    (d) Leak Testing Bench.

    (e) PVC Cutting Machine.

    (f) Tube Winding Machine (wherever necessary).

    (g) Welding Machine (wherever necessary).

An area of 30 m^2 for moulding and 15 m^2 for Assembling are recommended for basic installation. The assembling area shall be air-conditioned provided with HEPA filters. The moulding section, shall if necessary, have proper exhaust system.

Note : An additional area of 20 m^2 is recommended for any extra category.

(B) Sterile Disposable Hypodermic Syringes

(1) Moulding :

    (a) Granulator.

    (b) Injection Moulding Machine.

    (c) Air Compressor.

    (d) Weighing devices.

(2) Assembling :

    (a) Blister Pack Machine.

    (b) Vacuum Dust Cleaner.

    (c) Rubber-tip Washing-Machine.

    (d) Foil stamping or screen printing equipment.

An area of 30 m^2 for moulding and 15 m^2 for Assembling are recommended for basic installation. The assembling area shall be air-conditioned provided with HEPA filters. The moulding section shall, if necessary, have proper exhaust system.

Note : An additional area of 20 m^2 is recommended for any extra category.

(C) Sterile Disposable Hypodermic Needles

(1) Moulding :

(a) Needle grinding and levelling machine.

(b) Electropolishing Machine.

(c) Cutting Machine.

(d) Injection Moulding Machine.

(e) Needle Pointing Deburrine Machine.

(f) Air-compressor.

(2) Assembling :

(a) Needle cleaning Machine with Magnetic Separator.

(b) Blister Packing Machine.

(c) Needle Inspection Unit.

An area of 30 m^2 for Moulding and 15 m^2 for Assembling are recommended for basic installation. The assembling area shall be air-conditioned provided with HEPA filters. The moulding section shall, if necessary, have proper exhaust system.

Note : An additional area of 20 m^2 is recommended for any extra category.

3. Raw materials :

The licensee shall keep an inventory of all raw materials to be used at any stage of manufacture of devices and shall maintain records as per Schedule U. All such raw materials shall be identified and assigned control reference number. They shall be conspicuously labelled indicating the name of the material, control reference number, name of the manufacturer and be specifically labelled "Under Test" or "Approved" or "Rejected". The under test, approved or rejected materials shall appropriately be segregated. These shall be tested for complicance with required standards of quality.

A minimum area of 10 m^2 shall be provided for storage of raw materials.

4. Storage area :

The licensee shall provide separate storage facilities for quarantine and sterilized products.

An area not less than 10 m^2 shall be provided for each of them.

5. Washing, drying and sealing area :

The licensee shall provide wherever required adequate equipments like water distillation still, deionizer, washing machine, drying oven with trays for washing, drying and sealing of medical device.

An area not less than 10 m^2 shall be provided.

6. Sterilization :

The licensee shall provide requisite equipments with required controls and recording device for sterilization of medical devices by Ethylene Oxide Gas in his own premises or may make arrangements with some Institution approved by the Licensing Authority for sterilization. The products sterilized in this manner shall be monitored to assure acceptable levels of residual gas and its degradation products. An area of 10 m^2 is recommended for basic installation of such facility.

Provided that the above equipment may not be required in case the licensee opts for sterilization of medical devices by Ionising Radiation.

7. Testing facilities :

The licensee shall provide testing laboratory for carrying out Chemical and Physio-Chemical testing of medical devices and of raw materials used in its own premises :

Provided that the Licensing Authority shall permit the licensee in the initial stage to carry out testing of Sterility, Pyrogens, Toxicity on their products from the approved testing institutions but after one renewal period the licensee shall provide testing facilities of all such tests in their own premises.

8. Records :

The licensee shall maintain records of different manufacturing activities with regard to each stage of manufacture in-process controls, assembling, packing, batch records for the quantity of devices manufactured from each lot of blended granules, duration of work, hourly quantum of production in respect of each item as well as record of each sterilizing cycle of the gaseous method employed.

Note : The above requirements of machinery, equipments, space, qualifications are made subject to the modification at the discretional of the Licensing Authority, if he is of the opinion that having regard to the nature and extent of the manufacturing operations it is necessary to relax or alter them in the circumstances of a particular case.

SCHEDULE Y
[See rules 122A, 122B, 122D, 122DA, 122DAA and 122E]
REQUIREMENTS AND GUIDELINES FOR PERMISSION TO IMPORT AND / OR MANUFACTURE OF NEW DRUGS FOR SALE OR TO UNDERTAKE CLINICAL TRIALS

1. **APPLICATION FOR PERMISSION**
   (1) Application for permission to import or manufacture new drugs for sale or to undertake clinical trials shall be made in Form 44 accompanied with following data in accordance with the appendices, namely :
   (i) Chemical and pharmaceutical information as prescribed in item 2 of Appendix I;
   (ii) Animal pharmacology data as prescribed in item 3 of Appendix I and Appendix IV;
      (a) Specific pharmacological actions as prescribed in item 3.2 of Appendix I, and demonstrating, therapeutic potential for humans shall be described according to the animal models and species used. Wherever possible, dose-response relationships and ED 50s shall be submitted. Special studies conducted to elucidate mode of action shall also be described (Appendix IV);
      (b) General pharmacological actions as prescribed in item 3.3 of Appendix I and item 1.2 of Appendix IV;
      (c) Pharmacokinetic data related to the absorption, distribution, metabolism and excretion of the test substance as prescribed in item 3.5 of Appendix I. Wherever possible, the drug effects shall be corelated to the plasma drug concentrations;
   (iii) Animal toxicology data as prescribed in item 4 of Appendix I and Appendix III;
   (iv) Human Clinical Pharmacology Data a prescribed in items 5, 6 and 7 of Appendix I and as stated below :
      (a) For new drug substances discovered in India, clinical trials are required to be carried out in India right from Phase I and data should be submitted as required under items 1, 2, 3, 4, 5 (data, if any, from other countries), and 9 of Appendix I;
      (b) For new drug substances discovered in countries other than India, Phase I data as required under items 1, 2, 3, 4, 5 (data from other countries) and 9 of Appendix I should be submitted along with the application. After submission of Phase I data generated outside India to the Licensing Authority, permission may be granted to repeat Phase I trials and/or to conduct Phase II trials and subsequently Phase III trials concurrently with other global trials for that drug. Phase III trials are required to be conducted in India before permission to market the drug in India is granted;

(c) The data required will depend upon the purpose of the new drug application. The number of study subjects and sites to be involved in the conduct of clinical trial will depend upon the nature and objective of the study. Permission to carry out these trials shall generally be given in stages, considering the data emerging form earlier Phase(s);

(d) Application for permission to initial specific phase of clinical trial should also accompany Investigator's brochure, proposed protocol (Appendix X), case record from, study subject's informed consent document(s) (Appendix V), investigator's undertaking (Appendix VII) and ethics committee clearance, if available, (Appendix VIII);

(e) Reports of clinical studies submitted under items 508 of Appendix I should be in consonance with the format prescribed in Appendix II of this Schedule. The study report shall be certified by the Principal Investigator or, if no Principal Investigator is designated, then by each of the Investigators participating in the study. the certification should acknowledge the contents of the report, the accurate presentation of the study as undertaken, and express agreement with the conclusions. Each page should be numbered;

(v) Regulatory status in other countries as prescribed in item 9.2 of Appendix I, including Information in respect of restrictions imposed, if any, on the use of the drug in other countries, e.g. dosage limits, exclusion of certain age groups, warning about adverse drug reactions, etc. (item 9.2 of Appendix I). Likewise, if the drug has been withdrawn in any country by the manufacturer or by regulatory authorities, such information should also be furnished along with the reasons and their relevance, if any, to India. This information must continue to be submitted by the sponsor to the Licensing Authority during the course of marketing of the drug in India.

(vi) The full prescribing information should be submitted as part of the new drug application for marketing as prescribed in item 10 of Appendix I. The prescribing information (package insert) shall comprise the following sections : generic name; composition; dosage form/s, indication; does and method of administration; use in special populations (such as pregnant women, lactating women, pediatric patients, geriatric patients etc.); contraindications; warnings; precautions; drug interactions; undesirable effects; overdose, pharmacodynamic and pharmacokinetic properties; incompatibilities; shelf-life; packaging information; storage and handling instructions. All package inserts, promotional literature and patient education material subsequently produced are required to be consistent with the contents of the approval full prescribing information. The drafts of label and carton text should comply with provisions of rules 96 and 97. After submission and approval by the Licensing Authority, no changes in the package insert shall be effected without such changes being approved by the Licensing Authority; and

(vii) Complete testing protocols for quality control testing together with a Complete impurity profile and release specifications for the product as prescribed in item 11 of Appendix I should be submitted as part of new drug application for marketing. Samples of the pure drug substance and finished product are to be submitted when desired by the regulatory authority.

2. If the study drug is intended to be imported for the purposes of examination, test or analysis, the application for import of small quantities of drugs for such purpose should also be made in Form 12.

3. For drugs indicated in life threatening/serious diseases or diseases of special relevance to the Indian health scenario, the toxicological and clinical data requirements may be abbreviated, deferred or omitted, as deemed appropriate by the Licensing Authority.

2. CLINICAL TRIAL

(1) Approval for clinical trial :

(i) Clinical trial on a new drug shall be initiated only after the permission has been granted by the Licensing Authority under rule 21 (b), and the approval obtained from the respective ethics committee(s). The Licensing Authority as defined shall be informed of the approval of the respective institutional ethics committee(s) as prescribed in Appendix VIII, and the trial initiated at each respective site only after obtaining such an approval for that site. The trial site(s) may accept the approval granted to the protocol by the ethics committee of another trial site or the approval granted by an independent ethics committee (constituted as per Appendix VIII), provided that the approving ethics committee(s) is/are willing to accept their responsibilities for the study at such trial site(s) and the trial site(s) is/are willing to accept such an arrangement and that the protocol version is same at all trial sites.

(ii) All trial Investigator(s) should possess appropriate qualifications, training and experience and should have access to such investigational and treatment facilities as are relevant to the proposed trial protocol. A qualified physician (or dentist, when appropriate) who is an investigator or a sub-investigator for the trial, should be responsible for all trial-related medical (or dental) decisions. Laboratories used for generating data for clinical trials should be compliant with Good Laboratory Practices. If services of a laboratory or a facilities outside the country are to be availed, its/their name(s), address(s) and specific services to be used should be stated in the protocol to avail Licensing Authority's permission to send clinical trial related samples to such laboratory(ies) and/or facility(ies). In all cases, information about laboratory(ies) / facility[ies] to be used for the trial, if other than those at the investigation site(s), should be furnished to the Licensing Authority prior to initiation of trial at such site(s).

(iii) Protocol amendments if become necessary before initiation or during the course of a clinical trial, all such amendments should be notified to the Licensing Authority in writing along with the approval by the ethics committee which has granted the approval for the study. No deviations from or changes to the protocol should be implemented without prior written approval of the ethics committee and the Licensing Authority except when it is necessary to eliminate immediate hazards to the trial Subject(s) or when change(s) involve(s) only logistic or administrative aspects of the trial. All such exceptions must be immediately notified to the ethics committee as well as to the Licensing Authority. Administrative and/or logistic changes in the protocol should be notified to the Licensing Authority within 30 days

(2) Responsibilities of Sponsor :
(i) The clinical trial Sponsor is responsible for implementing and maintaining quality assurance systems to ensure that the clinical trial is conducted and data generated, documented and reported in compliance with the protocol and Good Clinical Practice (GCP) Guidelines issued by the Central Drugs Standard Control Organization, Directorate General of Health Services, Government of India as well as with all applicable statutory provisions. Standard operating procedures should be documented to ensure compliance with GCP and applicable regulations.

(ii) Sponsors are required to submit a status report on the clinical trial to the Licensing Authority at the prescribed periodicity.

(iii) In case of studies prematurely discontinued for any reason including lack of commercial interest in pursuing the new drug application, a summary report should be submitted within 3 months. The summary report should provide a brief description of the study, the number of patients exposed to the drug, dose and duration of exposure, details of adverse drug reactions (Appendix XI), if any, and the reason for discontinuation of the study or non-pursuit of the new drug application;

(iv) Any unexpected Serious Adverse Event (SAE) (as defined in GCP Guidelines) occurring during a clinical trial should be communicated promptly (within 14 calendar days) by the Sponsor to the Licensing Authority and to the other Investigator(s) participating in the study (see Appendix XI).

(3) Responsibilities of the Investigator(s) :
The Investigator(s) shall be responsible for the conduct of the trial according to the protocol and the GCP Guidelines and also for compliance as per the undertaking given in Appendix VII. Standard operating procedures are

required to be documented by the investigators for the tasks performed by them. During a subject's participation in a trial, the investigator should ensure that adequate medical care is provided to the participant for any adverse events. Investigator(s) shall report all serious and unexpected adverse events to the Sponsor within 24 hours and to the Ethics Committee that accorded approval to the study protocol within 7 working days of their occurrence.

(4) Informed Consent :
   (i) In all trials, a freely given, informed, written consent is required to be obtained from each study subject. The Investigator must provide information about the study verbally as well as using a patient information sheet, in a language that is non-technical and understandable by the study subject. The subject's consent must be obtained in writing using an 'Informed Consent Form'. Both the patient information sheet as well as the Informed Consent Form should have been approved by the ethics committee and furnished to the Licensing Authority. Any changes in the informed consent documents should be approved by the ethics committee and submitted to the Licensing Authority before such changes are implemented.
   (ii) Where a subject is not able to give informed consent (e.g. an unconscious person or a minor or those suffering from severe mental illness or disability), the same may be obtained from a legally acceptable representative (a legally acceptable representative is a person who is able to give consent for or authorize an intervention in the patient as provided by the law(s) of India). If the subject or his/her legally acceptable representative is unable to read/write - an impartial witness should be present during the entire informed consent process who must append his/her signatures to the consent form.
   (iii) A checklist of essential elements to be included in the study subject's informed consent document as well as a format for the Informed Consent Form for study subjects is given in Appendix V.

(5) Responsibilities of the Ethics Committee :
   (i) It is the responsibility of the ethics committee that reviews and accords its approval to a trial protocol to safeguard the rights, safety and well being of all trial subjects. The ethics committee should exercise particular care to protect the rights, safety and well being of all vulnerable subjects participating in the study, e.g., members of a group with hierarchical

structure (e.g. prisoners, armed forces personnel, staff and students of medical, nursing and pharmacy academic institutions), patients with incurable diseases, umemployed or impoverished persons, patients in emergency situation, ethnic minority groups, homeless persons, nomads, refugees, minors or others incapable of personally giving consent. Ethics committee(s) should get document 'standard operating procedures' and should maintain a record of its proceedings.

(ii) Ethics Committee(s) should make, at appropriate intervals, an ongoing review of the trials for which they review the protocol(s). Such a review may be based on the periodic study progress reports furnished by the investigators and/or monitoring and internal audit reports furnished by the Sponsor and/or by visiting the study sites.

(iii) In case an ethics committee revokes its approval accorded to a trial protocol, it must record the reasons for doing so and at once communicate such a decision to the Investigator as well as to the Licensing Authority.

(6) Human Pharmacology (Phase I) :

(i) The objective of studies in this Phase is the estimation of safety and tolerability with the initial administration of an investigational new drug into human(s). Studies in this Phase of development usually have non-therapeutic objectives and may be conducted in healthy volunteers subjects or certain types of patients. Drugs with significant potential toxicity e.g. cytotoxic drugs are usually studied in patients. Phase I trials should preferably be carried out by Investigators trained in clinical pharmacology with access to the necessary facilities to closely observe and monitor the Subjects.

(ii) Studies conducted in Phase I, usually intended to involve one or a combination of the following objectives :

(a) Maximum tolerated dose : To determine the tolerability of the dose range expected to be needed for later clinical studies and to determine the nature of adverse reactions that can be expected. These studies include both single and multiple dose administration.

(b) Pharmacokinetics : It is characterization of a drug's absorption, distribution, metabolism and excretion. Although these studies continue throughout the development plan, they should be performed to support formulation development and determine pharmacokinetic parameters in different age groups to support dosing recommendations.

(c) **Pharmacodynamics** : Depending on the drug and the endpoints studied, pharmacodynamic studies and studies relating to drug blood levels (pharmacokinetic/pharmacodynamic studies) may be conducted in healthy volunteer Subjects or in patients with the target disease. If there are appropriate validated indicators of activity and potential efficacy, pharmacodynamic data obtained from patients may guide the dosage and dose regimen to be applied in later studies.

(d) **Early measurement of drug activity** : Preliminary studies of activity or potential therapeutic benefit may be conducted in Phase I as a secondary objective. Such studies are generally performed in later Phases but may be appropriate when drug activity is readily measurable with a short duration of drug exposure in patients at this early stage.

(7) **Therapeutic Exploratory Trials (Phase II)** :
- (i) The primary objective of Phase II trials is to evaluate the effectiveness of a drug for a particular indication or indications in patients with the condition under study and to determine the common short-term side-effects and risks associated with the drug. Studies in Phase II should be conducted in a group of patients who are selected by relatively narrow criteria leading to a relatively homogeneous population. These studies should be closely monitored. An important goal for this Phase is to determine the dose(s) and regimen for Phase III trials. Doses used in Phase II are usually (but not always) less than the highest doses used in Phase I.
- (ii) Additional objectives of Phase II studies can include evaluation of potential study endpoints, therapeutic regimens (including concomitant medications) and target populations (e.g. mild versus severe disease) for further studies in Phase II or IIL These objectives may be served by exploratory analyses, examining subsets of data and by including multiple endpoints in trials.
- (iii) If the application is for conduct of clinical trials as a part of multi-national clinical development of the drug, the number of sites and the patients as well as the justification for undertaking such trials in India shall be provided to the Licensing Authority.

(8) **Therapeutic Confirmatory Trials (Phase III)** :
- (i) Phase III studies have primary objective of demonstration or confirmation of therapeutic benefit(s). Studies in Phase III are designed to confirm the preliminary evidence accumulated in Phase II that a drug is safe and effective for use in the intended indication and recipient population. These studies should be intended to provide an adequate basis for marketing

approval. Studies in Phase III may also further explore the dose-response relationships (relationships among dose, drug concentration in blood and clinical response), use of the drug in wider populations, in different stages of disease, or the safety and efficacy of the drug in combination with other drug(s).

(ii) For drugs intended to be administered for long periods, trials involving extended exposure to the drug are ordinarily conducted in Phase III, although they may be initiated in Phase II. These studies carried out in Phase III complete the information needed to support adequate instructions for use of the drug (prescribing information).

(iii) For new drugs approved outside India, Phase III studies need to be carried out primarily to generate evidence of effficacy and safety of the drug in Indian patients when used as recommended in the prescribing information. Prior to conduct of Phase III studies in Indian subjects, Licensing Authority may require pharmacokinetic studies to be undertaken to verify that the data generated in Indian population is in conformity with the data already generated abroad.

(iv) If the application is for the conduct of clinical trials as a part of multi-national clinical development of the drug, the number of sites and patients as well as the justification for undertaking such trials in India should be provided to the Licensing Authority along with the application.

(9) Post Marketing Trials (Phase IV) :

Post Marketing trials are studies (other than routine surveillance) performed after drug approval and related to the approved indication(s). These trials go beyond the prior demonstration of the drug's safety, efficacy and dose definition. These trials may not be considered necessary at the time of new drug approval but may be required by the Licensing Authority for optimizing the drug's use. They may be of any type but should have valid scientific objectives. Phase IV trials include additional drug-drug interaction (s), doseresponse or safety studies and trials designed to support use under the approved indication(s), e.g. mortality/morbidity studies, epidemiological studies, etc.

3. STUDIES IN SPECIAL POPULATIONS

Information supporting the use of the drug in children, pregnant women, nursing women, elderly patients, patients with renal or other organ systems failure, and those on specific concomitant medication is required to be submitted if relevant to the clinical profile of the drug and its anticipated usage pattern. Any claim sought to be made for the drug product that is not based on data submitted under preceding items of this Schedule should be supported by studies included under this item of the Schedule (Appendix 1, item 8.3).

(1) Geriatrics : Geriatric patients should be included in Phase III clinical trials (and in Phase II trials, at the Sponsor's option) in meaningful numbers, if

(a) the disease intended to be treated is characteristically a disease of aging; or

(b) the population to be treated is known to include substantial numbers of geriatric patients; or

(c) when there is specific reason to expect that conditions common in the elderly are likely to be encountered; or

(d) when the new drug is likely to alter the geriatric patient's response (with regard to safety or efficacy) compared with that of the non-geriatric patient.

(2) Paediatrics :

(i) The timing of paediatric studies in the new drug development program will depend on the medicinal product, the type of disease being treated, safety considerations, and the efficacy and safety of available treatments. For a drug expected to be used in children, evaluations should be made in the appropriate age group. When clinical development is to include studies in children, it is usually appropriate to begin with older children before extending the trial to younger children and then infants.

(ii) If the new drug is for diseases predominantly or exclusively affecting paediatric patients, clinical trial data should be generated in the paediatric population except for initial safety and tolerability data, which will usually be obtained in adults unless such initial safety studies in adults would yield little useful information or expose them to inappropriate risk.

(iii) If the new drug is intended to treat serious or life-threatening diseases, occurring in both adults and paediatric patients, for which there are currently no or limited therapeutic options, paediatric population should be included in the clinical trials early, following assessment of initial safety data and reasonable evidence of potential benefit. In circumstances where this is not possible, lack of data should be justified in detail.

(iv) If the new drug has a potential for use in paediatric patients - paediatric studies should be conducted. These studies may be initiated at various phases of clinical development or after post marketing survelliance in adults if a safety concern exists. In cases where there is limited paediatric data at the time of submission of application - more data in paediatric patients would be expected after marketing authorization for use in children is granted.

(v) The paediatric studies should include :

    (a) clinical trials,

    (b) relative bioequivalence comparisons of the paediatric formulation with the adult formulation performed in adults, and

    (c) definitive pharmacokinetic studies for dose selection across the age ranges of paediatric patients in whom the drug is likely to be used. These studies should be conducted in the paediatric patient population with the disease under study.

(vi) If the new drug is a major therapeutic advance for the paediatric population : The studies should begin early in the drug development, and this data should be submitted with the new drug application.

(vii) Paediatric Subjects are legally unable to provide written informed consent, and are dependent on their parent(s)/legal guardian to assume responsibility for their participation in clinical studies. Written informed consent should be obtained from the parent(s)/legal guardian. However, all paediatric participants should be informed to the fullest extent possible about the study in a language and in terms that they are able to understand. Where appropriate, paediatric participants should additionally assent to enrol in the study. Mature minors and adolescents should personally sign and date a separately designed written assent form. Although a participant's wish to withdraw from a study must be respected, there may be circumstances in therapeutic studies for serious or life-threatening diseases in which, in the opinion of the Investigator and parent(s)/ legal guardian, the welfare of a pediatric patient would be jeopardized by his or her failing to participate in the study. In this situation, continued parental/legal guardian consent should be sufficient to allow participation in the study.

(viii) For clinical trials conducted in the paediatric population, the reviewing ethics committee should include members who are knowledgeable about pediatric, ethical, clinical and psychosocial issues.

(3) Pregnant or nursing women :

    (i) Pregnant or nursing women should be included in clinical trials only when the drug is intended for use by pregnant/nursing women or foetuses/nursing infants and where the data generated from women who are not pregnant or nursing, is not suitable.

    (ii) For new drugs intended for use during pregnancy, follow-up data (pertaining to a period appropriate for that drug) on the pregnancy, fetus and child will be required. Where applicable, excretion of the drug or its metabolites into human milk should be examined and the infant should be monitored for predicted pharmacological effects of the drug.

(4) Post marketing surveillance :
  (i) Subsequent to approval of the product, new drugs should be closely monitored for their clinical safety once they are marketed. The applicants shall furnish Periodic Safety Update Reports (PSURs) in order to -
   (a) report all the relevant new information from appropriate sources;
   (b) relate these data to patient exposure;
   (c) summarize the market authorization status in different countries and any significant variations related to safety; and
   (d) indicate whether changes should be made to product information in order to optimize the use of the product.
  (ii) Ordinarily all dosage forms and formulations as well as indications for new drugs should be covered in one PSUR. Within the single PSUR separate presentations of data for different dosage forms, indications or separate population need to be given.
  (iii) All relevant clinical and non-clinical safety data should cover only the period of the report (interval data). The PSURs shall be submitted every six months for the first two years after approval of the drug is granted to the applicant. For subsequent two years - the PSURs need to be submitted annually. Licensing authority may extend the total duration of submission of PSURs if it is considered necessary in the interest of public health. PSURs due for a period must be submitted within 30 calendar days of the last day of the reporting period. However, all cases involving serious unexpected adverse reactions must be reported to the licensing authority within 15 days of initial receipt of the information by the applicant. If marketing of the new drug is delayed by the applicant after obtaining approval to market, such data will have to be provided on the deferred basis beginning from the time the new drug is marketed.
  (iv) New studies specifically planned or conducted to examine a safety issue should be described in the PSURs.
  (v) A PSUR should be structured as follows :
   (a) A title page stating : Periodic safety update report for the product, applicant's name, period covered by the report, date of approval of new drug, date of marketing of new drug and date of reporting,
   (b) Introduction,
   (c) Current worldwide market authorization status,
   (d) Update of actions taken for safety reasons,

(e) Changes to reference safety information,

(f) Estimated patient exposure,

(g) Presentation of individual case histories,

(h) Studies,

(i) Other information,

(j) Overall safety evaluation,

(k) Conclusion,

(l) Appendix providing material relating to indications, dosing, pharmacology and other related information.

(5) Special studies :

Bioavailability / Bioequivalence Studies :

(i) For drugs approved elsewhere in the world and absorbed systemically, bioequivalence with the reference formulation should be carried out wherever applicable. These studies should be conducted under the labelled conditions of administration. Data on the extent of systemic absorption may be required for formulations other than those designed for systemic absorption.

(ii) Evaluation of the effect of food on absorption following oral administration should be carried out. Data from dissolution studies should also be submitted for all solid oral dosage forms.

(iii) Dissolution and bioavailability data submitted with the new drug application must provide information that assures bioequivalence or establishes bioavailability and dosage correlations between the formulation(s) sought to be marketed and those used for clinical trials during clinical development of the product. (See items 8.1, 8.2 and 8.3 of Appendix I).

(iv) All bioavailability and bioequivalence studies should be conducted according to the Guidelines for Bioavailability and Bioequivalence studies as prescribed.

Note :

The data requirements stated in this Schedule are expected to provide adequate information to evaluate the efficacy, safety and therapeutic rationale of new drugs (as defined under rule 122-E) prior to the permission for sale. Depending upon the nature of new drugs and disease(s), additional information may be required by the Licensing Authority. The applicant shall certify the authencity of the data and documents submitted in support of an application for new drug. The Licensing Authority reserves the right to reject any data or any document(s) if such data or contents of such documents are found to be of doubtful integrity.

APPENDIX I
DATA TO BE SUBMITTED ALONG WITH THE APPLICATION TO CONDUCT CLINICAL TRIALS / IMPORT / MANUFACTURE OF NEW DRUGS FOR MARKETING IN THE COUNTRY

1. Introduction

    A brief description of the drug and the therapeutic class to which it belongs.

2. Chemical and pharmaceutical information

    2.1 Information on active ingredients

    Drug information (Generic Name, Chemical Name or INN)

    2.2 Physicochemical Data

    (a) Chemical name and Structure, Empirical formula, Molecular weight

    (b) Physical properties, Description, Solubility, Rotation, Partition coefficient, Dissociation constant.

    2.3 Analytical Data

    Elemental analysis

    Mass spectrum

    NMR spectra

    IR spectra

    UV spectra

    Polymorphic identification

    2.4 Complete monograph specification including

    Identification

    Identity/quantification of impurities

    Enantiomeric purity

    Assay

    2.5 Validations

    Assay method

    Impurity estimation method

    Residual solvent Other Volatile Impurities (OVI) estimation method

    2.6 Stability Studies (for details refer Appendix IX)

    Final release specification

    Reference standard characterization

    Material safety data sheet

2.7 Data on Formulation
- Dosage form
- Composition
- Master manufacturing formula
- Details of the formulation (including inactive ingredients)
- In-process quality control check
- Finished product specification
- Excipient compatibility study
- Validation of the analytical method
- Comparative evaluation with international brand(s) or approved Indian brands, if applicable
  - Pack presentation
  - Dissolution
  - Assay
  - Impurities
  - Content uniformity pH
- Force degradation study
- Stability evaluation in market intended pack at proposed storage conditions
- Packing specifications
- Process validation

When the application is for clinical trials only, the International Non-proprietary Name (INN) or generic name, drug category, dosage form and data supporting stability in the intended container-closure system for the duration of the clinical trial (information covered in item nos. 2.1, 2.3, 2.6, 2.7) are required.

3. Animal Pharmacology (for details refer Appendix IV)
   3.1 Summary
   3.2 Specific pharmacological actions
   3.3 General pharmacological actions
   3.4 Follow-up and Supplemental Safety Pharmacology Studies
   3.5 Pharmacokinetics : absorption, distribution; metabolism; excretion

4. Animal Toxicology (for details refer Appendix III)
   4.1 General Aspects
   4.2 Systemic Toxicity Studies
   4.3 Male Fertility Study

    4.4 Female Reproduction and Developmental Toxicity Studies
    4.5 Local Toxicity
    4.6 Allergenicity/Hypersensitivity
    4.7 Genotoxicity
    4.8 Carcinogenicity
5. Human/Clinical pharmacology (Phase I)
    5.1 Summary
    5.2 Specific Pharmacological effects
    5.3 General Pharmacological effects
    5.4 Pharmacokinetics, absorption, distribution, metabolism, excretion
    5.5 Pharmacodynamics / early measurement of drug activity
6. Therapeutic Exploratory Trials (Phase II)
    6.1 Summary
    6.2 Study report(s) as given in Appendix II
7. Therapeutic confirmatory trials (Phase III)
    7.1 Summary
    7.2 Individual study reports with listing of sites and Investigators.
8. Special Studies
    8.1 Summary
    8.2 Bio-availability / Bio-equivalence.
    8.3 Other studies e.g. geriatrics, paediatrics, pregnant or nursing women
9. Regulatory Status in other Countries
    9.1 Countries where the drug is
        (a) Marketed
        (b) Approved
        (c) Approved as IND
        (d) Withdrawn, if any, with reasons
    9.2 Restrictions on use, if any, in countries where marketed/approved.
    9.3 Free sale certificate or certificate of analysis, as appropriate.
10. Prescribing information
    10.1 Proposed full prescribing information
    10.2 Drafts of labels and cartons
11. Samples and Testing Protocols
    11.1 Samples of pure drug substance and finished product (an equivalent of 50 clinical doses, or more number of clinical doses if prescribed by the Licensing Authority), with testing protocol/s, full impurity profile and release specifications.

Notes :

(1) All items may not be applicable to all drugs. For explanation, refer text of Schedule Y.

(2) For requirements of data to be submitted with application for clinical trials refer text of this Schedule.

APPENDIX I-A

DATA REQUIRED TO BE SUBMITTED BY AN APPLICANT FOR GRANT OF PERMISSION TO IMPORT AND / OR MANUFACTURE A NEW DRUG ALREADY APPROVED IN THE COUNTRY

1. Introduction

   A brief description of the drug and the therapeutic class.

2. Chemical and pharmaceutical information

   2.1 Chemical name, code name or number, if any; non-proprietary or generic name, if any, structure; physico-chemical properties.

   2.2 Dosage form and its composition.

   2.3 Test specifications

   (a) active ingredients

   (b) inactive ingredients

   2.4 Tests for identification of the active ingredients and method of this assay.

   2.5 Outline of the method of manufacture of active ingredients

   2.6 Stability data

3. Marketing information

   3.1 Proposed package insert/promotional literature

   3.2 Draft specimen of the label and carton

4. Special studies conducted with approval of Licensing Authority

   4.1 Bioavailability/Bioequivalence and comparative dissolution studies for oral dosage forms.

   4.2 Sub-acute animal toxicity studies for intravenous infusions and injectables

APPENDIX II

STRUCTURE, CONTENTS AND FORMAT FOR CLINICAL STUDY REPORTS

1. **Title Page :**

   This page should contain information about the title of the study, the protocol code, name of the investigational product tested, development phase, indication studied, a brief description of the trial design, the start and end date of patient accrual and the names of the Sponsor and the participating Institutes (Investigators).

2. **Study Synopsis (1 to 2 pages) :** A brief overview of the study from the protocol development to the trial closure should be given here. This section will only summarize the important conclusions derived from the study.

3. Statement of compliance with the 'Guidelines for Clinical Trials on Pharmaceutical Products in India - GCP Guidelines' issued by the Central Drugs Standard Control Organization, Ministry of Health, Government of India.

4. **List of Abbreviations and Definitions**

5. **Table of contents**

6. **Ethics Committee :**

   This section should document that the study was conducted in accordance with the ethical principles of Declaration of Helsinki. A detailed description of the Ethics Committee constitution and date(s) of approvals of trial documents for each of the participating sites should be provided. A declaration should state that EC notifications as per Good Clinical Practice Guidelines issued by Central Drugs Standard Control Organization and Ethical Guidelines for Biomedical Research on Human Subjects, issued by Indian Council of Medical Research have been followed.

7. **Study Team :**

   Briefly describe the administrative structure of the study (Investigators, site staff, Sponsor/designates, Central laboratory etc.).

8. **Introduction :**

   A brief description of the product development rationale should be given here.

9. **Study Objective :**

   A statement describing the overall purpose of the study and the primary and secondary objectives to be achieved should be mentioned here.

10. **Investigational Plan :**

    This section should describe the overall trial design, the Subject selection criteria, the treatment procedures, blinding/randomization techniques if any, allowed/disallowed concomitant treatment, the efficacy and safety criteria assessed, the data quality assurance procedures and the statistical methods planned for the analysis of the data obtained.

11. **Trial Subjects :**

    A clear accounting of all trial Subjects who entered the study will be given here. Mention should also be made of all cases that were dropouts or protocol deviations. Enumerate the patients screened, randomised, and prematurely discontinued. State reasons for premature discontinuation of therapy in each applicable case.

12. Efficacy Evaluation :

The results of evaluation of all the efficacy variables will be described in this section with appropriate tabular and graphical representation. A brief description of the demographic characteristics of the trial patients should also be provided along with a listing of patients and observations excluded from efficacy analysis.

13. Safety Evaluation :

This section should include the complete list :

13.1 All serious adverse events, whether expected or unexpected and

13.2 Unexpected adverse events whether serious or not (complied from data received as per Appendix XI).

The comparison of adverse events across study groups may be presented in a tabular or graphical form. This section should also give a brief narrative of all important events considered related to the investigational product.

14. Discussion and overall Conclusion :

Discussion of the important conclusions derived from the trial and scope for further development.

15. List of References

16. Appendices :

List of Appendices to the Clinical Trial Report

(a) Protocol and amendments

(b) Specimen of Case Record Form

(c) Investigator's name(s) with contact addresses, phone, e-mail, etc.

(d) Patient data listings

(e) List of trial participants treated with investigational product

(f) Discontinued participants

(g) Protocol deviations

(h) CRFs of cases involving death and life threatening adverse event cases

(i) Publications from the trial

(j) Important publications referenced in the study

(k) Audit certificate, if available

(l) Investigator's certificate that he/she has read the report and that the report accurately describes the conduct and the results of the study.

APPENDIX III
ANIMAL TOXICOLOGY (NON-CLINICAL TOXICITY STUDIES)

1. General Principles

Toxicity studies should comply with the norms of Good Laboratory Practice (GLP). Briefly, these studies should be performed by suitably trained and qualified staff employing properly calibrated and standardized equipment of adequate size and capacity. Studies should be done as per written protocols with modifications (if any) verifiable retrospectively. Standard Operating Procedures (SOPs) should be followed for all managerial and laboratory tasks related to these studies. Test substances and test systems (in-vitro or in-vivo) should be properly characterized and standardized. All documents belonging to each study, including its approved protocol, raw data, draft report, final report, and histology slides and paraffin tissue blocks should be preserved for a minimum of 5 years; after marketing of the drug.

Toxicokinetic studies (generation of pharmacokinetic data either as an integral component of the conduct of non-clinical toxicity studies or in specially designed studies) should be conducted to assess the systemic exposure achieved in animals and its relationship to dose level and the time course of the toxicity study. Other objectives of toxicokinetic studies include obtaining data to relate the exposure achieved in toxicity studies to toxicological findings and contribute to the assessment of the relevance of these findings to clinical safety, to support the choice of species and treatment regimen in non-clinical toxicity studies and to provide information which, in conjunction with the toxicity findings, contributes to the design of subsequent non-clinical toxicity studies.

1.1 Systemic Toxicity Studies

1.1.1 Single-dose Toxicity Studies :

These studies (see Appendix I item 4.2) should be carried out in 2 rodent species (mice and rats) using the same route as intended for humans. In addition, unless the intended route of administration in humans is only intravenous, at least one more route should be used in one of the species to ensure systemic absorption of the drug. This route should depend on the nature of the drug. A limit of 2 g/kg (or 10 times the normal dose that is intended in humans, whichever is higher) is recommended for oral dosing. Animals should be observed for 14 days after the drug administration, and Minimum Lethal Dose (MLD) and Maximum Tolerated Dose (MTD) should be established. If possible, the target organ of toxicity should also be determined. Mortality should be observed for upto 7 days after parenteral administration and upto 14 days after oral administration. Symptoms, signs and mode of death should be reported, with appropriate macroscopic and microscopic findings where necessary. LD_{10} and LD_{50} should be reported preferably with 95% confidence limits. If $LD_{50}S$ cannot be determined, reasons for the same should be stated.

The dose causing severe toxic manifestations or death should be defined in the case of cytotoxic anticancer agents, and the post-dosing observation period should be to 14 days. Mice should first be used for determination of MTD. Findings should then be confirmed in rat for establishing linear relationship between toxicity and body surface area. In case of non-linearity, data of the more sensitive species should be used to determine the Phase I starting dose. Where rodents are known to be poor predictors of human toxicity (e.g., antifolates), or where the cytotoxic drug acts by a novel mechanism of action, MTD should be established in non-rodent species.

1.1.2 Repeated-dose Systemic Toxicity Studies :

These studies (see Appendix I, item 4.2) should be carried out in at least two mammalian species, of which one should be a non-rodent. Dose ranging studies should precede the 14-, 28-, 90- or 180- day toxicity studies. Duration of the final systemic toxicity study will depend on the duration, therapeutic indication and scale of the proposed clinical trial. (see Item 1.8). If a species is known to metabolize the drug in the same way as humans, it should be preferred for toxicity studies.

In repeated-dose toxicity studies the drug should be administered 7 days by the route intended for clinical use. The number of animals required for these studies, i.e. the minimum number of animals on which data should be available, is shown in Item 1.9.

Wherever applicable, a control group of animals given the vehicle alone should be included, and three other groups should be given graded doses of the drug. The highest dose should produce observable toxicity; the lowest dose should not cause observable toxicity, but should be comparable to the intended therapeutic dose in humans or a multiple of it. To make allowance for the sensitivity of the species the intermediate dose should cause some symptoms, but not gross toxicity or death, and should be placed logarithmically between the other two doses.

The parameters to be monitored and recorded in long-term toxicity studies should include behavioural, physiological, biochemical and microscopic observations. In case of parenteral drug administration, the sites of injection should be Subjected to gross and microscopic examination. Initial and final electrocardiogram and fundus examination should be carried out in the non-rodent species.

In the case of cytotoxic anticancer agents dosing and study design should be in accordance with the proposed clinical schedule in terms of days of exposure and number of cycles. Two rodent species may be tested for initiating Phase I trials. A non-rodent species should be added if the drug has a novel mechanism of action, or if permission for Phase II, III or marketing is being sought.

For most compounds, it is expected that single dose tissue distribution studies with sufficient sensitivity and specificity will provide an adequate assessment of tissue distribution and the potential for accumulation. Thus, repeated dose tissue distribution studies should not be required uniformly for all compounds and should only be conducted when appropriate data cannot be derived from other sources. Repeated dose studies may be appropriate under certain circumstances based on the data from single dose tissue distribution studies, toxicity and toxicokinetic studies. The studies may be most appropriate for compounds which have an apparently long half life, incomplete elimination or unanticipated organ toxicity.

Notes :

(i) **Single dose toxicity study :** Each group should contain at least 5 animals of either sex. At least four graded doses should be given. Animals should be exposed to the test substance in a single bolus or by continuous infusion or several doses within 24 hours. Animals should be observed for 14 days. Signs of intoxication, effect on body weight, gross pathological changes should be reported. It is desirable to include histo-pathology of grossly affected organs, if any.

(ii) **Dose-ranging study :** Objectives of this study include the identification of target organ of toxicity and establishment of MTD for subsequent studies.

(a) **Rodents :** Study should be performed in one rodent species (preferably rat) by the proposed clinical route of administration. At least four graded doses including control should be given, and each dose group as well as the vehicle control should consist of a minimum of 5 animals of each sex. Animals should be exposed to the test substance daily for 10 consecutive days. Highest dose should be the maximum tolerated dose of single-dose study. Animals should be observed daily for signs of intoxication (general appearance, activity and behaviour, etc.), and periodically for the body weight and laboratory parameters. Gross examination of viscera and microscopic examination of affected organs should be done.

(b) **Non-rodents :** One male and one female are to be taken for ascending Phase MTD study. Dosing should start after initial recording of cage-side and laboratory parameters. Starting dose may be 3 to 5 times the extrapolated effective dose or MTD (whichever is less), and dose escalation in suitable steps should be done every third day after drawing the samples fbr laboratory parameters. Dose should be lowered appropriately when clinical or laboratory evidence of toxicity are observed. Administration of test substance should then continue for 10 days at the well-tolerated dose level following which, samples for laboratory parameters should be taken. Sacrifice, autopsy and microscopic examination of affected tissues should be performed as in the case of rodents.

(iii) **14-28 days repeated-dose toxicity studies :** One rodent (6-10/sex/group) and one non-rodent (2-3/sex/group) species are needed. Daily dosing by proposed clinical route at three dose levels should be done with highest dose having observable toxicity, middose between high and low dose, and low dose. The doses should preferably be multiples of the effective dose and free from toxicity. Observation parameters should include cage-side observations, body weight changes, food/water intake, blood biochemistry, haematology, and gross and microscopic studies of all viscera and tissues.

(iv) **90-days repeated-dose toxicity studies :** One rodent (15-30/sex/group) and one non-rodent (4-6/sex/group) species are needed. Daily dosing by proposed clinical route at three graded dose levels should be done. In addition to the control a "high-dose reversal" group and its control group should be also included. Parameters should include signs of intoxication (general appearance, activity and behaviour, etc.), body weight, food intake, blood biochemical parameters, haematological values, urine analysis, organ weights, gross and microscopic study of viscera and tissues. Half the animals in "reversal" groups (treated and control) should be sacrificed after 14 days of stopping the treatment. The remaining animals should be sacrificed after 28 days of stopping the treatment or after the recovery of signs and/or clinical pathological changes - whichever comes later, and evaluated for the parameters used for the main study.

(v) **180-days repeated-dose toxicity studies :** One rodent (15-30/sex/group) and one non--rodent (4-6/sex/group) species are needed. At least 4 groups, including control, should be taken. Daily dosing by proposed clinical route at three graded dose levels should be done. Parameters should include signs of intoxication, body weight, food intake, blood biochemistry, haematology, urine analysis, organ weights, gross and microscopic examination of organs and tissues.

1.2 Male Fertility Study

One rodent species (preferably rat) should be used. Dose selection should be done from the results of the previous 14 or 28 days toxicity study in rat. Three dose groups, the highest one showing minimal toxicity in systemic studies, and a control group should be taken. Each group should consist of 6 adult male animals. Animals should be treated with the test substance by the intended route of clinical use for minimum 28 days and maximum 70 days before they are paired with female animals of proven fertility in a ratio of 1: 2 for mating.

Drug treatment of the male animals should continue during pairing. Pairing should be continued till the detection of vaginal plug or 10 days, whichever is earlier. Females getting thus pregnant should be examined for their fertility index after day 13 of gestation. All the male animals should be sacrificed at the end of the study. Weights of each testis and epididymis should be separately recorded. Sperms from one epididymis should be examined for their motility and morphology. The other epididymis and both testes should be examined for their histology.

1.3 Female Reproduction and Developmental Toxicity Studies

These studies (see Appendix I, item 4.4) need to be carried out for all drugs proposed to be studied or used in women of child bearing age. Segment I, II and III studies (see below) are to be performed in albino mice or rats, and segment II study should include albino rabbits also as a second test species.

On the occasion, when the test article is not compatible with the rabbit (e.g. antibiotics which are effective against gram positive, anaerobic organisms and protozoas) the Segment II data in the mouse may be substituted.

1.3.1 Female Fertility Study (Segment I) : The study should be done in one rodent species (rat preferred). The drug should be administered to both males and females, beginning a sufficient number of days (28 days in males and 14 days in females) before mating. Drug treatment should continue during mating and, subsequently, during the gestation period. Three graded doses should be used, the highest dose (usually the MTD obtained from previous systemic toxicity studies) should not affect general health of the parent animals. At least 15 males and 15 females should be used per dose group. Control and the treated groups should be of similar size. The route of administration should be the same as intended for therapeutic use.

Dams should be allowed to litter and their medication should be continued till the weaning of pups. Observations on body weight, food intake, clinical signs of intoxication, mating behaviour, progress of gestation/parturition periods, length of gestation, parturition, post-partum health and gross pathology (and histopathology of affected organs) of dams should be recorded. The pups from both treated and control groups should be observed for general signs of intoxication, sex-wise distribution in different treatment groups, body weight, growth parameters, survival, gross examination, and autopsy. Histopathology of affected organs should be done.

1.3.2 Teratogenicity Study (Segment II) : One rodent (preferably rat) and one non-rodent (rabbit) species are to be used. The drug should be administered throughout the period of organogenesis, using three dose levels as described for segment I. The highest dose should cause minimum maternal toxicity and the lowest one should be proportional to the proposed dose for clinical use in humans or a multiple of it. The route of administration should be the same as intended for human therapeutic use.

The control and the treated groups should consist of at least 20 pregnant rats (or mice) and 12 rabbits, on each dose level. All foetuses should to be subjected to gross examination, one of the foetuses should be examined for skeletal abnormalities and the other half for visceral abnormalities. Observation parameters should include : (Dams) signs of intoxication, effect on body weight, effect on food intake, examination of uterus, ovaries and uterine contents, number of corpora lutea, implantation sites, resorptions (if any); and for the foetuses, the total number, gender, body length, weight and gross/visceral skeletal abnormalities, if any.

1.3.3 Perinatal Study (Segment III) : This study is specially recommended if the drug is to be given to pregnant or nursing mothers for long periods or where there are indications of possible adverse effects on foetal development. One rodent species (preferably rat) is needed. Dosing at levels comparable to multiples of human dose should be done by the intended clinical route. At least 4 groups (including control), each consisting of 15 dams should be used. The drug should be administered throughout the last trimester of pregnancy (from day 15 of gestation) and then the dose that causes low foetal loss should be continued throughout lactation and weaning. Dams should then be sacrificed and examined as described below.

One male and one female from each litter of F_1 generation (total 15 males and 15 females in each group) should be selected at weaning and treated with vehicle or test substance (at the dose levels described above) throughout their periods of growth to sexual maturity, pairing, gestation, parturition and lactation. Mating performance and fertility of F_1 generation should thus be evaluated to obtain the F_2 generation whose growth parameters should be monitored till weaning. The criteria of evaluation should be the same as described earlier.

Animals should be sacrificed at the end of the study and the observation parameters should include (Dams) body weight, food intake, general signs of intoxication, progress of gestation/parturition periods and gross pathology (if any); and for pups, the clinical signs, sex-wise distribution in dose groups, body weight, growth parameters, gross examination, survival and autopsy (if needed) and where necessary, histopathology.

1.4 Local toxicity

These studies (see Appendix I, item 4.5) are required when the new drug is proposed to be used by some special route (other than oral) in humans. The drug should be applied to an appropriate site (e.g., skin or vaginal mucous membrane) to determine local effects in a suitable species. Typical study designs for these studies should include three dose levels and untreated and/or vehicle control, preferably use of 2 species, and increasing group size with increase in duration of treatment. Where dosing is restricted due to anatomical or human reasons, or the drug concentration cannot be increased beyond a certain level due to the problems of solubility, pH or tonicity, a clear statement to this effect should be given. If the drug is absorbed from the site of application, appropriate systemic toxicity studies will also be required.

Notes:

(i) **Dermal toxicity study:** The study should be done in rabbit and rat. Daily topical (dermal) application of test substance in its clinical dosage form should be done. Test material should be applied on shaved skin covering not less than 10% of the total body surface area. Porous gauze dressing should be used to hold liquid material in place. Formulations with different concentrations (at least 3) of test substance, several fold higher than the clinical dosage form should be used. Period of application may vary from 7 to 90 days depending on the clinical duration of use. Where skin irritation is grossly visible in the initial studies, a recovery group should be included in the subsequent repeated-dose study. Local signs (erythema, oedema and eschar formation) as well as histological examination of sites of application should be used for evaluation of results.

(ii) **Photo-allergy or dermal photo-toxicity:** It should be tested by Armstrong/Harber Test in guinea pig. This test should be done if the drug or a metabolise is related to an agent causing photosensitivity or the nature of action suggests such a potential (e.g., drugs to be used in treatment of leucoderma). Pretest in 8 animals should screen 4 concentrations (patch application for 2 hours ± 15 min.) with and without UV exposure (10 J/cm^2). Observations recorded at 24 and 48 hours should be used to ascertain highest non-irritant dose. Main test should be performed with 10 test animals and 5 controls. Induction with the dose selected from pretest should use 0.3 ml/patch for 2 hour ± 15 min. followed by 10 J/cm^2 of UV exposure. This should be repeated on day 0, 2, 4, 7, 9 and 11 of the test. Animals should be challenged with the same concentration of test substance between day 20 to 24 of the test with a similar 2-hours application followed by exposure to 10 J/cm^2 of UV light. Examination and grading of erythema and oedema formation at the challenge sites should be done 24 and 48 hours after the challenge. A positive control like musk ambrett or psoralin should be used.

(iii) **Vaginal toxicity test:** Study is to be done in rabbit or dog. Test substance should be applied topically (vaginal mucosa) in the form of pessary, cream or ointment. Six to ten animals per dose group should be taken. Higher concentrations or several daily applications of test substance should be done to achieve multiples of daily human dose. The minimum duration of drug treatment is 7 days (more according to clinical use), subject to a maximum of 30 days. Observation parameters should include swelling, closure of introitus and histopathology of vaginal wall.

(iv) **Rectal tolerance test :** For all preparations meant for rectal administration this test may be performed in rabbits or dogs. Six to ten animals per dose group should be taken. Formulation in volume comparable to human dose (or the maximum possible volume) should be applied once or several times daily, per rectally, to achieve administration of multiples of daily human dose. The minimum duration of application is 7 days (more according to clinical use), Subject to a maximum of 30 days. Size of suppositories may be smaller, but the drug content should be several fold higher than the proposed human dose. Observation parameters should include clinical signs (sliding on backside), signs of pain, blood and/or mucous in faeces, condition of anal region/sphincter, gross and (if required) histological examination of rectal mucosa.

(v) **Parenteral drugs :** For products meant for intravenous or intramuscular or subcutaneous or intradermal injection the sites of injection in systemic toxicity studies should be specially examined grossly and microscopically. If needed, reversibility of adverse effects may be determined on a case to case basis.

(vi) **Ocular toxicity studies (for products meant for ocular instillation) :** These studies should be carried out in two species, one of which should be the albino rabbit which has a sufficiently large conjunctival sac. Direct delivery of drug onto the cornea in case of animals having small conjunctival sacs should be ensured. Liquids, ointments, gels or soft contact lenses (saturated with drug) should be used. Initial single dose application should be done to decide the exposure concentrations for repeated-dose studies and the need to include a recovery group. Duration of the final study will depend on the proposed length of human exposure Subject to a maximum of 90 days. At least two different concentrations exceeding the human dose should be used for demonstrating the margin of safety. In acute studies, one eye should be used for drug administration and the other kept as control. A separate control group should be included in repeated-dose studies.

Slit-lamp examination should be done to detect the changes in cornea, iris and aqueous humor. Fluorescent dyes (sodium fluorescein, 0.25 to 1.0%) should be used for detecting the defects in surface epithelium of cornea and conjunctive. Changes in intra-ocular tension should be monitored by a tonometer. Histological examination of eyes should be done at the end of the study after fixation in Davidson's or Zenker's fluid.

(vii) **Inhalation toxicity studies :** The studies are to be undertaken in one rodent and one non-rodent species using the formulation that is to be eventually proposed to be marketed. Acute, subacute and chronic toxicity studies should be performed according to the intended duration of human exposure. Standard systemic toxicity study designs (described above) should be used. Gases and vapours should be given in whole body exposure chambers; aerosols are to be given by nose-only method. Exposure time and concentrations of test substance (limit dose of 5 mg/l) should be adjusted to ensure exposure at levels comparable to multiples of intended human exposure. Three dose groups and a control (plus vehicle control, if needed) are required. Duration of exposure may vary Subject to a maximum of 6 hours per day and five days a week. Food and water should be withdrawn during the period of exposure to test substance.

Temperature, humidity and flow rate of exposure chamber should be recorded and reported. Evidence of exposure with test substance of particle size of 4 micron (especially for aerosols) with not less that 25% being 1 micron should be provided. Effects on respiratory rate, findings of bronchial ravage fluid examination, histological examination of respiratory passages and lung tissue should be included along with the regular parameters of systemic toxicity studies or assessment of margin of safety.

1.5 Allergenicity/ Hypersensitivity :

Standard tests include Guinea Pig Maximization Test (GPMT) and Local Lymph Node Assay (LLNA) in mouse. Any one of the two may be done.

Notes :

(i) **Guinea Pig Maximization Test :** The test is to be performed in two steps; first, determination of maximum non-irritant and minimum irritant doses, and second, the main test. The initial study will also have two components. To determine the intradermal induction dose, 4 dose levels should be tested by the same route in a batch of 4 male and 4 female animals (2 of each sex should be given Freund's adjuvant). The minimum irritant dose should be used for induction. Similarly, a topical minimum irritant dose should be determined for challenge. This should be established in 2 males and 2 females. A minimum of 6 male and 6 female animals per group should be used in the main study. One test and one control group should be used. It is preferable to have one more positive control group. Intradermal induction (day 1) coupled with topical challenge (day 21) should be done. If there is no response, rechallenge should be done 7-30 days after the primary challenge. Erythema and oedema (individual animal scores as well as maximization grading) should be used as evaluation criteria.

(ii) **Local Lymph Node Assay :** Mice used in this test should be of the same sex, either only males or only females. Drug treatment is to be given on ear skin. Three graded doses, the highest being maximum non-irritant dose plus vehicle control should be used. A minimum of 6 mice per group should be used. Test material should be applied on ear skin on three consecutive days and on day 5, the draining auricular lymph nodes should be dissected out 5 hours after i.v. 3H-thymidine or bromo-deoxy-uridine (BrdU). Increase in 3H-thymidine or BrdU incorporation should be used as the criterion for evaluation of results.

1.6 Genotoxicity

Genotoxic compounds, in the absence of other data, shall be presumed to be trans-species carcinogens, implying a hazard to humans. Such compounds need not be Subjected to long-term carcinogenicity studies. However, if such a drug is intended to be administered for chronic illnesses or otherwise over a long period of time - a chronic toxicity study (upto one year) may be necessary to detect early tumorigenic effects.

Genotoxicity tests are in-vitro and in vivo-tests conducted to detect compounds which induce genetic damage directly or indirectly. These tests should enable a hazard identification with respect to damage to DNA and its fixation.

The following standard test battery is generally expected to be conducted :

(i) A test for gene mutation in bacteria.
(ii) An in-vitro test with cytogenetic evaluation of chromosomal damage with mammalian cells.
(iii) An in-vivo test for chromosomal damage using rodent hematopoietic cells.

Other genotoxicity tests e.g. tests for measurement of DNA adducts, DNA strand breaks, DNA repair or recombination serve as options in addition to the standard battery for further investigation of genotoxicity test results obtained in the standard battery. Only under extreme conditions in which one or more tests comprising the standard battery cannot be employed for technical reasons, alternative validated tests can serve as substitutes provided sufficient scientific justification should be provided to support the argument that a given standard battery test is not appropriate.

Both in-vitro and in-vivo studies should be done. In-vitro studies should include Ame's Salmonella assay and chromosomal aberrations (CA) in cultured cells. In-vivo studies should include micronucleus assay (MNA) or CA in rodent bone marrow. Data analysis of CA should include analysis of 'gaps.'

Cytotoxic anticancer agents : Genotoxicity data are not required before Phase I and II trials. But these studies should be completed before applying for Phase III trials.

Notes :

Ame's Test (Reverse mutation assay in Salmonella) : S. typhimurium tester strains such as TA98, TA100, TA102, TA1535, TA97 or Escherichia coli WP2 uvrA or Escherichia coli WP2 uvrA (pKM101) should be used.

(i) In-vitro exposure (with and without metabolic activation, S9 mix) should be done at a minimum of 5 log dose levels. "Solvent" and "positive" control should be used. Positive control may include 9-amino-acridine, 2-nitrofluorine, sodium azide and mitomycin C, respectively, in the tester strains mentioned above. Each set should consist of at least three replicates. A 2.5 fold (or more) increase in number of revertants in comparison to spontaneous revertants would be considered positive.

(ii) **In-vitro cytogenetic assay :** The desired level of toxicity for in-vitro cytogenetic tests using cell lines should be greater than 50% reduction in cell number or culture confluency. For lymphocyte cultures, an inhibition of mitotic index by greater than 50% is considered sufficient. It should be performed in CHO cells or on human lymphocyte in culture. In-vitro exposure (with and without metabolic activation, S9 mix) should be done using a minimum of 3 log doses. "Solvent" and "positive" control should be included. A positive control like Cyclophosphamide with metabolic activation and Mitomycin C for without metabolic activation should be used to give a reproducible and detectable increase clastogenic effect over the background which demonstrates the sensitivity of the test system. Each set should consist of at least three replicates. Increased number of aberrations in meta Phase chromosomes should be used as the criteria for evaluation.

(iii) **In-vivo micronucleus assay :** One rodent species (preferably mouse) is needed. Route of administration of test substance should be the same as intended for humans. Five animals per sex per dose groups should be used. At least three dose levels, plus "solvent" and "positive" control should be tested. A positive control like mitomycin C or cyclophosphamide should be used. Dosing should be done on day 1 and 2 of study followed by sacrifice of animals 6 hours after the last injection. Bone marrow from both the femora should be taken out, flushed with foetal bovine serum (20 min.), pelletted and smeared on glass slides. Giemsa-May Gruenwald staining should be done and increased number of micronuclei in polychromatic erythrocytes (minimum 1000) should be used as the evaluation criteria.

(iv) **In-vivo cytogenetic assay :** One rodent species (preferably rat) is to be used. Route of administration of test substance should be the same as intended for humans. Five animals/sex/dose groups should be used. At least three dose levels, plus "solvent" and "positive" control should be tested. Positive control may include cyclophosphamide. Dosing should be done on day 1 followed by intra-peritoneal colchicine administration at 22 hours. Animals should be sacrificed 2 hours after colchicine administration. Bone marrow from both the femora should be taken out, flushed with hypotonic saline (20 min.), pelletted and resuspended in Carnoy's fluid. Once again the cells should be pelletted and dropped on clean glass slides with a Pasteur pipette. Giemsa staining should be done and increased number of aberrations in meta Phase chromosomes (minimum 100) should be used as the evaluation criteria.

1.7 Carcinogenicity (see Appendix I, item 4.8)

Carcinogenicity studies should be performed for all drugs that are expected to be clinically used for more than 6 months as well as for drugs used frequently in an intermittent manner in the treatment of chronic or recurrent conditions. Carcinogenicity studies are also to be performed for drugs if there is concern about their carcinogenic potential emanating from previous demonstration of carcinogenic potential in the product class that is considered relevant to humans or where structure-activity relationship suggests carcinogenic risk or when there is evidence of preneoplastic lesions in repeated dose toxicity studies or when long-term tissue retention of parent compound or metabolise(s) results in local tissue reactions or other pathophysiological responses. For pharmaceuticals developed to treat certain serious diseases, Licensing Authority may allow carcinogenicity testing to be conducted after marketing permission has been granted.

In instances where the life-expectancy in the indicated population is short (i.e., less than 2 - 3 years) - no long-term carcinogenicity studies may be required. In cases where the therapeutic agent for cancer is generally successful and life is significantly prolonged there may be later concerns regarding secondary cancers. When such drugs are intended for adjuvant therapy in tumour free patients or for prolonged use in non-cancer indications, carcinogenicity studies may be/are needed. Completed rodent carcinogenicity studies are not needed in advance of the conduct of large scale clinical trials, unless there is special concern for the patient population.

Carcinogenicity studies should be done in a rodent species (preferably rat). Mouse may be employed only with proper scientific justification. The selected strain of animals should not have a very high or very low incidence of spontaneous tumors.

At least three dose levels should be used. The highest dose should be sub-lethal, and it should not reduce the life span of animals by more than 10% of expected normal. The lowest dose should be comparable to the intended human therapeutic dose or a multiple of it, e.g. 2.5x; to make allowance for the sensitivity of the species. The intermediate dose to be placed logarithmically between the other two doses. An untreated control and (if indicated) a vehicle control group should be included. The drug should be administered 7 days a week for a fraction of the life span comparable to the fraction of human life span over which the drug is likely to be used therapeutically. Generally, the period of dosing should be 24 months for rats and 18 months for mice.

Observations should include macroscopic changes observed at autopsy and detailed histopathology of organs and tissues. Additional tests for carcinogenicity (short-term bioassays, neonatal mouse assay or tests employing transgenic animals) may also be done depending on their applicability on a case to case basis.

Note :

Each dose group and concurrent control group not intended to be sacrificed early should contain atleast 50 animals of each sex. A high dose satellite group for evaluation of pathology other than neoplasia should contain 20 animals of each sex while the satellite control group should contain 10 animals of each sex. Observation parameters should include signs of intoxication effect on body weight, food intake, clinical chemistry parameters, haematology parameters, urine analysis, organ weights, gross pathology and detailed histopathology. Comprehensive descriptions of benign and malignant tumor development, time of their detection, site, dimensions, histological typing etc. should be given.

1.8 Animal Toxicity Requirements for Clinical Trials and Marketing of a New Drug

Systemic Toxicity Studies			
Route of administration	Duration of proposed human administration	Human Phase(s) for which study is proposed to be conducted	Long term toxicity requirements
Oral or Parenteral or Transdermal	Single dose or several doses in one day, Upto 1 wk	I, II, III	2 sp; 2 wk
	> 1 wk but upto 2 wk	I, II, III	2 sp; 4 wk
	> 2 wk but upto 4 wk	I, II, III	2 sp; 12 wk
	Over 1 mo	I, II, III	2 sp; 24 wk
Inhalation (general anaesthetics, aerosols)	Upto 2 wk	I, II, III	2 sp; 1 mo; (Exposure time 3h/d, 5d/wk)
	Upto 4 wk	I, II, III	2 sp; 12 wk, (Exposure time 6h/d, 5d/wk)
	> 14 wk	I, II, III	2 sp; 24 wk, (Exposure time 6h/d, 5d/wk)
Local Toxicity Studies			
Dermal	Upto 2 wk	I, II	1 sp; 4 wk
		III	2 sp; 4 wk
	< 2 wk	I, II, III	2 sp; 12 wk
Ocular or Octic or Nasal	Upto 2 wk	I, II	1 sp; 4 wk
		III	2 sp; 4 wk
	< 2 wk	I, II, III	2 sp; 12 wk
Vaginal or Rectal	Upto 2 wk	I, II	1 sp; 4 wk
		III	2 sp; 4 wk
	> 2 wk	I, II, III	2 sp; 12 wk

Special Toxicity Studies

Male Fertility Study :
- Phase I II III in male volunteers/patients

Female Reproduction and Developmental Toxicity Studies :
- Segment II studies in 2 species; Phase II, III involving female patients of child bearing age.
- Segment I study; Phase III involving female patients of child-bearing age.
- Segment III study; Phase III for drugs to be given to pregnant or nursing mothers for long periods or where there are indications of possible adverse effects on foetal development.

Allergenicity/Hypersensitivity :
- Phase I, II, III - when there is a cause of concern or for parenteral drugs (including dermal application)

Photo-allergy or dermal photo-toxicity :
- Phase I, II, III - if the drug or a metabolite is related to an agent causing photosensitivity or the nature of action suggests such a potential.

Genotoxicity :
- In-vitro studies - Phase I
- Both in-vitro and in-vivo - Phase II, III

Arcinogenicity :
- Phase III - when there is a cause for concern, or when the drug is to be used for more than 6 months.

Abbreviations : sp-species; mo-month; wk-week; d-day; h-hour; I, II, III - Phases of clinical trial;

Notes :
1. Animal toxicity data generated in other countries may be accepted and may not be asked to be repeated/duplicated in India on a case to case basis depending upon the quality of data and the credentials of the laboratory(ies) where such data has been generated.
2. Requirements for fixed dose combinations are given in Appendix VI.

1.9 Number of Animals required for Repeated-dose Toxicity Studies

Group	14-28 days				84-182 days			
	Rodent (Rat)		Non-rodent (Dog or Monkey)		Rodent (Rat)		Non-rodent (Dog or Monkey)	
	M	F	M	F	M	F	M	F
Control	6-10	6-10	2-3	2-3	15-30	15-30	4-6	4-6
Low dose	6-10	6-10	2-3	2-3	15-30	15-30	4-6	4-6
Intermediate	6-10	6-10	2-3	2-3	15-30	15-30	4-6	4-6
High dose	6-10	6-10	2-3	2-3	15-30	15-30	4-6	4-6

1.10 Laboratory Parameters to be Included in Toxicity Studies :

Haematological Parameters :

- Haemoglobin
- Total RBC count
- Haematocrit
- Reticulocyte
- Total WBC count
- Differential WBC Count
- Platelet Count
- Terminal Bone Marrow Examination
- ESR (Non-rodents only)
- General Blood Picture : A special mention of abnormal and immature cells should be made.
- Coagulation Parameters (Non-rodents only) : Bleeding Time, Coagulation Time, Prothrombin Time, Activated Partial thromboplastin Time

Urinalysis Parameters :

- Colour
- Appearance
- Specific Gravity
- 24-hours urinary output
- Reaction pH
- Albumin
- Sugar
- Acetone
- Bile pigments
- Urobilinogen
- Occult Blood
- Microscopic examination of urinary sediment

Blood Biochemical Parameters :

- Glucose
- Cholesterol
- Triglycerides
- HDL Cholesterol (Non-reodents only)
- LDL Cholesterol (Non-rodents only)
- Bilirubin
- SGPT (ALT)
- SGOT (AST)
- Alkakine Phosphatase (ALP)
- GGT (Non-rodents only)
- Blood Urea Nitrogen
- Creatinine
- Total Proteins
- Albumin
- Globulin (Calculated values)
- Sodium
- Potassium
- Phosphorus
- Calcium

Gross and Microscopic Pathology :

- Brain*; Cerebrum, Cerebellum, Midbrain
- (Spinal Cord)
- Eye
- (Middle Ear)
- Thyroid
- (Parathyroid)
- Spleen*
- Thymus
- Adrenal*
- (Pancreas)
- (Trachea)
- Lung*

2. Chemical and Pharmaceutical Information

Most of the data under this heading (see Appendix I, item 2) are required with the application for marketing permission. When the application is for clinical trials only, information covered in items 2.1 to 2.3 of Appendix I will usually suffice.

3. Animal Toxicology

3.1 Acute Toxicology : Acute toxicity studies (see Appendix I item 4.2) should be carried out in at least two species usually mice and rats using the same route as intended for humans. In addition, at least one more route should be used to ensure systemic absorption of drug; this route may depend on the nature of the drug. Mortality should be looked for upto 72 hours after parenteral administration and upto 7 days after oral administration. Symptoms, signs and mode of death should be reported, with appropriate macroscopic and microscopic findings where necessary. LD 50s should be reported preferably with 95% confidence limits if it cannot be determined reasons for this should be stated.

3.2 Long Term Toxicity : Long term toxicity (see Appendix I, item 1.3) should be carried out in at least two mammalian species, of which one should be a non-rodent. The duration of study will depend on whether the application is for marketing permission or for clinical trial, and in the latter case, on the phases of trials (see Appendix III). If a species is known to metabolize the drug in the same way as humans, it should be preferred.

In long term toxicity studies the drug should be administered 7 days a week by the route intended for clinical use in humans. The number of animals required for these studies, i.e., the minimum number on which data should be available, is shown in Appendix IV.

A control group of animals given the vehicle alone should be included, and three other groups should be given graded doses of the drug; the highest dose should produce observable toxicity, the lowest dose should not cause observable toxicity, but should be comparable to the intended therapeutic dose in humans or a multiple of it e.g. 2.5 to make allowance for the sensitivity of the species; the intermediate dose should cause some symptoms, but not gross toxicity or death, and may be placed logarithmical between the other two doses.

The variables to be monitored and recorded in long-term toxicity studies should include behavioural, physiological, biochemical, and microscopic observations.

3.3 Reproduction studies : Reproduction studies (see Appendix I, item 4.4) need to be carried out only if the new drug is proposed to be studied or used in women of child bearing age. Two species should generally be used, one of them being a non-rodent if possible.

(a) **Fertility Studies :** The drugs should be administered to both males and females, beginning a sufficient number of days before mating. In females the medication should be continued after mating and the pregnant one should be treated throughout pregnancy. The highest dose used should not effect general health or growth of the animals. The route of administration should be the same as for therapeutic use in humans. The control and the treated group should be of similar size and larger enough to give at least 20 pregnant animals in the control group of rodents and at least 8 pregnant animals in the control group of non-rodents. Observations should include total examination of the litters from both the groups, including spontaneous abortions, if any.

(b) **Teratogenicity Studies :** The drugs should be administered throughout the period of organogenesis, using three dose levels. One of the doses should case minimum material toxicity and one should be the proposed dose for clinical use in human or a multiple of it. The route of administration should be the same as for human therapeutic use. The control and the treated groups should consist of at least 20 pregnant females in case of non-rodents, on each dose used. Observations should include the number of implantation sites; resorptions if any; and the number of foetuses with their sexes, weights and malformations, if any.

(c) **Perinatal studies :** The drugs should be administered throughout the last third of pregnancy and then through lactation to weaning. The control of each treated group should have at least 12 pregnant females and the dose which causes low foetal loss should be continued throughout lactation weaning. Animals should be sacrificed and observations should include macroscopic autopsy and where necessary, histopathology.

3.4 Local Toxicity : These studies (see Appendix I, Item 4.5) are required when the new drug is proposed to be used topically in humans. The drug should be applied to an appropriate site to determine local effects in a suitable species such as guinea-pigs or rabbits, if the drug is absorbed from the site of applications, appropriate systemic toxicity studies will be required.

3.5 Mutagenicity and Carcinogenicity : These studies (see Appendix 1, item 4.6) are required to be carried out if the drug or its metabolite is related to a known carcinogen or when the nature and action of the drug is such as to suggest a carcinogenic/mutagenic potential. For carcinogenicity studies, at least halo species should be used. These species should not have a high incidence of spontaneous tumors and should preferably be known to metabolize the drug in the same manner as humans. At least three dose levels should be used; the highest dose should be sublethal but cause observable toxicity; the lowest dose should be comparable to the intended human therapeutic dose or a multiple of it, e.g. 2.5x; to make intermediate dose to be placed logarithmically between the other two doses. A control group should always be included. The drug should be administered 7 days a week or a fraction of the life span comparable to the fraction of human life span over which the drug is likely to be used therapeutically. Observations should include macroscopic changes observed at autopsy and detailed histopathology.

4. Animal Pharmacology

Specific pharmacological actions (see Appendix I, item 3.2) are those with therapeuticpotential for humans. These should be described according to the animals models and species used. Wherever possible, dose-response relationships and ED 50s should be given. Special studies to elucidate mode of action may also be described.

General pharmacological action (see Appendix I, item 3.3) are effects on other organs and systems, especially cardiovascular, respiratory and central nervous systems.

Pharmacokinetic data help relate drug effect to plasma concentration and should be given to the extent available.

5. Human/Clinical Pharmacology (Phase I)

The objective of phase I trials (see Appendix 1, item 5) is to determine the maximum tolerated dose in humans; pharmacodynamic effects, adverse reactions, if any, with their nature and intensity; and pharmacokinetic behaviour of the drug as far as possible. These studies are carried out in healthy adult males, using clinical, physiological and biochemical observations. At least 2 subjects should be used on each dose.

Phase I trials are usually carried out by investigators trained in clinical pharmacology and having the necessary facilities to closely observe and monitor the subjects. These may be carried out at one or two centres.

6. Exploratory Trials (Phase II)

In phase II trial (see Appendix I, item 6) a limited number of patients are studied carefully to determine possible therapeutic uses, effective dose range and further evaluation of safety and pharmacokinetics. Normally 10-12 patients should be studied at each dose level. These studies are usually limited to 3-4 centres and carried out by clinicians specialized in the concerned therapeutic areas and having adequate facilities to perform the necessary investigations for efficacy and safety.

7. Confirmatory Trials (Phase III)

The purpose of these trials (see Appendix I, item 7) is to obtain sufficient evidence about the efficacy and safety of the drug in a larger number of patients, generally in comparison with a standard drug and/or a placebo as appropriate. These trials may be carried out by clinicians in the concerned therapeutic areas, having facilities appropriate to the protocol. If the drug is already approved /marketed in other countries, phase III data should generally be obtained on at least 100 patients distributed over 3-4 centres primarily to confirm the efficacy and safety of the drug, in Indian patients when used as recommended in the product monograph for the claims made.

If the drug is a new drug substance discovered in India and not marketed in any other country, phase III data should be obtained on at least 500 patients distributed over 10-15 centres. In addition, data on adverse drug reactions observed during clinical use of the drug should be collected in 1000-2000 patients; such data may be collected through clinicians who give written consent to use the drug as recommended and to provide a report on its efficacy and adverse drug reactions in the treated patients. The selection of clinicians for such monitoring and supply of drug to them will need approval of the licensing authority under Rule 21.

8. Special Studies

(A) These include studies on oral solid dosage forms, such as, bioavailability and dissolution studies. These are required to be submitted on the formulations manufactured in the country. (See Appendix I, items 8.2 and 8.3).

(B) These include studies to explore additional aspects of the drug, e.g. use in elderly patients or patients with renal failure, secondary or ancillary effects, interactions, etc. (see Appendix I, items 8.1 and 8.2).

9. Submission of Reports (Appendix II)

The reports of completed clinical trials shall be submitted by the applicant duly signed by the investigator within a stipulated period of time. The applicant should do so even if he is no longer interested to market the drug in the country unless there are sufficient reasons for not doing so.

10. Regulatory Status in other Countries

It is important to state if any restrictions have been placed on the use of the drug in any other country, e.g. dosage limits, exclusion of certain age groups, warning about adverse drug reactions, etc. (see Appendix I, item 9.2).

Likewise, if the drug has been withdrawn from any country specially by a regulatory directive, such information should be furnished along with reasons and their relevance, if any, to India (see Appendix I, item 9.1(d)].

11. Marketing Information

The product monograph should comprise the full prescribing information necessary to enable a physician to use the drug properly. It should include description, actions, indications, dosage precaution, drug interactions, warnings and adverse reactions.

The draft of label and carton texts should comply with provisions of Rules 96 and 97 of the said rules.

12. Post-marketing Surveillance Study

On approval of a new drug, the importer or the manufacturer shall conduct post marketing surveillance study of that new drug after getting the protocols and the names of the investigators approved by the Licensing Authority as defined under clause (b) of rule 21 during the initial period of two years of marketing.

DRUGS & COSMETIC ACT, 1940
Provisions relating to (Ayurvedic, Unani & Siddha Drugs)
[Ayurvedic, Unani & Siddha Drugs Technical Advisory Board]

(I) The Central Government shall, by notification in the Official Gazette and with effect from such date as may be specified therein, constitute a Board(to be called the {Ayurvedic, Unani & Siddha Drugs Technical Advisory Board}) to advise the Central Government and the State Governments on technical matters arising out of this chapter and to carry out the other functions assigned to it by this chapter.

   (A) Te Board Shall consist of the following members, namely:-
   - (i) The Director-General of Health Services, ex officio;
   - (ii) The Drugs Controller, India, ex officio;
   - (iii) The principal officer dealing with Indian system of medicine in the Ministry of Health, ex officio;
   - (iv) The Director of the Central Drugs Laboratory, Calcutta, ex officio;
   - (v) One person holding the appointment of Govt. Analyst under section 34-F, to be nominated by the Central Govt.;
   - (vi) One Pharmacognocist to be nominated by Central Govt.;
   - (vii) One Phyto-chemist to be nominated the Central Govt.
   - (viii) Four persons to be nominated by Central Govt., two from amongst the members of the Ayurvedic Pharmacopoeia Committee, one from amongst the members of the Unani Pharmacopoeia Committee and one from amongst the members of the Siddha Pharmacopoeia Committee;
   - (ix) One teacher in Darvyaguna, and Bhaishajya Kalpana, to be nominated by the Central Government;
   - (x) One teacher in ILM-UL-ADVIA and TAKLIS-WA DAWASZAI, to be nominated by the Central Government;
   - (xi) One teacher in Gunapadam to be nominated by Central Government;
   - (xii) Three persons, one each to represent the Ayurvedic, Siddha & Unani drug industry, to be nominated by the Central Government;
   - (xiii) Three persons, one each from among the practitioners of Ayurvedic, Siddha & Unani Tibb systems of medicine to be nominated by the Central Government;
   - (xiv) Three persons, one each from among the practitioners of Ayurvedic, Siddha & Unani Tibb systems of medicine to be nominated by the Central Government.

(B)
- (i) The Central Govt. shall appoint a member of the Board as its Chairman.
- (ii) The nominated members of the Board shall hold office for three years but shall be eligible for renomination.
- (iii) The Board may, subject to the previous approval of Central Govt. make bye-laws fixing a quorum and regulating its own procedure and conduct of all business to be transacted by it.
- (iv) The functions of the Board may be exercised not withstanding any vacancy therein.
- (v) The Central Govt. shall appoint a person to be Secretary of the Board and shall provide the Board with such clerical and other staff as the Central Govt. considers necessary.

The Ayurvedic, Siddha & Unani Durgs Consultative Committee :

1. The Central Govt. may constitute an advisory committee to be called the Ayurvedic, Siddha and Unani Drugs Consultative Committee to advise the Central Govt., the State Govt. and the Ayurvedic, Siddha and Unani Drugs Technical Advisory Board on any matter for the purpose of securing uniformity throughout India in the administration of this Act in so far as it relates to Ayurvedic, Siddha and Unani Drugs.
2. The Ayurvedic, Siddha and Unani Drugs Consultative Committee shall consist of two persons to be nominated by the Central Govt. as representatives of that Govt. and not more than one representative of each State to be nominated by the State Govt. concerned.
3. The Ayurvedic, Siddha and Unani Drugs Consultative Committee shall meet when required to do so by the Central Govt. and shall regulate is own procedure.

MANUFACTURE FOR SALE OF AYURVEDIC (INCLUDING SIDDHA) OR UNANI DRUGS

1. **Manufacture on more than one set of premises :** If Ayurvedic (including Siddha) or Unani drugs are manufactured on more than one set of premises, a separate application shall be made and a separate license shall be obtained in respect of each such set of premises.
2. **Licensing authorities :** For the purpose of this part the State Govt. shall appoint such licensing authorities and for such areas as may be specified in this behalf by notification in the Official Gazette.
3. **Application for license to manufacture Ayurvedic (including Siddha) or Unani Drugs :**
   - (i) An application for the grant or renewal of a license to manufacture for sale any Ayurvedic (including Siddha) or Unani drugs shall be made in Form 24-D to the licensing authority along with a fee of rupees sixty:

Provided that in case of renewal the applicant may apply for the renewal of the license before its expiry or within one month of such expiry.

Provided further that the applicant may apply for renewal after the expiry of one month but within three months of such expiry in which case of fee payable for renewal of such license shall be rupees sixty plus additional fee of rupees thirty.

(ii) A fee of rupees fifteen shall be payable for a duplicate copy of a license issued under this rule, if the original license is defaced, damaged or lost.

4. **Form of license to manufacture Ayurvedic (including Siddha) or Unani drugs :**
   (i) Subject to the conditions of Rule 157 being fulfilled, a license to manufacture for sale any Ayurvedic (including Siddha)or Unani system shall be issued in Form 25-D. The license shall be issued within a period of three months from the date of receipt of the application.
   (ii) A license under this rule shall be granted by the licensing authority after consulting such expert in Ayurvedic (including Siddha) or Unani system of medicine, as the case may be, which the State Govt. may approve in this behalf.

5. **Form of loan license to manufacture for sale Ayurvedic(including Siddha) or Unani drugs :**
   (i) A loan license to manufacture for sale any Ayurvedic (including Siddha) or Unani drugs shall be issued in Form 25-E.
   (ii) A license under this rule shall be granted by the licensing authority after consulting such expert in Ayurvedic (including Siddha) or Unani system of medicine, as the case may be, which the State Govt. may approve in this behalf.
   (iii) The licensing authority shall, before the grant of a loan license. Satisfy himself that the manufacturing unit has adequate equipment, staff, capacity for manufacture and facilities for testing, to undertake the manufacture on behalf of the applicant for a loan license.

6. **Certificate of renewal** : The certificate of renewal of a license in Form 25-D shall be issued in Form 26-D.

7. **Conditions for the grant or renewal of a license in Form 25-D :** Before a license in Form 25-D is granted or renewed in Form 26-D the following conditions shall be complied with by the applicant, namely:-
   (i) The manufacture of Ayurvedic (including Siddha) or Unani drugs shall be carried out in such premises and under such hygienic conditions as are specified in schedule T.

(ii) The manufacture of Ayurvedic (including Siddha) or Unani drugs shall be conducted under the direction and supervision of competent technical staff consisting at least of one person, who is a whole-time employee and who possesses the following qualifications, namely:-
   (a) A degree in Ayurveda or Ayurvedic Pharmacy, Siddha or Unani systems of medicine, as the case may be, conferred by a University, a State Govt. or Statutory Facilities, Councils and Boards of Indian Systems of Medicine recognized by the Central Govt. or a State Govt. for this purpose, or
   (b) A diploma in Ayurveda, Siddha or Unani System of medicine granted by a State Govt. or an Institution recognized by the Central Govt. for this purpose, or
   (c) A graduate in Pharmacy or Pharmaceutical Chemistry or Chemistry or Botany of a University recognized by the Central Govt. with experience of at least two years in the manufacture of drugs pertaining to the Ayurvedic or Siddha or Unani system of medicine, or
   (d) A Vaid or Hakim registered in a State Register of Practitioners of indigenous system of medicines having experience of at least four years in the manufacture of Siddha or Unani drugs, or
   (e) A qualification as Pharmacist in Ayurvedic (including Siddha) or Unani system of medicine, possessing experience of not less than eight years in the manufacture of Ayurvedic or Siddha or Unani Drugs as may be recognized by the Central Govt.
(iii) The competent technical staff to direct and supervise the manufacture of Ayurvedic drugs shall have qualifications in Ayurveda and the competent technical staff to direct and supervise the manufacture of Siddha drugs and Unani drugs shall have qualifications in Siddha or Unani, as the case may be.

8. **Conditions of license** : A license in Form 25-D shall be subject to the conditions stated therein and to the following further conditions, namely :
The license shall maintain proper records of the details of manufacture and of the tests, if any, carried out by him, or by any other person on his behalf, of the raw materials and finished products.
The license shall allow an Inspector appointed under the Act to enter any premises where the manufacture of a substance in respect of which the license is issued is carried on, to inspect the premises, to take samples of the raw materials as well as the finished products, and to inspect the records maintained under these rules.
The license shall maintain an Inspection Book in Form 35 to enable an Inspector to record his impressions and the defects noticed.

9. **Cancellation and suspension of licenses :**
   (i) The licensing authority may, after giving the licensee an opportunity to show cause, within a period which shall not be less than fifteen days from the date of receipt of such notice, why such an order should not be passed, by an order in writing stating the reasons therefore, cancel a license issued under this part or suspend it for such period as he thinks fit, either wholly or in respect of some of the drugs to which it relates, if in his opinion, the licensee has failed to comply with any of the conditions of the license or with any provisions of the Act or the rules made thereunder.
   (ii) A licensee whose license has been suspended or cancelled may appeal to the State Government within a period of three months from the date of receipt of the order, which shall, after considering the appeal, decide the same.
10. **Identification of raw materials :** Raw material used in the preparation of Ayurvedic(including Siddha) or Unani drugs shall be identified and tested, wherever tests are available for their genuineness, and records of such tests as are carried out for the purpose and the methods thereof shall be maintained.

GOOD MANUFACTURING PRACTICES FOR AYURVEDIC, SIDDHA AND UNANI MEDICINES NOTIFIED UNDER DRUGS & COSMETIC ACT 1940 ON 23rd JUNE 2000

The Good Manufacturing Practices are prescribed to ensure that:
(i) Raw materials used in the manufacture of drugs are authentic, of prescribed quality and are free from contamination.
(ii) The manufacturing process is as has been prescribed to maintain the standards.
(iii) Adequate quality control measures are adopted and
(iv) The manufactured drug which is released for sale is of acceptable quality.
(v) To achieve the objectives listed above, each licencee shall evolve methodology and procedures for following the prescribed process of manufacture of drugs which should be documented as a manual and kept for reference and inspection. However, teaching institutions and registered qualified Vaidyas, Siddhas and Hakeems who prepare medicines on their own to dispense to their patients and not selling such drugs in the market are exempted from the purview of G.M.P.

PART I
GOOD MANUFACTURING PRACTICES

Factory Premises :
The manufacturing plant should have adequate space for:-
(i) Receiving and storing raw material.
(ii) Manufacturing process Areas

(iii) Quality control section.
(iv) Finished goods store
(v) Office
(vi) Rejected goods/drugs store

(I) General Requirements

1. **Location and surroundings :** The factory buildings for manufacture of Ayurveda, Siddha and Unani medicines shall be so situated and shall have such construction as to avoid contamination from open sewrage, drain, public lavatory or any factory which produces disagreeable or obnoxious odour or fumes or excessive soot, dust or smoke.

2. **Buildings :** The building used for factory shall be such as to permit production of drugs under hygenic conditions and should be free from cobwebs and insects/rodents. It should have adequate provision of light and ventilation. The floor and the walls should not be damp or moist. The premises used for manufacturing, processing, packaging and labeling will be in conformity with the provisions of the Factory Act. It shall be located so as to be:
   (i) Compatible with other manufacturing operations that may be carried out in the same or adjacent premises.
   (ii) Adequately provided with working space to allow orderly and logical placement of equipment and materials to avoid the risk of mix up between different drugs or components thereof and control the possibility of cross contamination by other drugs or substances and avoid the risk of omission of any manufacturing or control step:
   (iii) Designed, constructed and maintained to prevent entry of insects and rodents. Interior surface (walls, floors and ceilings) shall be smooth and free from cracks and permit easy cleaning and disinfection. The walls of the room in which the manufacturing operations are carried out shall be impervious to and be capable of being kept clean. The flooring shall be smooth and even and shall be such as not to permit retention or accumulation of dust or waste products.
   (iv) Provided with proper drainage system in the processing area. The sanitary fitting and electrical fixtures in the manufacturing area shall be proper and safe.
   (v) Furnace/Bhatti section could be covered with tin roof & proper ventilation, but sufficient care should be taken to prevent flies and dust.
   (vi) There should be fire safety measures and proper exits should be there.

3. **Water Supply :** The water used in manufacture shall be pure and of potable quality. Adequate provision of water for washing the premises shall be made.

4. **Disposal of Waste :** From the manufacturing sections and laboratories the waste water & the residues which might be prejudicial to the workers or public health shall be disposed off after suitable treatment as per guidelines of pollution control authorities to render them harmless.
5. **Container's Cleaning :** In factories where operations involving the use of containers such as bottles, vials and jars are conducted, there shall be adequate arrangements separated from the manufacturing operations for washing, cleaning and drying of such containers.
6. **Stores :** Storage should have proper ventilation and shall be free from dampness. It should provide independent adequate space for storage of different types of material, such as raw material, packaging material & finished products.
7. (a) **Raw Materials :** All raw materials procured for manufacturing will be stored in the raw materials store. The manufacture based on the experience and the characteristics of the particular raw material used in Ayurveda, Siddha and Unani system shall decide the use of appropriate containers which would protect.

    Quality of the raw material as well as prevent it from damage due to dampness, microbiological contamination or rodent and insect infestation, etc. If certain raw materials require such controlled environmental conditions, the raw materials stores may be sub-divided with proper enclosures to provide such conditions by suitable cabinization. While designing such containers, cabins or areas in the raw materials store, care may be taken to handle the following different categories of raw material:-
    (i) Raw material of metallic origin.
    (ii) Raw material of mineral origin.
    (iii) Raw material from animal source.
    (iv) Fresh Herbs.
    (v) Dry Herbs or plant parts.
    (vi) Excipients etc.
    (vii) Volatile oils/perfumes & flavours.
    (viii) Plant extracts and exudates/resins.

    Each container used for raw material storage shall be properly identified with the label which indicates name of the raw material, source of supply and will also clearly state the status of raw material such as 'Under Test' or 'Approved' or 'Rejected'. The labels shall further indicate the identify of the particular supply in the form of batch No. or lot No. and the date of receipt of the consignment.

All the raw materials shall be sampled and got tested either by the in house Ayurvedic, Siddha and Unani experts (Quality control technical person) or by the laboratories approved by the Government and shall be used only on approval after verifying. The rejected raw material should be removed from other raw material store and should be kept in separate room. Procedure of 'First in first out' should be adopted for raw materials wherever necessary. Records of the receipt, testing and approval or rejection and use of raw material shall be maintained.

(b) **Packaging Materials :** All packaging materials such as bottles, jars, capsules etc. shall be stored properly. All containers and closure shall be adequately cleaned and dried before packing the products.

(c) **Finished Goods Stores :** The finished goods transferred from the production area after proper packaging shall be stored in the finished goods stores within an area marked "Quarantine". After the quality control laboratory and the experts have checked the correctness of finished goods with reference to its packing/labeling as well as the finished product quality as prescribed, then it will be moved to "Approved Finished Goods Stock" area. Only approved finished goods shall be dispatched as per marketing requirements. Distribution records shall be maintained as required.

If any Ayurvedic, Siddha and Unani drug needs special storage conditions, finished goods store shall provide necessary environmental requirements.

(d) **Working space :** The manufacturing area shall provide adequate space (manufacture and quality control) for orderly placement of equipment and material used in any of the operations for which these are employed so as to facilitate easy and safe working and to minimize or to eliminate any risk of mix-up between different drugs, raw materials and to prevent the possibility of cross contamination of one drug by another drug that is manufactured, stored or handled in the same premises.

(e) **Health Clothing, Sanitation and Hygiene of Workers :** All workers employed in the Factory shall be free from contagious diseases. The clothing of the workers shall consist of proper uniform suitable to the nature of work and the climate and shall be clean. The uniform shall also include cloth or synthetic covering for hands, feet and head wherever required. Adequate facilities for personal cleanliness such as clean towels, soap and scrubbing brushes shall be provided. Separate provision shall be made for lavatories to be used by men and women, and such lavatories shall be located at places separated from the processing rooms. Workers will also be provided facilities for changing their clothes and to keep their personal belongings.

(f) Medical Services : The Manufacturer shall also provide:-
  (i) Adequate facilities for first aid;
  (ii) Medical examination of workers at the time of employment and periodical check up thereafter by a physician once a year, with particular attention being devoted to freedom from infections. Records thereof shall be maintained.

(g) Equipment : For carrying out manufacturing depending on the size of operation and the nature of product manufactured, suitable equipment either manually operated or operated semi-automatically (Electrical or steam based) or fully automatic machinery shall be made available. These may include machines for use in the process of manufacture such as crushing, grinding, powdering, boiling, mashing, burning, roasting, filtering, drying filling, labeling and packing etc. To ensure ease in movement of workers and orderliness in operations a suitably adequate space will be ensured between two machines or rows of machines. These Equipments have to be properly installed and maintained with proper cleaning.

Proper standard operational procedures (SOPs) for cleaning, maintaining & performance of every machine should be laid down.

(h) Batch Manufacturing Records : The licencee shall maintain batch manufacturing record of each batch of Ayurvedic, Siddha and Unani drugs manufactured irrespective of the type of product manufactured (classical preparation or patent and proprietary medicines). Manufacturing records are required to provide an account of the list of raw materials and their quantities obtained from the store, tests conducted during the various stages of manufacture like taste, colour, physical characteristics and chemical tests as may be necessary or indicated in the approved books of Ayurveda, Siddha and Unani mentioned in the First Schedule of the Drugs and Cosmetic Act, 1940 (23 of 1940). These tests may include any in-house or pharmacopoeial test adopted by the manufacturer in the raw material or in the process material and in the finished product. These records shall be duly signed by Production and Quality Control Personnel respectively. Details of transfer of manufactured drug to the finished products store including dates and quantity of drugs transferred along with record of testing of the finished product, if any, and packaging, records shall be maintained. Only after the manufactured drugs have been verified and accepted quality shall be allowed to be cleared for sale.

It should be essential to maintain the record of date, manpower, machine and equipments used and to keep in process record of various shodhana, Bhavana, burning in fire and specific grindings in terms of internal use.

(i) **Distribution Records :** Records of sale and distribution of each batch of Ayurveda, Siddha and Unani Drugs shall be maintained in order to facilitate prompt and complete recall of the batch, if necessary.

(j) **Record of Market Complaints :** Manufacturers shall maintain a register to record all reports of market complaints received regarding the products sold in the market. The manufacturer shall enter all data received on such market complaints, investigations carried out by the manufacturers regarding the complaint as well as any corrective action initiated to prevent recurrence of such market complaints shall also be recorded. Once in a period of six months the manufacturer shall submit the record of such complaints to the licensing authority. The Register shall also be available for inspection during any inspection of the premises.

Reports of any adverse reaction resulting from the use of Ayurvedic, Siddha and Unani drugs shall also be maintained in a separate register by each manufacturer. The manufacturer shall investigate any of the adverse reaction to find if the same is due to any defect in the product, and whether such reactions are already reported in the literature or it is a new observation.

(k) **Quality Control :** Every licensee is required to provide facility for quality control section in his own premises or through Government approved testing laboratory. The test shall be as per the Ayurveda, Siddha and Unani pharmacopoeial standard. Where the tests are not available, the test should be performed according to the manufacturers specification or other information available. The quality control section shall verify all the raw materials, monitor in process, quality checks and control the quality of finished product being released to finished goods store/ware house. Preferably for such Quality control there will be a separate expert. The quality control section shall have the following facilities:

(i) There should be 150 sq. feet area for quality control section.
(ii) For identification of raw drugs, reference books and reference samples should be maintained.
(iii) Manufacturing record should be maintained for the various processes.
(iv) To verify the finished products, controlled samples of finished products of each batch will be kept for 3 years.
(v) To supervise and monitor adequacy of conditions under which raw materials, semi-finished products and finished products are stored.
(vi) Keep record in establishing shelf life and storage requirements for the drugs.

(vii) Manufacturers who are manufacturing patent proprietary Ayuveda Siddha, and Unani medicines shall provide their own specification and control references in respect of such formulated drugs.

(viii) The record of specific method and procedure of preparation, that is, "Bhavana", "Mardana" and "Puta" and the record of every process carried out by the manufacturer shall be maintained.

(ix) The standards for identity, purity and strength as given in respective pharmacopoeias of Ayurveda, Siddha and Unani systems of medicines published by Government of India shall be complied with.

(x) All raw materials will be monitored for fungal, bacterial contamination with a view to minimise such contamination.

(xi) Quality control section will have a minimum of :
  (a) one person with Degree qualification in Ayurveda/Siddha/Unani (A.S.U.) as per Schedule II of Indian Medicine Central Council Act, 1970 (84 of 1970) of a recognized university or Board.
  (b) Provided that Bachelor of Pharmacy, Pharmacognosy and Chemistry may be associated with the quality control section.

(II) Requirement for Sterile Product :
(A) Manufacturing Areas

For the manufacture of sterile Ayurvedic, Unani and Siddha drugs, separate enclosed areas specifically designed for the purpose shall be provided. These areas shall be provided with air locks for entry and shall be essentially dust free and ventilated with an air supply. For all areas where aseptic manufacture has to be carried out, air supply shall be filtered through bacteria retaining filters (HEPA Filters) and shall be at a pressure higher than in the adjacent areas. The filters shall be checked for performance on installation and periodically thereafter the record of checks shall be maintained. All the surfaces in sterile manufacturing areas shall be designed to facilitate cleaning and disinfection. For sterile manufacturing routine microbial counts of all Ayurvedic, Siddha and Unani drug manufacturing areas shall be carried out during operations. Results of such count shall be checked against established in-house standards and record maintained.

Access to manufacturing areas shall be restricted to minimum number of authorised personnel. Special procedure to be followed for entering and leaving the manufacturing areas shall be written down and displayed.

For the manufacturing of Ayurvedic, Siddha and Unani drug that can be sterilised in their final containers, the design of the areas shall preclude the possibility of the products intended for sterilisation being mixed with or taken to be products already sterilised. In case of terminally sterilised products, the design of the areas shall preclude the possibility of mix up between non-sterile and sterile products.

(B) Precautions against contamination and mix :

(i) Carrying out manufacturing operations in a separate block of adequately isolated building or operating in an isolated enclosure within the building.

(ii) Using appropriate pressure differential in the process area.

(iii) Providing a suitable exhaust system.

(iv) Designing laminar flow sterile air systems for sterile products.

(v) The germicidal efficiency of UV lamps shall be checked and recorded indicating the burning hours or checked using intensity.

(vi) Individual containers of liquids, and opthalmic solutions shall be examined against black-white background fitted with diffused light after filling to ensure freedom from contamination with foreign suspended matter.

(vii) Expert technical staff approved by the Licensing Authority shall check and compare actual yield against theoretical yield before final distribution of the batch.

All process controls as required under master formula including room temperature relative humidity, volume filled, leakage and clarity shall be checked and recorded.

PART – II

(A) LIST OF MACHINERY, EQUIPMENT AND MINIMUM MANUFACTURING PERMISES REQUIRED FOR THE MANUFACTURE OF VARIOUS CATEGORIES OF AYURVEDIC, SIDDHA SYSTEM OF MEDICINES

Sr. No	Category of Medicine	Minimum manufacturing space required	Machinery/ equipment recommended
		1200 Square feet covered area with separate cabins partitions for each activity. If Unani medicines are manufactured in same Premises an additional Area of 400 sq. feet will be required.	

1.	Anjana/Pisti	100 Sq. feet	Karel/mechnised/motorised, kharel, End runner/ Ball-Mill Sieves/Shifter
2.	Churna/Nasya Kwath Churn	200 Sq.feet	Grinder/ Disintegrator/ Manjan/Lepa Pulverisar/Powder mixer/ sieves/shifter
3.	Pills/Vatti/Gutika Matirai	100 Sq.feet	Ball Mill, Mass mixer powder mixer pill/vati cutting machine, stainless steel trays/ Containers for Storage. Driers/Mechanised chattee (for mixing guggul) where required.
4.	Tablets	100 Sq.feet	Ball Mill, Mass Mixer/Powdermixer Granulator drier, Tablet compressing Machine and sugar-Coating, foliching pay in case of sugar coated tablets, mechanisedchattee (for mixing of guggulu) where required.
5.	Kupi pakva/ Ksara/Parpati/ Lavana Bhasma Satva/Sindura Karpu/Uppu/Param	150 Sq.feet	Bhatti, Karahi/Stainless Steel Vessels/Patila Flask, Multani Matti/Plaster of Paris,Copper Rod, Earthen container, Gaj Put Bhatti, Muffle furnace (Electrically Operated) End/Edge Runner, Exhaust Fan, Wooden/S.S. Spatula.
6.	Kajal	100 Sq. feet	Earthen lamps for Collection of Kajal, Tipple Roller Mill, End Runner, Sieves, S.S. Patila, Filling/packing and manufacturing room should be provided with exhaust fan & ultra violet lamps
7.	Capsules	100 Sq.feet	Air Conditioner, De humidifier, hygrometer, Thermo-meter, Capsule filling Machine and chemical balance.
8.		100 Sq.feet	Tube filling Pasai machine, Crimping Medicine/Ointment Mixer, End Runner /Mill (Where required), S.S. Storage Container S.S. Patila
9.		100 Sq.feet	Bhatti section fitted with Exhaust fan and should be fly proof, Iron Kadahi/S.S. Patila and S.S. Storage container

10.	Panak Syrup/Pravahi	150 Sq.feet	Tinctum press, Kwath Manapaku exhaust fan fitted and fly proof, Bhatti section, Bottle washing Machine, filter press/Grav filter Liquid filling tank with tap/liquid filling machine, P.P. Copping Machine.
11	Asava/Aristha	200 Sq.feet	Same as mentioned above. Fermentation tanks containers and Distillation Plant where necessary, Filter Press
12	Sura	100 Sq.feet	Same as mentioned above plus Distillation plant and Transfer pump
13.	Ark Tinir	100 Sq.feet	Maceration tank, Distillation plant, Liquid filling tank with tap/Gravity filter/Filter press, Visual inspection box.
14.	Tail/Ghrit Ney	100 Sq.feet	Bhatti, Kadahi/S.S. Patila S.S. Storage Containers, Filtration equipment, filling tank with tap/Liquid filling machine.
15.	Aschyotan/ Netra Malham Panir	100 Sq.feet	Hot air oven electrically heated with thermostatic control, cettle gas or electrically heated with suitable mixing arrangements collation mill or ointment mill, tube filling equipment, mixing and storage tanks of stainless steel or of other suitable material sintered glass funnel, seitz filter or filter candle, liquid filling equipment, autoclave.
16		200 Sq.feet	Each manufacturing unit will have a separate area for Bhatti, furnaces, boilers, puta, etc. This will have proper ventilation, removal of smoke, prevention of flies, insects, dust etc. The furnace section could have tin roof.

(B) LIST OF MACHINERY, EQUIPMENT AND MINIMUM MANUFACTURING PERMISES REQUIRED FOR THE MANUFACTURE OF VARIOUS CATEGORIES OF UNANI SYSTEM OF MEDICINES.

Sr. No.	Category of Medicine	Minimum manufacturing space required equipment	Machinery/recommended
		1200 square feet covered area with separate abins, Partitions for each activity. If Ayurveda/Siddha, Medicines are also manufactured in same premises an additional areas of 400 square feet will be required	
1.	Itrifal Tiryao/majoon/Laooq/Jawarish Khamiras	100 Sq.feet	Grinder/Pulveriser, Sieves, powder mixer (if required), S.S. Patilas, Bhatti and Other accessories, Planter mixer for Khamiras
2.	Arq.	100 Sq.feet	Distillation Plant (garembic) S.S. Storage Tank, Boiling Vessel, Gravity filter, Bottle Filling machine, Bottle washing machine, Bottle drier.
3.	Habb (Pills)	100 Sq.feet	Grinder/Pulversier, Seives, Powder Mixer, (Where required) Trays.
4	Sufoof (Powder)	100 Sq. feet	Grinder/pulversier, Seives, Trays, Sccops, Powder mixer, (Where required).
5.	Raughan (oils) (Crushing & Boiling)	100 Sq.feet	Oil Expeller, S.S. Patilas Oil filter Bottle, filling Machine, Bottle drier, Bhatti
6.	Shiyaf, Surma, Kajal	100 Sq. feet	End runner, mixing S.S. Vessel
7.	Marham, Zimad, Ointment)	100 Sq.feet	Kharal (Bhatti, End runner, Grinder, Pulveriser, Tripple Roller Mill (if needed).

8.	Qurs(Tab)	100 Sq.feet	Grinder/Pulveriser, Sieves, Powder mixer (Where needed), Granulator, Drier, Tablet Compressing Machine, Die punches Trays, O.T. Apparatus, Balance with weights, Scoops, Sugar Coating Pan, polishing pan, Heater.
9.	Kushta	100 Sq.feet	Bhatti, Kharal, Sil Batta, Eartern pots.
10.	Murabba	100 Sq.feet	Aluminium Vessels 50-100 kgs. Capacity, Gendna, Bhatti.
11.	Capsule	100 Sq.feet	Pulveriser, Powder mixer (Where needed), capsule filling machine, Air Conditioner, Dehumidifier Balance with weights, storage-containers, ooo glass.
12.	Sharbat & Jushanda	100 Sq.feet	Tinctum Press, exhausted fan fitted, Bhatti section, Bottle Washing machine, Filter Press Gravity Filter, Liquid filling tank with tap/ liquid filling Machine, PP capping machine, air oven electrically heated with Thermostatic control, cettle.
13.	Qutoor Chasm and Marham(Eye drops Eye ointment	100 Sq.feet	Hot air oven electrically heated with Thermostatic control, Cettle.
14.	Each manufacturing unit will have a separate area for Bhatti, furnaces, boilers, putta, etc. This will have proper ventilation, removal of smoke, prevention of flies, insects, dust etc.	200 Sq.feet	

Ref. : Some of the contents are from the website of Department of Ayurveda, Yoga and Naturopathy, Unani, Siddha and Homoeopathy (AYUSH).

Chapter 14...

USEFUL INFORMATION

List of Drugs Banned for Marketing in India

The Government of India vide notifications published in the Gazette of India vide G.S.R. No. 578 (E) dated 23/07/1983 and subsequent amendments, made under Section 26 A of Drugs and Cosmetics Act, 1940 has prohibited the manufacture, sale and distribution of the following categories of fixed dose combinations which do not have any therapeutic justification or are likely to involve risk to human beings :

G.S.R. No. 578 (E) dt 23-07-1983

1. Amidopyrine.
2. Fixed dose combinations of vitamins with anti-inflammatory agents and tranquilizers.
3. Fixed dose combinations of Atropine and Analgesic and Antipyretics.
4. Fixed dose combinations of Strychnine and Caffeine in tonics.
5. Fixed dose combinations of Yohimbine and Strychnine with Testosterone and Vitamins.
6. Fixed dose combinations of Iron with Strychnine, Arsenic and Yohimbine.
7. Fixed dose combinations of Sodium Bromide/chloral hydrate with other drugs.
8. Phenacetin.
9. Fixed dose combinations of antihistaminic with anti-diarrhoeals.
10. Fixed dose combinations of Penicillin with Sulphonamides.
11. Fixed dose combinations of Vitamins with Analgesics.
12. Fixed dose combinations of Tetracycline with Vitamin C.

G.S.R. No. 793 (E) dt 13-12-1995

13. Fixed dose combinations of Hydroxyquinoline group of drugs with any other drug except for preparations meant for external use only.

G.S.R. No. 1057 (E) dt 03-11-1988

14. Fixed dose combinations of Corticosteroids with any other drug for internal use.
15. Fixed dose combinations of Chloramphenicol with any other drug for internal use.

G.S.R. No. 304 (E) dt 07-06-1991

16. Fixed dose combinations of crude Ergot preparation except those containing Ergotamine, Caffeine, analgesics, antihistamines for the treatment of migraine, headache.
17. Fixed dose combinations of Vitamins with Anti TB drugs except combination of Isoniazid with Pyridoxine Hydrochloride (Vitamin B_6).
18. Penicillin skin/eye Ointment.
19. Tetracycline Liquid Oral preparations.
20. Nialamide.
21. Practolol.
22. Methapyrilene, its salts.

G.S.R. No. 49 (E) dt 31-01-1984

23. Methaqualone.

G.S.R. No. 322 (E) dt 03-05-1984

24. Oxytetracycline Liquid Oral preparations.
25. Demeclocycline Liquid Oral preparations.

G.S.R. No. 863 (E) dt 22-11-1985

26. Combination of anabolic Steroids with other drugs.
27. Fixed dose combination of Oestrogen and Progestin (other than oral contraceptives) containing per tablet Oestrogen content of more than 50 mcg (equivalent to Ethinyl Estradiol) and Progestin content of more than 3 mg (equivalent to Norethisterone Acetate) and all fixed dose combination injectable preparations containing synthetic Oestrogen and Progesterone. (Subs. By Noti. No. 743 (E) dt 10-08-1989)

G.S.R. No. 999 (E) dt 26-12-1990

28. Fixed dose combinations of Sedatives/ hypnotics/anxiolytics with analgesics-antipyretics.
29. Fixed dose combinations of Pyrazinamide, other anti-tubercular drugs except combination of Pyrazinamide with Rifampicin and INH per recommended daily dose given below:

Drugs	Minimum	Maximum
Rifampicin	450 mg	600 mg
INH	300 mg	400 mg
Pyrazinamide	1000 mg	1500 mg

30. Fixed dose combination of Histamine H-2 receptor antagonists with antacids except for those combinations approved by Drugs Controller, India.

31. The patent and proprietary medicines of fixed dose combinations of essential oils with alcohol having percentage higher than 20% proof except preparations given in the Indian Pharmacopoeia.
32. All Pharmaceutical preparations containing chloroform exceeding 0.5% w/w or v/v whichever is appropriate.

G.S.R. No. 69 (E) dt 11-02-1991
33. Fixed dose combination of Ethambutol with INH other than the following: INH Ethambutol 200 mg. 600 mg., 300 mg. 800 mg.
34. Fixed dose combination containing more than one antihistamine.
35. Fixed dose combination of anthelmintic with cathartic/purgative except for piperazine.
36. Fixed dose combination of Salbutamol or any other bronchodilator with centrally acting anti-tussive and/or antihistamine.
37. Fixed dose combination of laxatives and/or anti-spasmodic drugs in enzyme preparations.
38. Fixed dose combination of Metoclopramide with systemically absorbed drugs except fixed dose combination of metoclopramide with aspirin/paracetamol.

G.S.R. No. 395 (E) dt 19-05-1999
39. Fixed dose combination of centrally acting, antitussive with antihistamine, having atropine like activity in expectorants.
40. Preparations claiming to combat cough associated with asthma containing centrally acting antitussive and/ or an antihistamine.
41. Liquid oral tonic preparations containing glycerophosphates and/or other phosphates and / or central nervous system stimulant and such preparations containing alcohol more than 20% proof.
42. Fixed dose combination containing Pectin and/or Kaolin with any drug which is systemically absorbed from GI tract except for combination of Pectin and/or Kaolin with drugs not systemically absorbed.

G.S.R. No. 304 (E) dt 07-06-1991
43. Chloral Hydrate as a drug.

G.S.R. No. 612 (E) dt 09-08-1994
44. Dovers Powder I.P.
45. Dover's Powder Tablets I.P.

G.S.R. No. 731 (E) dt 30-09-1994
46. Antidiarrhoeal formulations containing Kaolin or Pectin or Attapulgite or Activated Charcoal.

47. Antidiarrhoeal formulations containing Phthalyl Sulphathiazole or Sulphaguanidine or Succinyl Sulphathiazole.
48. Antidiarrhoeal formulations containing Neomycin or Streptomycin or Dihydrostreptomycin including their respective salts or esters.
49. Liquid Oral antidiarrhoeals or any other dosage form for pediatric use containing Diphenoxylate or Atropine or Belladona including their salts or esters or metabolites Hyoscyamine or their extracts or their alkaloids.
50. Liquid Oral antidiarrhoeals or any other dosage form for pediatric use containing halogenated hydroxyquinolines.
51. Fixed dose combination of antidiarrhoeals with electrolytes.

G.S.R. No. 57 (E) dt 07-02-1995

52. Patent and proprietary oral rehydration salts other than those conforming to the following parameters :
    (a) Patent and proprietary oral rehydration salts on reconstitution to one litre shall contain : Sodium - 50 to 90 millimoles. Total osmolarity : 240 - 290 milli osmoles. Dextrose : Sodium molar ratio should not less than 1:1 and not more than 3:1.
    (b) Patent and proprietary cereal based oral rehydration salts on reconstitution to one litre shall contain :- Total osmolarity - Not more than 2900 milli osmoles. Precooked rice- not less than 50 gm and not more than 80 gm as total replacement of Dextrose.
    (c) Patent and proprietary Oral Rehydration Salts (ORS) may contain aminoacids in addition to Oral Rehydration Salt conforming to the parameters specified above and labeled with the indication for "Adult Choleratic Diarrhoea" only.
    (d) Patent and Proprietary oral rehydration salts shall not contain Mono or Polysaccharides or saccharin sweetening agent.

G.S.R. No. 633 (E) dt 30-09-1995, GSR No. 123 (E) dt 11-03-1996 and GSR No. 230 (E) dt 04-06-1996

53. Fixed dose combination of Oxyphenbutazone or Phenylbutazone with any other drug.

G.S.R. No. 405 (E) dt 03-06-1996

54. Fixed dose combination of Analgin with any other drug.

    Clarification : Fixed dose combination of Analgin with any drug other than antispasmodics were banned by the Government of India vide G.S.R. No. 633(E), dated 13.09.1995. However, the Drug Action Forum contended before the Supreme Court that the preparations of Analgin and antispasmodics should also be banned. Dr. J.S. Bajaj, being directed by the court, submitted his report supporting these contentions.

On 17th Dec. 1996, a learned solicitor submitted that the Central Government has decided that all State/U.T. Drug Licensing Authorities will be given directions by the Government under Section 33-P of the Drugs and Cosmetics Act, to suspend manufacturing licenses of all fixed dose formulations of Analgin including Analgin with Antispasmodics till further notice. Accordingly, the Government of India, under letter dated 17th Dec. 1996, issued such directives. In view of the above directives, the manufacture, sale and distribution of fixed dose combinations of Analgin and antispasmodics is prohibited.

55. Fixed dose combination of dextropropoxyphene with any other drug other than anti-spasmodics and/or non-steriodal anti-inflammatory drugs (NSAIDS).
56. Fixed dose combination of a drug, standards of which are prescribed in the Second Schedule to the said Act with an Ayurvedic, Siddha or Unani drug.

G.S.R. No. 93 (E) dt 25-02-1997

57. Parenteral preparations containing fixed dose combination of streptomycin with penicillins with effect from 01-01-1998.

G.S.R. No. 499 (E) dt 14-08-1998

58. Mepacrine Hydrochloride (Quinacrine and its salts) in any dosage form for use for female sterilization or contraception.
59. Fenfluramine and Dexfenfluramine.
60. Fixed dose combination of haemoglobin in any form (natural or synthetic).
61. Fixed dose combination of Pancreatin and Pancrelipase containing amylase, protease, and lipase with any other enzyme.

(Both 59 & 60 added by G.S.R. 590 (E) dt. 17-8-1999.

Sr. No. 59 & 60 omitted by G.S.R. 704(E) dt. 20-10-1999.)

G.S.R. No. 702 (E) dt 20-10-1999

62. Fixed dose combination of Vitamin B_1, Vitamin B_6 and Vitamin B_{12} for human use with effect from 01-01-2001

G.S.R. No. 814 (E) dt 16-12-1999 (w.e.f. 01-09-2000)

63. Fixed dose combination of haemoglobin in any form (natural or synthetic).
64. Fixed dose combination of Pancreatin and Pancrelipase containing amylase, protease and lipase with any other enzyme.

G.S.R. No. 169 (E) dt 12-03-2001

65. Fixed dose combination of Diazepam and Diphenhydramine Hydrochloride.

G.S.R. No. 170 (E) dt 12-03-2001 (with effect from 01-01-2002)

66. Fixed dose combination of Nitrofurantoin and trimethoprim.
67. Fixed dose combination of Phenobarbitone with any anti-asthmatic drug.
68. Fixed dose combination of Phenobarbitone with Hyoscin and/or Hyoscyamine.
69. Fixed dose combination of Phenobarbitone with Ergotamine and/or Belladona.
70. Fixed dose combination of Haloperidol with any anti-cholinergic agent including Propantheline Bromide.
71. Fixed dose combination of Nalidixic Acid with any anti-amoebic including Metronidazole.
72. Fixed dose combination of Loperamide Hydrochloride with Furazolidone.
73. Fixed dose combination of Cyproheptadine with Lysine or Peptone.

G.S.R 603 (E) dt 13-08-2001 (with effect from 01-09-2002)

74. Fixed dose combination of Metoclopramide with other drugs except combination of Metoclopramide with Aspirin/Paracetamol with effect from 1st September, 2002.

G.S.R. No. 732 (E) dt 29-10.2002, Amended vide GSR 191(E) dt 05-03-2003 (with effect from 01-04-2003)

75. Astemizole Terfinadine

G.S.R 100 (E) dt 11-02-2003 (with effect from 11-02-2003)

76. Fixed dose combination of Rifampicin, Isoniazid and Pyrazinamide, except those which provide daily adult dose given below :

Drugs	Minimum	Maximum
Rifampicin	450 mg	600 mg
Isoniazid	300 mg	400 mg
Pyrazinamide	1000 mg	1500 mg

G.S.R. No. 780 (E) dt 01-10-2003 (with effect from 01-10-2003)

77. Phenformin for human use.

G.S.R. No. 810 (E) dt 13-12-2004 (with effect from 13-12-2004)

78. Rofecoxib and its formulations for human use.

G.S.R. No. 510 (E) dt 25-7-2005 (with effect from 25-7-2005)

79. Valdecoxib and its formulations for human use.

G.S.R. No. 499 (E) dt 4/5-7-2008 (with effect from 4/5-7-2008)

80. Diclofenac and its formulations for animal use.

(Ref. : website www.drugcontrol.org)

DRUGS AND COSMETICS (AMENDMENT) RULES, 2005

MINISTRY OF HEALTH AND FAMILY WELFARE

NOTIFICATION

New Delhi, the 24th February, 2005

G.S.R. 105(E) : The following draft of certain rules further to amend the Drugs and Cosmetics Rules, 1945, which the Central Government proposes to make, after consultation with the Drugs Technical Advisory Board, in exercise of the powers conferred by Section 12 and Section 33 of the Drugs and Cosmetics Act, 1940 (23 of 1940), is hereby published as required by the said sections for the information of all persons likely to be affected thereby and notice is hereby given that the said draft rules will be taken into consideration after the expiry of a period of forty-five days from the date on which the copies of the Official Gazette in which this notification is published, are made available to the public.

Any objection or suggestions which may be received from any person with respect to the said draft rules before the expiry of the period as specified above will be taken into consideration by the Central Government which may be addressed to the Secretary (Health), Ministry of Health and Family Welfare, Government of India, Nirman Bhawan, New Delhi-110 011.

DRAFT RULES

1. (a) These rules may be called the **Drugs and Cosmetics (Amendment) Rules, 2005.**

    (b) They shall come into force on the date of their publication in the Official Gazette.

2. In the Drugs and Cosmetics Rules, 1945, for Schedule H, the following Schedule shall be substituted, namely:-

SCHEDULE H

(See Rules 65 and 97)
(Prescription Drugs)

1. Abacavir
2. Abciximab
3. Acamprosate Calcium
4. Acebutol Hydrochloride
5. Aclarubicin Injection
6. Alclometasone Dipropionate
7. Actilyse
8. Acyclovir
9. Adenosine
10. Adrenocorticotrophic Hormone
11. Alendronate Sodium
12. Allopurinol
13. Alphachymotrypsin
14. Alprazolam
15. Alprostadil
16. Amantadine Hydrochloride
17. Amifostine
18. Amikacin
19. Amiloride Hydrochloride
20. Amineptine
21. Aminoglutethimide
22. Aminosalicylic acid
23. Amiodarone Hydrochloride
24. Amitriptyline its salts
25. Amlodipine Besylate
26. Amoscanate
27. Amoxapine
28. Amrinone Lactate
29. Analgin
30. Androgenic, Anabolic, Oestrogenic & Progestational Substances
31. Antibiotics
32. Apraclonidine
33. Aprotinin
34. Organic Compound of Arsenic for Injection
35. Arteether
36. Artemether

37. Artesunate
38. Articaine Hydrochloride
39. Atenolol
40. Atracurium Besylate Injection
41. Atorvastatin
42. Auranofin
43. Azathioprine
44. Aztreonam
45. Bacampicillin
46. Baclofen
47. Balsalazide
48. Bambuterol
49. Barbituric Acid, its Salts / Derivatives of Barbituric Acid
50. Basiliximab
51. Benazepril Hydrochloride
52. Benidipine Hydrochloride
53. Benserazide Hydrochloride
54. Betahistine Dihydrochloride
55. Bethanidine Sulphate
56. Bezafibrate
57. Bicalutamide
58. Biclotymol
59. Bifonazole
60. Bimatoprost
61. Biperiden Hydrochloride
62. Biphenyl Acetic Acid
63. Bitoscanate
64. Bleomycin Oil Suspension
65. Primonidine Tartrate
66. Bromhexine Hydrochloride
67. Bromocriptine Mesylate
68. Budesonide
69. Bulaquine
70. Bupivacaine Hydrochloride
71. Bupropion
72. Buspirone
73. Butenafine Hydrochloride
74. Butorphanol Tartrate
75. Cabergoline
76. Calcium Dobesilate
77. Candesartan
78. Capecitabine
79. Captopril

80. Carbidopa
81. Carbocisteine
82. Carboplatin Injection
83. Carboquone
84. Carisoprodol
85. L-Carnitine
86. Carteolol Hydrochloride
87. Carvedilol
88. Cefadroxyl
89. Cefatoxime Sodium
90. Cefazolin Sodium
91. Cefdinir
92. Cefepime Hydrochloride
93. Cefetamet Pivoxil
94. Cefpirome
95. Cefpodoxime Poxetil
96. Ceftazidime Pentahydrate
97. Ceftizoxime Sodium Sterile
98. Cefuroxime
99. Celecoxib
100. Centchroman
101. Centbutindole
102. Centpropazine
103. Chlordiazepoxide its Salts
104. Chlormezanone
105. Chlopromazine its Salts
106. Chlorzoxazone
107. Ciclopirox Olamine
108. Cimetidine
109. Cinnarizine
110. Ciprofloxacin Hydrochloride Monohydrate/Lactate
111. Citalopram Hydrobromide
112. Clarithromycin
113. Clavulanic Acid
114. Clidinium Bromide
115. Clindamycin

116. Clobazam
117. Clobetasol Propenate
118. Clobetasone 17-Butyrate
119. Clofazimine
120. Clofibrate
121. Clonazepam
122. Clonidine Hydrochloride
123. Clopamide
124. Clopidogrel Bisulphate
125. Clostebol Acetate
126. Clotrimazole
127. Clozapine
128. Codeine, its Salts & Derivatives
129. Colchicine
130. Corticosteroids, their Esters, their Derivatives & their Dosage Forms
131. Cotrimoxazole
132. Cyclandelate
133. Cyclosporin Oral Solution
134. Daclizumab
135. Danazol
136. Dapsone, its Salts and Derivatives
137. Desloratadine
138. Desogestrole
139. Dexrazoxane
140. Dextranomer
141. Dextropropoxyphene, its Salts
142. Diazapam
143. Diazoxide
144. Diclofenac Sodium / Potassium/ Acid
145. Didanosine
146. Digoxine
147. Dilazep Hydrochloride
148. Diltiazem
149. Dinoprostone
150. Diphenoxylate, its Salts
151. Dipivefrin Hydrochloride

152. Di-Sodium Pamidronate
153. Disopyramide
154. Docetaxel
155. Domperidone
156. Donepezil Hydrochloride
157. Dopamine Hydrochloride
158. Dothiepin Hydrochloride
159. Doxapram Hydrochloride
160. Doxazosin Mesylate
161. Doxepin Hydrochloride
162. Drotrecogin-Alpha
163. Ebastine
164. Econozole
165. Efavirenz
166. Enalapril Meleate
167. Enfenamic Acid
168. Epinephrine, its Salts
169. Epirubicine Injection
170. Eptifibatide
171. Ergot, Alkaloids of, Whether Hydrogenated or not, their Homologues, Salts
172. Esomeprazole
173. Estradiol Succinate
174. Estramustine Phosphate Capsule
175. Etanercept
176. Ethacridine Lactate
177. Ethambutol Hydrochloride
178. Ethamsylate
179. Ethinyloestradiol
180. Ethionamide
181. Etidronate Disodium
182. Etodolac
183. Etomidate
184. Etoposide Capsule and Injection
185. Exemestane
186. Famciclovir
187. Famotidine

188. Fenofibrate
189. Fexofenadine
190. Finasteride
191. Flavoxate Hydrochloride
192. Fludarabine
193. Flufenamic Acids, its Salts/esters
194. Flunarizine Hydrochloride
195. Fluoxetine Hydrochloride
196. Flupenthixol
197. Fluphenazine Enanthate and Decanoate
198. Flurazepam
199. Flurbiprofen
200. Flutamide
201. Fluticasone Propionate
202. Fluvoxamine Maleate
203. Formestane
204. Fosinopril Sodium
205. Fosphenytoin Sodium
206. Fotemustine
207. Gabapentin
208. Calanthamine Hydrobromide
209. Gallamine, its Salts, its Quaternary Compound
210. Gancyclovir
211. Ganirelix
212. Gatifloxacin
213. Gemcitabine
214. Gemfibrozil
215. Gemtuzumab
216. Genodeoxycholic Acid
217. Gliclazide
218. Glimepiride
219. Glucagon
220. Glycopyrrolate
221. Glydiazinamide
222. Gosereline Acetate
223. Granisetron

224. Guanethidine
225. Gugulipid
226. Halogenated Hydroxyquinolines
227. Haloperidol
228. Heparin
229. Hepatitis B. Vaccine
230. Hyaluronidase
231. Hydrocorisone 17-Butyrate
232. Hydrotalcite
233. Hydroxyzine, its Salts
234. Ibuprofen
235. Idebenone
236. Iindapamide
237. Imipramine, its Salts
238. Indinavir Sulphate
239. Indomethacin, its Salts
240. Insulin Human
241. Interferon Injection
242. Intravenous Fat Emulsion
243. Iobitridol
244. Iohexol Injection
245. Iopamidol Injection
246. Iomeprol
247. Iopromide
248. Irbesartan
249. Irinotecan Hydrochloride
250. Iron Preparation for Parenteral use
251. Isepamicine
252. Isocarboxside
253. Isoflurane
254. Isonicotnic Acid Hydrazine and other-Hydragine Derivatives of Isonicotinic Acid
255. Isosorbide Dinitrate / Mononitrate
256. Isotretinoin
257. Isoxsuprinc
258. Itopride
259. Ketamine Hydrochloride

260. Ketoconazole Acetate
261. Ketoprofen
262. Ketorolac Tromethamine
263. Labetalol Hydrochloride
264. Lacidipine
265. Lamivudine
266. Lamotrigine
267. Latanoprost
268. Lefunomide
269. Lercanidipine Hydrochloride
270. Letrozole
271. Leuprolide Acetate
272. Levarterenol, its Salts
273. Levobunolol
274. Levocetirizine
275. Levodopa
276. Levofloxacin
277. Levovist
278. Lidoflazine
279. Linezolid
280. Lithium Carbonate
281. Lofepramine Decanoate
282. Loperamide
283. Lorazepam
284. Losartan Potassium
285. Loteprednol
286. Lovastatin
287. Loxapine
288. Mebendazole
289. Mebeverine Hydrochloride
290. Medroxy Progesterone Acetate Tablets
291. Mefenamic Acid, its Salts, its Esters, their Salts
292. Mefloquine Hydrochloride
293. Megestrol Acetate
294. Meglumine Iocarmate
295. Melagenina Lotion

296. Melitracen Hydrochloride
297. Meloxicam
298. Mephenesin, its Esters
299. Mephentermine
300. Meropenam
301. Mesterolone
302. Metaxalone
303. Methicillin Sodium
304. Methocarbamol
305. Metoclopramide
306. Metoprolol Tartrate
307. Metrizamide
308. Metronidazole
309. Mexiletine Hydrochloride
310. Mianserin Hydrochloride
311. Miconazole
312. Midazolam
313. Mifepristone
314. Milrinone Lactate
315. Miltefosine
316. Minocycline
317. Minoxidil
318. Mirtazapine
319. Misoprostol
320. Mitoxantrone Hydrochloride
321. Mizolastine
322. Moclobemide
323. Mometasone Furoate
324. Montelukast Sodium
325. Morphazinamide Hydrochloride
326. Mosapride
327. Moxifloxacin
328. Mycophenolate Mofetil
329. Nadifloxacin
330. Nadolol
331. Nafareline Acetate

332. Nalidixic Acid
333. Naproxen
334. Narcotic Drugs Listing in Narcotic Drugs & Psychotropic Substances Act, 1985
335. Natamycin
336. Nateglinide
337. N-Butyl-2-Cyanoacrylate
338. Nebivolol
339. Nebumetone
340. Nelfinavir Mesilate
341. Netilmicine Sulphate
342. Nevirapine
343. Nicergoline
344. Nicorandil
345. Nifedipine
346. Nimesulide
347. Nimustine Hydrochloride
348. Nitrazepam
349. Nitroglycerin Injection
350. Norethisterone Enanthate Injection
351. Norfloxacin
352. Octylonium Bromide
353. Ofloxacin
354. Olanzapine
355. Ornidazole
356. Orphenadrine, its Salts
357. Orthoclone Sterile
358. Oxazepam
359. Oxazolidine, its Salts
360. Oxcarbazepine
361. Oxethazaine Hydrochloride
362. Oxiconazole
363. Oxolinic Acid
364. Oxprenolol Hydrochloride
365. Oxybutynin Chloride
366. Oxyfedrine
367. Oxymetazoline

368. Oxyphenbutazone
369. Oxytocin
370. Ozothine
371. Pancuronium Bromide
372. Pantoprazole
373. Para-Amino Benzene Sulphonamide, its Salts & Derivatives
374. Para-Amino Salicylic Acid, its Salts, its Derivatives
375. Parecoxib
376. Paroxetine Hydrochloride
377. D-penicillamine
378. Pentazocine
379. Pentoxifylline
380. Pepleomycin Injection
381. Phenelzine, its Salts
382. Phenobarbital
383. Phenothiazine, Derivatives of and Salts of its Derivatives
384. Phenylbutazine, its Salts
385. Pimozide
386. Pindolol
387. Pioglitazone Hydrochloride
388. Piracetam
389. Piroxicam
390. Pituitory Gland, Active Principles of, not otherwise specified in this Schedule and their Salts
391. Polidocanol Injection
392. Polyestradiol Phosphate Injection
393. Poractant Alfa
394. Praziquantel
395. Prednimustine Tablets
396. Prednisolone Stearoylglycolate
397. Prenoxdiazine Hydrochloride
398. Promazine Hydrochloride
399. Promegestone
400. Propafenon Hydrochloride
401. Propanolol Hydrochloride
402. Propofol Injection

403. Protristyline Hydrochloride
404. Pyrazinamide
405. Pryvinium, its Salts
406. Quetiapine Fumerate
407. Quinapril
408. Quinidine Sulphate
409. Rabeprazole
410. Racecadotril
411. Raloxifene Hydrochloride
412. Ranitidine
413. Rauwolfia, Alkaloids of, their Salts, Derivatives of the Alkaloids or Rauwolfia
414. Reboxetine
415. Repaglinide
416. Reproterol Hydrochloride
417. Rilmenidine
418. Riluzole
419. Risperidone
420. Ritonavir
421. Ritodrine Hydrochloride
422. Rituximab
423. Rivastigmine
424. Rocuronium Bromide
425. Ropinirole
426. Rosoxacin
427. Rosiglitazone Maleate
428. Salbutamol Sulphate
429. Salicyl-Azo-Sulphapyridine
430. Salmon Calcitonin
431. Saquinavir
432. Satranidazole
433. Septopal Beads & Chains
434. Serratiopeptidase
435. Sertraline Hydrochloride
436. Sibutramine Hydrochloride
437. Sildenafil Citrate
438. Simvastatin

439. Sirolimus
440. Sisomicin Sulphate
441. S-Neominophagen-C Injection
442. Sodium Picosulphate
443. Sodium Cromoglycate
444. Sodium Hyaluronate Solution
445. Sodium Valproate
446. Sodium and Maglumine Iothalamates
447. Somatostatin
448. Somatotropin
449. Sotalol
450. Sparfloxacin
451. Spectinomycin Hydrochloride
452. Spironolactone
453. Stavudine
454. Sucralfate
455. Sulphadoxine
456. Sulphamethoxine
457. Sulphamethoxypyridazine
458. Sulphaphenazole
459. Sulpiride
460. Sulprostone Hydrochloride
461. Sumatriptan
462. Tacrine Hydrochloride
463. Tamsulosin Hydrochloride
464. Trapidil
465. Tegaserod Maleate
466. Teicoplanin
467. Telmisartan
468. Temozolamide
469. Terazosin
470. Terbutaline Sulphate
471. Terfenadine
472. Terizidone
473. Terlipressin
474. Testosterone Undecoanoate
475. Teratolol Hydrochloride
476. Thalidomide
477. Thiacetazone
478. Thiocolchicoside
479. Thiopropazate, its Salts

480. Thymogene
481. Thymosin-Alpha 1 Injection
482. Tiaprofenic Acid
483. Tibolone
484. Timolol Maleate
485. Tinidazole
486. Tabramycin
487. Tolfenamic Acid
488. Topiramate
489. Topotecan Hydrochloride
490. Tranexamic Acid
491. Tranycypromine, its Salts
492. Trazodone
493. Tretinoin
494. Trifluperazine
495. Trifluperidol Hydrochloride
496. Triflusal
497. Trimetazidine Dihydrochloride
498. Trimipramine
499. Tripotassium Dicitrate Bismuthate
500. Tromantadine Hydrochloride
501. Urokinase
502. Valdecoxib
503. Valsartan
504. Vasopressin
505. Vecuronium Bromide Injection
506. Venlafaxine
507. Verapamil Hydrochloride
508. Verteporfin
509. Vindesine Sulphate
510. Vinorelbine Tatrate
511. Xipamide
512. Zidovudine Hydrochloride
513. Ziprasidone Hydrochloride
514. Zoledronic Acid
515. Zolpidem
516. Zopiclone
517. Zuclopenthixol

Note :
1. Preparations exempted under proviso to para 2 of Note to Schedule X shall also be covered by this Schedule.

2. Preparations containing the above substances excluding those intended for topical or external use (except ophthalmic and ear/nose preparations containing antibiotics and/or steroids) are also covered by this Schedule. This inclusion of a substance in this Schedule dose not imply or convey that the substance is exempted from the provisions of "Rule 122A/122B".

[No. X-11014/3/2004-DMS & PFA]

RITA TEOTIA, Jt. Secy.

FORM 19

[See Rule 59(2)]

Application for grant or renewal of a licence to sell, stock, exhibit or offer for sale, or distribute drugs other than those specified in Schedule X

1. I/We.. hereby apply for licence to sale by wholesale/retail drugs specified in Schedule C and C(1) and excluding those Specified in Schedule X* and / or drugs other than those specified in Schedule C, C(1) and X to the Drugs and Cosmetics Rules, 1945* and also to operate a pharmacy on the premises situated at ....

2. $ The sale and dispensing of drugs will be made under the personal supervision of the registered pharmacist / competent person namely :

    ....(Name) .... (Qualification)

    ....(Name) .... (Qualification)

3. Categories of drugs to be sold.

4. + Particulars for special storage accommodation.

5. A fee of rupees ....has been credited to the Government under the head of account ....

    ....

Date : ....

Signature : ....

* Delete whichever is not applicable.

$ To be deleted if drugs will be sold only by wholesale.

+ Required only if products requiring special storage are to be sold.

FORM 19-A

[See Rule 59(2)]

Application for grant or renewal of a restricted licence to sell, stock or exhibit or offer for sale, or distribute drugs by retail by dealers who do not engage the service of a qualified person

1. I/We.......................... of .... hereby apply for a licence to sell by retail.

   (i) Drugs other than those specified in Schedules C, C(1) and X or (ii) Drugs specified in Schedule C (1), on the premises situated at .... as vender in the area ....

2. Sales shall be restricted to such drugs as can be sold without the supervision of a registered pharmacist under the Drugs and Cosmetics Rules.

3. Names or classes of drugs proposed to be sold ....

*4. Particulars of the storage accommodation for the storage of Schedule C (1) drugs on the premises referred to above.

+5. The drugs for sale will be purchased from the following dealers and such other dealers as may be endorsed on the licence by the licensing authority from time to time.

   Name of the dealers ....

   Licence No. ....

6. A fee of rupees.. has been credited to Government under the Head of account ....

Date : ....

Signature : ....

* Delete if not required.

+ Applies only to an itinerant vendor.

FORM 19-AA
[See Rule 62-C]

Application for grant or renewal of a licence to sell, stock or exhibit or offer for sale by wholesale or distribute drugs from a motor vehicle

1. I/We...of............................ hereby apply for licence to sell, stock or exhibit or offer for sale by wholesale or distribute drugs specified in Schedule C and C (1) and/ or drugs other than those specified in Schedule C and C (1) from the vehicle bearing registration No. .... assigned under Motor Vehicle Act, 1939.
2. Categories of drugs to be sold/distributed.
   ....
   ....
   ....
3. A fee of rupees .... has been credited to Government under the head of account ....
*4. Particulars of the storage accommodation for the storage of drugs specified in Schedule C and C (1) on the vehicle referred to above.

Date : ....
Signature : ....
* Delete if not required.

FORM 19-B
[See Rule 67-A]

Application for licence to sell, stock or exhibit or offer for sale, or distribute Homoeopathic Medicines

1. I/We .... of .... hereby apply for a licence to sell by *wholesale / *retail Homoeopathic Medicine on the premises situated at ....
+2. The sale and dispensing of Homoeopathic medicines shall be made under the personal supervision of the following competent person in-charge.
   Name ....
   Name ....
3. A fee of rupees .... has been credited to the Government under the head of account ....

Date : ....
Signature : ....
*Delete whichever is not applicable.
+To be deleted if Homoeopathic medicine will be sold by wholesale.

FORM 19-C
[See Rule 59(2)]

Application for grant or renewal of a licence to sell, stock, exhibit or offer for sale, or distribute drugs specified in Schedule X

1. I/We .... of .... hereby apply for a licence to sell by *wholesale/retail drugs specified in schedule X to the Drugs and Cosmetic Rule, 1945. We operate a pharmacy on the premises, situated at ....

2. +The sale and dispensing of drugs will be made under the personal supervision of the qualified person mentioned below :
   .... (Name) .... (Qualification)
   .... (Name) .... (Qualification)

3. Name of the drugs to be sold.
4. ++Particulars of storage accommodation.
5. A fee of rupees............has been credited to Government account under the head of account...........................

Date : ....
Signature : ....

*Delete whichever is not applicable.
+To be deleted if drugs will be sold only on wholesale.
++Required only if products requiring special storage are to be sold.

FORM- 24
[See Rule 69]

Application for the grant of or renewal of a licence to manufacture for sale or for distribution of drugs other than those specified in [Schedule C, C (1) and X]

1. I/We .... of .... hereby apply for the grant/renewal of a licence to manufacture on the premises situated at............ .... the following drugs being drugs other than those specified in Schedules C, C(1) and X to the Drugs and Cosmetics Rules, 1945.

2. Names of Drugs categorized according to Schedule M ....
3. Names, qualifications and experience of technical staff employed for manufacture and testing.

   ....
   ....
   ....
   ....
   ....

4. A fee of rupees .... has been credited to Government under the head of account ....

Date : ....
Signature : ....
Note : The application should be accompanied by a plan of the premises.

FORM 24-A

[See Rule 69-A]

Application for grant or renewal of a loan licence to manufacture for sale or for distribution of drugs other than those specified in Schedule C, C (1) and X

1. I/We* .... of! ....hereby apply for the grant/ renewal of a loan licence to manufacture on the premises situated at .... C/O# .... the under mentioned drugs, other than those specified in Schedules C, C(1) and X to the Drugs and Cosmetics Rules, 1945. Names of drugs (each substance to be separately specified).

2. The names, qualifications and experience of the expert staff actually connected with the manufacture and testing of the specified products in the manufacturing premises.

3. I/We enclose

    (a) A true copy of a letter from me/us to the manufacturing concern whose manufacturing capacity is intended to be utilized by me/us.

    (b) A true copy of a letter from the manufacturing concern that they agree to lend the services of their expert staff, equipment and premises for the manufacture of each item required by me/us and that they will analyse every batch of finished product and maintain the registers of raw materials, finished products and reports of analysis separately in this behalf.

    (c) Specimens of labels, cartons of the products proposed to be manufactured.

4. A fee of rupees .... has been credited to Government under the head of account ....

Date : ....

Signature : ....

*Enter here the name of proprietor, partners or Managing Director as the case may be.

!Enter here the name of the applicant firm and the address or the principal place of business.

#Enter here the name and address of the manufacturing concern where the manufacture will be actually carried out and also the licence number under which the latter operates.

FORM 24-B
[See Rule 69]

Application for grant or renewal of a licence to repack for sale or distribution of drugs, being drugs other than those specified in Schedule C and C (1) excluding those specified in Schedule X

1. I/We .... of .... hereby apply for grant/renewal of a licence to repack the following drugs at the premises situated at ....
2. Names of the drugs to be repacked ....
   ....
   ....
3. Name, qualification and experience of competent staff.
   ....
   ....
   ....
   ....
4. A fee of rupees ....has been credited to Government under the head of account ....

Date : ....
Signature of applicant : ....
Note : The application shall be accompanied by a plan of the premises.

Form 24-C
[See Rule 85-B]

Application for the grant or renewal of a licence to manufacture for sale [or for distribution] of Homoeopathic medicines or a licence to manufacture potentised preparations from back potencies by licensees holding licence in Form 20-C

1. I/We .... of .... holder of licence No. .... in Form 20-C hereby apply for grant/renewal of licence to manufacture the under mentioned Homoeopathic Mother Tincture/Potentised and other preparations on the premises situated at ....
   Names of the Homoeopathic preparations .... (Each item to be separately specified).
2. Names, qualifications and experience of technical staff employed for manufacture and testing of Homoeopathic Medicines.
3. A fee of rupees .... has been credited to Government under head of account ....

Date : ....
Signature : ....
Notes : 1. Delete whichever portion is not applicable.
    2. The application should be accompanied by a plan of the premises.

FORM 24-E

[See Rule 154-A]

Application for grant or renewal of a loan licence to manufacture for sale Ayurvedic (including Siddha) or Unani Drugs

1. I/We* ………………….............of+…………………….............. hereby apply for the grant /renewal of loan licence to manufacture Ayurvedic (including Siddha)or Unani Drugs on the premises situated at…………………….............. C/O** …………………

2. Names of drugs to be manufactured (with details). ……………………..............

3. The names, qualifications and experience of technical staff actually connected with the manufacture and testing of Ayurvedic (including Siddha) or Unani drugs in the manufacturing premises.

4. I/We enclose

    (a) A true copy of a letter from me/us to the manufacturing concern whose manufacturing capacity is intended to be utilised by me/us.

    (b) A true copy of a letter from the manufacturing concern that they agree to lend the services of their competent technical staff, equipment, and Premises for the manufacture of each item required by me/us and that they shall maintain the registers of raw materials and finished products separately in this behalf.

    (c) Specimen of labels, cartons of the drugs proposed to be manufactured.

5. A fee of Rs……………………..............has been credited to Government under the head of account ……………………............. and the relevant Treasury Challan is enclosed herewith.

Date………………............. Signature…………………….

(Applicant)

* Enter here the name of the Proprietor, partners or Managing Director as the case

+ Enter here the name of the applicant firm and the address of the principal place of business.

** Enter here the name and address of the manufacturing concern where the manufacture will be actually carried out and also the licence number under which the latter operates.

FORM 24-F

[See Rule 69]

Application for grant or renewal of a licence to manufacture for sale or for distribution of drugs specified in Schedule X and not specified in Schedule C and C(1)

1. I/We.. of .... hereby apply for the grant/renewal of licence to manufacture on premises situated at .... the under mentioned drugs, specified in Schedule X to the Drugs and Cosmetics Rules, 1945.

2. Names of Drugs :

   ....
   ....
   ....

3. Names, qualifications and experience of technical staff employed for manufacture and testing.

   ....
   ....
   ....
   ....
   ....

4. A fee of rupees .... has been credited to Government account under the head of account ....

Date : ....
Signature : ....
Designation : ....

FORM 27

Application for grant or renewal of a licence to manufacture for sale or for distribution of drugs specified in Schedule C and C (1) excluding those specified in part XB and Schedule X

1. I/We.. hereby apply for the grant/renewal of a licence to manufacture on the premises situated at .... the under mentioned drugs, being drugs specified in Schedule C and C(1), excluding those specified in part XB and Schedule X to the Drugs and Cosmetics Rules, 1945.

    Names of Drugs :

    ....

    ....

    ....

    (each item to be separately specified).

2. The names, qualifications and experience of the expert staff responsible for the manufacture and testing of the above-mentioned drugs:

    (a) Name(s) of staff responsible for test:

    ....

    ....

    ....

    (b) Name(s) of staff responsible for manufacture:

    ....

    ....

    ....

3. The premises and plan are ready for inspection/will be ready for inspection on ....

4. A fee of rupees .... and an inspection fee of rupees .... has been credited to Government under the head of account..

    Date : ....
    Signature : ....
    Designation : ....

    Note : The application shall be accompanied by a plan of the premises.

FORM 27-A
[See Rule 75-A]

Application for grant or renewal of a loan licence to manufacture for sale or for distribution of drugs specified in Schedule C and C (1) excluding those specified in part XB and Schedule X

1. I/We*.. of .... hereby apply for the grant/renewal of loan licence to manufacture on the premises situated at .... C/O# .... the under mentioned drugs, being drugs specified in Schedules C and C(1) excluding those specified in part XB and Schedule X to the Drugs and Cosmetics Rules, 1945. Names of Drugs (each substance to be separately specified).

   ....
   ....
   ....

2. The names, qualifications and experience of the expert staff actually connected with the manufacture and testing of the specified products in the manufacturing premises.
   (a) Name(s) of expert staff responsible for manufacture ....
   (b) Name(s) of expert staff responsible for testing ....

3. I/We enclose :
   (a) A true copy of a letter from me/us to the manufacturing concern whose manufacturing capacity is intended to be utilized by me/us.
   (b) A true copy of a letter from the manufacturing concern that they agree to lend the services of their expert staff, equipment and premises for the manufacture of each item required by me/us and that they will analyse every batch of finished products and maintain the registers of raw materials, finished products and reports of analysis separately on this behalf.
   (c) Specimens of labels, cartons of the products proposed to be manufactured.

4. A fee of rupees .... has been credited to Government under the head of account ....

Date : ....
Signature : ....

* Enter here name of the proprietor, partners or Managing Director as the case may be.

! Enter here name of the applicant firm and the address of the principal place of business.

Enter here the name and address of the manufacturing concern where the manufacture will be actually carried out and also the licence number under which the latter operates.

FORM 27-B

Application for grant or renewal of a licence to manufacture for sale or for distribution of drugs specified in Schedules C, C (1) and X.

1. I/We .... of .... hereby apply for the grant/renewal of a licence to manufacture on the premises situated at .... the under mentioned drugs, specified in Schedules C, C(1) and X to the Drugs and Cosmetics Rules, 1945.

2. Names of Drugs.

   ....

   ....

   ....

3. The names, qualifications and experience of the expert staff responsible for the manufacture and testing of the above mentioned drugs.

   (a) Name(s) of staff responsible for test.

   ....

   (b) Name(s) of staff responsible for manufacture.

   ....

4. The premises and plant* are ready for inspection/will be ready for inspection on ....

5. A fee of rupees .... and an inspection fee of rupees .... has been credited to the Government under the head of account ....

Date : ....

Signature : ....

The application shall be accompanied by a plan of the premises.

*Delete whichever is not applicable.

FORM 27-C
[See Rule 122-F]

Application for grant/renewal of licence for the operation of a Blood Bank for processing of whole blood and / or preparation of blood components.

1. I/We .... of M/S. .... hereby apply for the grant of licence / renewal of licence number .... dated .... to operate a Blood Bank, for processing of whole blood and / or* for preparation of its components on the premises situated at
....
....

2. Name(s) of the item(s):
   (1) ....
   (2) ....
   (3) ....

3. The name(s), qualification and experience of competent Technical Staff are as under :
   (a) Name(s) of Medical Officer.
   ....
   ....
   ....

   (b) Name(s) of Technical Supervisor.
   ....
   ....
   ....

   (c) Name(s) of Registered Nurse.
   ....
   ....
   ....

   (d) Name(s) of Blood Bank Technician.
   ....
   ....
   ....

4. The premises and plant are ready for inspection/will be ready for inspection on ....

5. A licence fee of rupees .... and an inspection fee of rupees .... has been credited to the Government under the head of account .... (receipt enclosed).

Date:................
Signature................
Name and Designation ......
* Delete whichever is not applicable.

Notes :
1. The application shall be accompanied by a plan of the premises, list of machinery and equipment for collection, processing, storage and testing of whole blood and its components, memorandum of association/ constitution of the firm, copies of certificate relating to educational qualifications and experience of the competent technical staff and documents relating to ownership or tenancy of the premises.
2. Copy of the application together with the relevant enclosures shall also be sent to the Central Licence Approving Authority and to the concerned Zonal / Sub-Zonal Officers of the Central Drugs Standard Control Organization.

FORM 27-D

[See Rule 75]

Application for grant or renewal of a licence to manufacture for sale or for distribution of Large Volume Parenterals/Sera and Vaccines excluding those specified in Schedule X

1. I/We.................................... of .... hereby apply for the grant/renewal of a licence to manufacture for sale or distribution on the premises situated at .... the under mentioned Large Volume Parenterals/Sera and Vaccines, specified in Schedule C and C(1), to the Drugs and Cosmetics Rules, 1945.

2. Name(s) of Drug(s)

   ....
   ....
   ....

   (each item to be separately specified).

3. The name(s), qualification and experience of the competent technical staff responsible for the manufacture of the above-mentioned drugs.

   (a) Name(s) of staff responsible for testing :

   ....
   ....

   (b) Name(s) of staff responsible for manufacturing :

   ....
   ....

4. The premises and plant are ready for inspection/will be ready for inspection on ....
   ....

5. A fee of rupees .... and an inspection of rupees ....has been credited to Government under the head of account ....

Date:................ Signature..................

Designation ....

Notes :

1. The application is to be accompanied by a plan of the premises, list of equipment and machinery to be employed for manufacture and testing; memorandum of association / constitution of the firm; copies of qualification and experience of competent technical staff and documents relating to ownership or tenancy of the premises.

2. A copy of the application together with relevant enclosures shall also be sent each to Central Licence Approving Authority and concerned Zonal / Sub-Zonal Officers of the Central Drugs Standard Control organisation.

FORM 27-E
[See Rule 122-F]
Application for grant /renewal* of licence to manufacture blood products for sale or distribution

1. I/We .... of M/s............................... hereby apply for the grant of licence/renewal of licence number .... dated .... to manufacture products on the premises situated at
....
....

2. Name(s) of item(s).
   1. ....
   ....
   2. ....
   ....
   3. ....
   ....
   4. ....
   ....

3. The name(s), qualification and experience of competent technical staff as under.
   (a) responsible for manufacturing
   (b) responsible for testing
   1 .... 1 ....
   2 .... 2 ....
   3 .... 3 ....

4. The premises and Plant are ready for inspection/will be ready for inspection on
....

5. A licence fee of rupees .... and an inspection fee of rupees .... has been credited to the Government under the head of account .... (receipt enclosed).

Dated : ....
Signature : ....
Name & Designation : ....
* Delete whichever is not applicable.

Notes :
1. The application shall be accompanied by a plan of the premises, list of machinery and equipments for manufacture of blood products, memorandum of association /constitution of the firm, copies of certificate relating to educational qualification and experience of the competent technical staff and documents relating to ownership or tenancy of the said premises.
2. A copy of the application together with the relevant enclosures shall also be sent to the Central Licence Approving Authority and to the concerned Zonal/Sub Zonal Officers of the Central Drugs Standard Control Organization.

FORM 30
[See Rule 90]

Application for licence to manufacture drugs for purpose of examination, test or analysis

I .... of .... by occupation .... hereby apply for a licence to manufacture the drugs specified below for purposes of examination, test or analysis at .... and I undertake to comply with the conditions applicable to the licence.

Names of drug :

....
....
....
....
....

Date : ....
Signature : ....

FORM 31
[See Rule 139]

Application for grant or renewal of a licence to manufacture cosmetics for sale or for distribution

1. I/We .... of .... hereby apply for the grant/renewal of a licence to manufacture on the premises situated at .... the following cosmetics :

2. Names of cosmetics.

   ....
   ....

3. Names, qualifications and experience of technical staff employed for manufacture and testing :

   ....
   ....
   ....

4. A fee of rupees .... has been credited to Government under the head of account ....

Date : ....
Signature : ....

Note : The application should be accompanied by a plan of the premises.

FORM 31-A
(See Rule 138-A)
Application for grant or renewal of a loan licence to manufacture cosmetics for sale [or for distribution]

1. I/We.. of .... hereby apply for grant/renewal of a loan licence to manufacture cosmetics, for sale, on the premises situated at ....

2. ....
   C/O .... the following cosmetics :

2. Names of cosmetics.

   ....
   ....

3. The names, qualifications and experience of the expert staff actually connected with the manufacture and testing of the specified products in the manufacturing premises.

   ....
   ....
   ....

4. I/We enclose
   (a) A true copy of a letter from me/us to the manufacturing concern whose manufacturing capacity is intended to be utilized by me/us.
   (b) A true copy of a letter from the *manufacturing concern that they agree to lend the services of their expert staff, equipment and premises for the manufacture of each item required by me/us and they will analyse every batch of and maintain the registers of raw materials, finished products and reports of analysis separately in this behalf.
   (c) Specimens of labels, cartons of the products proposed to be manufactured.

5. A fee of rupees ....has been credited to Government under the head of account ....

Date : ....
Signature : ....
*Enter here the name and address of the manufacturing concern where the manufacture will be actually carried out and also their licence number.

FORM 36
[See Rule 150-B]
Application for grant or renewal of approval for carrying out tests drugs/cosmetics or raw materials used in the manufacture thereof on behalf of licensees for manufacture for sale of drugs/ cosmetics

1. I/We .... of .... hereby apply for the grant or renewal of approval for carrying out tests of identity, purity, quality and strength on the following categories of drugs / items of cosmetics or raw materials used in the manufacture thereof on behalf of licensees for manufacture for sale of drugs/ cosmetics.
2. *Categories of drugs, items of cosmetics :
   (a) Drugs other than those specified in Schedule C and C(1)and also excluding Homoeopathic Drugs :
      (i) Crude vegetable drugs.
      (ii) Mechanical contraceptives.
      (iii) Surgical dressings.
      (iv) Drugs requiring the use of ultraviolet/ Infra Red Spectrophotometer or Chromatography.
      (v) Disinfectants.
      (vi) Other Drugs.
   (b) Drugs specified in Schedules C and C(1) :-
      (i) Sera, Vaccines, Antigens, Toxins, Antitoxins, Toxoids, Bacteriophages and similar Immunological Products.
      (ii) Antibiotics.
      (iii) Vitamins.
      (iv) Parenteral preparations.
      (v) Sterilized surgical ligature / suture.
      (vi) Drugs requiring the use of animals for their test.
      (vii) Drugs requiring microbiological tests.
      (viii) Drugs requiring the use of Ultraviolet/Infra Red Spectrophotometer or Chromatography.
      (ix) Other drugs.
   (c) Homoeopathic Drugs.
   (d) Cosmetics.
3. Names, qualifications and experience of expert staff employed for testing and the person-in-charge of testing.
4. List of testing equipment provided.
5. I / We enclose a plan of the testing premises showing the location and area of the different sections thereof.
6. An inspection fee of rupees .... has been credited to Government under the head of account ....

Date : ....
Signature : ....
*Delete whichever is not applicable.

FORM 44

(See rules 122A, 122B, 122D and 122 DA)

Application for grant of permission to import or manufacture a New Drug or to undertake clinical trial

I/We*………………………………………. of M/s ……………………..………….. (address) hereby apply for grant of permission for import of and/or clinical trial or for approval to manufacture a new drug or fixed dose combination or subsequent permission for already approved new drug. The necessary information / data is given below :

1. Particulars of new drug :
   (1) Name of the drug.
   (2) Dosage form.
   (3) Composition of the formulation :
   (4) Test specification : (i) active ingredients. (ii) inactive ingredients.
   (5) Pharmacological classification of the drug.
   (6) Indications for which proposed to be used.
   (7) Manufacturer of the raw material (bulk drug substances).
   (8) Patent status of the drug.

2. Data submitted along with the application (as per Schedule Y with indexing and page numbers:)
   A. Permission to market a new drug :
      (1) Chemical and Pharmaceutical information.
      (2) Animal Pharmacology.
      (3) Animal Toxicology.
      (4) Human / Clinical Pharmacology (Phase I).
      (5) Exploratory Clinical Trials (Phase II).
      (6) Confirmatory Clinical Trials (Phase III) (including published review articles)
      (7) Bio-availability, dissolution and stability study data.
      (8) Regulatory status in other countries.
      (9) Marketing information :
         (a) Proposed product monograph.
         (b) Drafts of labels and cartons.
      (10) Application for test licence.

B. Subsequent approval / permission for manufacture of already approved new drug :
   (a) Formulation :
      (1) Bio-availability / bio-equivalence protocol.
      (2) Name of the investigator/center.
      (3) Source of raw material (bulk drug substances) and stability study data.
   (b) Raw material (bulk drug substances) :
      (1) Manufacturing method.
      (2) Quality control parameters and/or analytical specification, stability report.
      (3) Animal toxicity data.
C. Approval / Permission for fixed dose combination :
   (1) Therapeutic Justification.
      (authentic literature in pre-reviewed journals/text books)
   (2) Data on pharmacokinetics/pharmacodynamics combination.
   (3) Any other data generated by the applicant on the safety and efficacy of the combination.
D. Subsequent Approval or approval for new indication - new dosage form :
   (1) Number and date of Approval / permission already granted.
   (2) Therapeutic justification for new claim / modified dosage form
   (3) Data generated on safety, efficacy and quality parameters.

A total fee of rupees .... (in words) .... has been credited to the Government under the Head of Account .... (Photocopy of receipt is enclosed).

Date : ....
Signature : ....…..
Designation : ....
*Delete whichever is not applicable.

ANNEXURE

ARUNACHAL PRADESH Drugs Controller, Directorate of Health Services, Naharlagun-791119 (Arunachal Pradesh) Phone: 0360-2244248(0)2244182(8) Fax:2244105	**ASSAM** Drugs Controller, Directorate of Health Services, Dispur, Hengrabari, Guwahati-38' Phone: 0361-22665276, 22200245(R), Fax: 2261630
BIHAR Drugs Controller, Directorate of Health Services. 4th Floor. Vikas Bhawan. New Secretariat. Patna-800015 Phone: 0612-22211 10/ 671389(8), 9431278474(M)	**CHANDIGARH** Drugs Controller& Licensing Authority, Chandigarh Admn., Chandigarh Phone:780781; 265640(R) i Fax: 780781
CHATTISGARH Drugs Controller, FDA, CGO Nursing Hostel, Near Mantralaya, Raipur-492001 Chattisgarh Phone: 0771-2235226, 2221025 5038202 (R) Fax:2221625	**DAMAN** Drugs Licence Authority, Director, Medical & Health Services, Primary Health Centre, Moti Daman, Daman-396220 Phone: 0260-250847/ 254870 Fax:250870
GOA Director, Foods and Drugs Control Administration, Old G M C Building, Panji Goa-403001 Phone: 0832-2224639, 2220245, 2430948 Resi: 2224638, Fax:2224639	**GUJARAT** Commissioner FDCA Gujarat State, Old Sachivalya, Block No.8, 1st Floor, Dr. Jivraj Mehta Bhavan, Gandhi Nagar-382010 Phone: 079-23253400, 9825049232, 26851817(8) Fax:079-23252417
HARAYANA Drugs Controller, Directorate General of Health Services, Sector 20, Punchkula, Haryana Phone:0172-2551081 / 2584999(8) , 9814916180 (M)	**HIMACHAL PRADESH** Drugs Controller, Health & FW Deptt. SDA Complex, Kasumpati, Shimla-170009 (HP) Phone: 0177-2621842/ 2621224/ 2621466 Extn.232/ 01792-221107(R) Fax:222508. 9816030033 (M)

JHARKHAND Drugs Controller cum licensing Authority, Jharkhand directorate of Health Services, Jagarnthpur High School Bldg., Sector -3, Dhurva, Ranchi-834004 Phone: 0651-441886/ 0651-245850(R)	**JAMMU & KASHMIR** The Controller, Drugs & Food Control Organisation, Patoli Magotrian PP Janipur Jammutavi- 180001 Phone:080-2538527 2597445
KARNATAKA Drugs Controller, Drugs Control Department, State of Karnataka P B No. 5377, Next to Carito House, Palace Road,Bangalore-560001 Phone: 080-22262846/22870943/ 23356134 (R) Fax: 22286492 Email: drugscontroller(&,vsnl.net	**KERALA** Drugs Controller & licensing Authority, Kerala, Public Health Lab. Campus, Red Cross Road, Thiruvananthpuram-695035 Phone: 0471-247325 6/ 2471896/ 2472178(R) Fax:0471-2473256, 9820710993 (M)
MADHYA PRADESH Controller Food & Drugs Admn. Idgah Hills, Bhopal-462001 Phone:0755-2665385/5299372(R) Fax: 2665385	**MAHARASHTRA** Commissioner, Food & Drugs Admn., Opp. RBI Building, Bandra, Mumbai-400051 Phone: 26590548/ 22844903(R) Fax: 26591959. 26591820, 9820530690 (M)
MANIPUR Drugs Controller & Director, Medical & Health Services, Lamphlept, Imphal-795004 Manipur Phone: 0385-2310283/ 2221848 (R) Fax:2310964	**MEGHALAYA** Director of Health Services, Government of Meghalaya, Shillong-793001, Meghalya Phone: 0364-2225709/ 225375 (R) Fax:2228493
MIZORAM Director of Health Services, Mizoram, Chaltlang, Aizwal-796001 Phone: 0389-2323452/ 2328053(R) Fax:2320169	**NAGALAND** Dy. Drugs Controller, Directorate of Health Services, Nagaland, Kohima-797001 Phone: 0370-2222626/ 2243409 (R) Fax:2243887

NEW DELHI Drugs Controller, Drugs Control Department, Govt. of National Capital Territory of Delhi, 15, Sham Nath Marg, Delhi-110054 Phone: 011-233922018/26492365(R) Fax:22393704	**ORISSA** Drugs Controller, New Nandankanan Road, Bhubaneshwar-751017 Phone: 067-2300494/ 2564878 (R) Fax: 2300494
PONDICHERRY Asstt. Commissioner, FDA, 102-C, Chellan Nagar, Pond icherry-605011 Phone: 0443-340193/332849(R)	**PUNJAB** State Drug Controlling Authority, Sector 34-E, Chandigarh-160016 Phone:0172-604657 Extn.,399 Fax : 609142
RAJASTHAN Drugs Controller, Directorate of Medical & Health Services, Swasthya Bhawan, Tilak Marg, Jaipur-302004 Phone: 0141-2381670/ 2336280 (R) Fax: 2310447	**SIKKIM** State Drugs Controller, Deptt. Of Health & FW, Govt. of Sikkim, Gangtok-737101 Phone: 03592-222633 Fax: 224481
SILVASSA Asstt. Drugs Controller, Medical & Public Health Department, Dadra & Nagar Haveli, Silvassa-396230 Phone: 0260-2642961/ 642940/ 642947(R)/ 642264(R) Fax: 64961	**TAMILNADU** Drugs Controller, 258-261, Anna Salai, Tahampet, Chennai-600006 Phone:044-24321830/ 22440043 (R) Fax: 24321830

EUROPEAN REGULATORY BODIES

European Agency Medicines (EMEA)
http://www.emea.europa.eu

Heads of Medicines Agencies (HMA)
http://www.hma.eu

DG Enterprises - Pharmaceuticals - Regulatory Framework and Market Authorisations
http://www.ec.europa.eu/enterprise/pharmaceuticals/index en.htm

Austria Osterreichische Agentur fur Gesundheit und Ernahrungssicherheit GmbH
http://www.aqes.at

Belgium : Federal Public Service - Health, Food chain safety and Environment
http://www.afiqp.fqov.be

Bulgaria : Bulgarian Drug Agency (BDA)
http://www.bda.bq

Cyprus : Ministry of Health
http://www.pio.qov.cy

Czech Republic : State Institute for Drug Control (SUKL)
http://www.sukl.cz

Denmark : Laegemiddelstyrelsen (DKMA)
http://www.dkma.dk

Estonia : State Agency of Medicines
http://www.sam.ee

Finland : National Agency for Medicines
http://www.nam.fi

France : Agence Frangaise de Sécurité Sanitaire des Produits de Sante (AFSSAPS)
http://www.afssaps.sante.fr

Germany : Bundesinstitut für Arzneimittel und Medizinprodukte (BfArM)
http://www.bfarm.de/de/index.php

Greece : National Organization for Medicines
http://www.eof.gr

Hungary : National Institute of Pharmacy
http://www.oqyi.hu

Iceland : Icelandic Medicines Control Agency (IMCA)
http://www.imca.is

Ireland: Irish Medicines Board (IMB)
http://www.imb.ie

Italy : Agenzia Italiana del Farmaco (AIFA)
http://www.aqenziafarmaco.it/aifa/servlet/section.ktml...

Latvia : State Agency of Medicines
http://zaale.vza.qov.lv

Lithuania : State Medicines Control Agency
http://www.vvkt.lt

Luxembourg : Ministere de la Sante
http://www.etat.lu/MS

Netherlands : College ter Beoordeling van Geneesmiddelen
httpa/www.cbq-meb.nl

Norway : Statens Legemiddelverk
http://www.leqemiddelverket.no

Poland : The Office for Registration of Medicinal Products, Medical Devices and Biocidal Products
http://www.urpl.qov.pl

Portugal : National Medicines and Health Products Authority (INFARMED)
http://www.infarmed.pt

Romania : National Medicines Agency (NMA)
http://www.anm.ro

S'ovak Republic : State Institute for Drug Control (SIDC)
http://www.sukl.sk

Slovenia : Agency for Medicinal Products and Medical Devices of the Republic of Slovenia
http://www2.gov.si/mz/mz-splet.nsf

Spain : Agencia Española de Medicamentos y Productos Sanitarios
http://www.agemed.es

United Kingdom : Medicines and Healthcare Products Regulatory Agency (MHRA)
http://www.mhra.qov.uk

INTERNATIONAL REGULATORY BODIES

Australian Government Department of Health and Ageing (TGA)
http://www.health.qov.au

Canada
Health Canada - Health Products and Food Branch
http://www.hc-sc.qc.ca

Japan
Ministry of Health, Labour and Welfare
http://www.mhlw.qo.ip/english

New Zealand
Ministry of Health
http://www.moh.qovt.nz

Switzerland
Swissmedic,Schweizerisches Heilmittelinstitut
http://www.swissmedic.ch

USA
Food and Drug Administration (FDA) Center for Drug Evaluation and Research (CDER)
http://www.fda.gov/cder

EUROPEAN AND INTERNATIONAL BODIES AND INSTITUTIONS

Drug3k - Online Drug Encyclopedia
http://www.druq3k.com

Association of the British Pharmaceutical Industry (ABPI)
http://www.abpi.orq.uk

Association of the European Self-Medication Industry (AESGP)
http://www. aesq p. be

BioIndustry Association (BIA)
http://www. bioindustrV.orq

British Generic Manufacturers Association (BGMA)
http://www.britishqenerics.co.uk

Drug Information Association (DIA)
http://www.diahome.orq

European Directorate for the Quality of Medicines and Healthcare (EDQM)
http://www.edqm.eulsite/paqe 628.php

European Generic Medicines Association (EGA)
http:1/www.eqaqenerics.com

European Federation of Pharmaceutical Industries and Associations (EFPIA)
http://www.efpia.orq

European Pharmaceutical Legislation
http://www.ec.europa.eu/enterprise/pharmaceuticals/index en.htm

Heads of Medicines Agencies (HMA)
http//www.hma.eu
International Conference on Harmonization of Technical Requirements for Registration of Pharmaceuticals for Human Use (ICH)
http://www.ich.orq

International Federation of Pharmaceutical Manufacturers and Associates (IFPM)
http://www.ifpma.orq

nCADREAC - New Collaboration Agreement between Drug Regulatory Authorities in Central and Eastern European Countries
http://www.newcadreac.orq/cadreac.html

Pharmaceutical Information & Pharmacovigilance Association
http://www.aiopi.orq.uk

The Organisation for Professionals in Regulatory Affairs (TOPRA)
http://www.topra.orq

The Proprietary Association of Great Britain
http://www.paqb.orq.uk

■ ■ ■

www.ingramcontent.com/pod-product-compliance
Lightning Source LLC
Chambersburg PA
CBHW081144230426
43664CB00018B/2799